THE AUTHOR

Born in 1919, Burnett James was originally
intended for a naval career, but a disabling
attack of polio at the age of fifteen, while he
was a cadet at the Nautical College,
Pangbourne, put a sudden end to that.
Always keen on music (he played bugle and
alto saxophone in the Pangbourne bands),
he subsequently turned to the study of music
and became a professional critic and musical
journalist, specialising in record reviewing
and magazine editorial work as well as
writing books on music and composers. He
has worked on the editorial staff of a number
of prominent monthly and weekly magazines,
including *Audio Record Review, John
O'London's, Time and Tide, Audio* and *Jazz
Journal*. He was broadcast on BBC Radio
and television. His books include, *Beethoven
and Human Destiny, Brahms: A Critical
Study, Ravel: His Life and Times, Manuel
de Falla and the Spanish Musical Renaissance,
Living Forwards* (autobiography), *An
Adventure in Music, Essays on Jazz* and
Music on Record (with Peter Gammond). He
currently has in preparation, or in the press,
books on Sibelius, Mahler and Elgar. He is
married with two sons (one a classical
guitarist) and has lived some years earlier
in Switzerland where he expanded his
general musical experience. His hobbies are
photography and watching cricket (active
participation in the latter having been
scuppered by the polio, like the ambition in
youth towards admiralty). He regards his
friend the late Sir Neville Cardus as his
principal mentor as a writer and critic.

WAGNER
and the Romantic Disaster

BURNETT JAMES

MIDAS BOOKS
HIPPOCRENE BOOKS
New York

In the Composers – Life and Times Series

BACH	Tim Dowley
BARTOK	Hamish Milne
BEETHOVEN	Ateş Orga
BERLIOZ	Robert Clarson-Leach
BRAHMS	Paul Holmes
CHOPIN	Ateş Orga
DVORAK	Neil Butterworth
ELGAR	Simon Mundy
HAYDN	Neil Butterworth
MAHLER	Edward Seckerson
MENDELSSOHN	Mozelle Moshansky
MOZART	Peggy Woodford
OFFENBACH	Peter Gammond
PAGANINI	John Sugden
RACHMANINOFF	Robert Matthew-Walker
RAVEL	Burnett James
ROSSINI	Nicholas Till
SCHUBERT	Peggy Woodford
SCHUMANN	Tim Dowley
SHOSTAKOVICH	Eric Roseberry
TCHAIKOVSKY	Wilson Strutte
VERDI	Peter Southwell-Sander

Composers – Special anniversary editions

Double Life	Miklos Rozsa
John Ireland	Muriel Searle
Wagner and the Romantic Disaster	Burnett James

First published UK in 1983 by
MIDAS BOOKS
12 Dene Way, Speldhurst, Tunbridge Wells, Kent TN3 0NX

ISBN 0 85936 106 3 (UK)

© Burnett James 1983

First published USA in 1983 by
HIPPOCRENE BOOKS
171 Madison Avenue, New York, NY 10016

ISBN 0 88254 667 8 (US)

Printed and bound in Great Britain at Nene Litho and Woolnough Bookbinding, Wellingborough, Northants.

CONTENTS

INTRODUCTION

To the writing of books on Wagner there is apparently no end. The centenary of his death is unlikely to stem the flow. And it is right and understandable that it should be so. The impact of Richard Wagner, his theories and his dramas, upon not only the German but the entire European mind and consciousness has been immense and profound. That is to say, he remains one of the most controversial figures in the history of the last two hundred years or so – not because of his ideas, some of which to our way of thinking are disagreeable, if not outright offensive; not because his music necessarily either attracts or repels with a force and a contrary tension not exceeded by that of any comparable figure; but quite simply because he achieved his main object, which was to make the unconscious articulate. He may not have specifically intended it that way, but that is how it came out and why he continues to excite the imagination and compel the attention even of those who would rather he did not. It has always been so.

All true art reverberates in the unconscious. Perhaps that is the simple distinction between art and entertainment, properly so called. The lines are not, and cannot be, rigid; there is always a crossing of the frontiers, and much true art may also be justly called entertainment. Not everything that resonates in the unconscious lays claim to being called art; but if it does not, then it cannot be seen as true art at all. It is because Wagner's art resonates at the deepest levels and then draws the resonance deliberately to the surface that he became even before his death, and has remained ever since, a figure of fascinating – some would say snake-like – compulsion, his power essentially hypnotic.

He has also exerted a greater influence over his successors than any other composer except Arnold Schoenberg. And that influence has been largely deplorable. If that of Schoenberg has been slightly less deplorable (and there are many who would dispute that), it is because, as Hanslick discerned, Wagner's methods were suitable only to Wagner and could not be transplanted into another soil or personality, while Schoenberg's theories and system had wider application. But the deplorable nature of 'influence' remains. As Hemingway said, the individual is all you ever have and all schools only serve to categorize their members as failures. The Wagnerian failures have been legion in their time.

To attempt to bring a historical character into clear focus is always a perilous undertaking; it leads down a path that is strewn with bear traps and bottomless pits. The main difficulty is that of perspective. The years between tend to cloud rather than clarify the essential material. Perhaps the most tempting trap, and the commonest, is that of judging past ages and their characters by what we think of them instead of what they thought of themselves. Their lights may not be our lights; but unless we make the attempt first to see them in their own light, even if it seems to us dim, we can never see them clear and in the round. And in the case of a man like Wagner, who bestrode his age, stamping an indelible mark upon it in many areas and leaving a legacy of dubious if unintended consequences, the temptation is much exaggerated.

So far as Wagner, Hitler, the Nazis and the Second World War are concerned, we have still not gone very far. It is recognized and understood better on the Continent, especially inside Germany; but in Britain and America it is still largely evaded. Yet it is important because of the deep psychological and emotional affinity between Wagner's music and dramas and the German psyche. It has to be dealt with and disposed of, not necessarily in order to cleanse Wagner of the charge of having 'inspired' Hitler and Nazism or of making it stick, but simply to clear the undergrowth so that we can again (or maybe at last) obtain an uninterrupted view of the subject itself. Most of the associations of Wagner and the Nazis are not only unperceptive but trite. We have still not got far beyond the stage of labouring the obvious. In any film documentary dealing with the war and the Nazis, whenever a German army group is surrounded or a German battleship sunk, we are sure to be bludgeoned with bleeding chunks of *Götterdämmerung*, however wildly inappropriate. And it has long become clear that the Berlin bunkers in 1945 fell not to Russian or American projectiles but to Wagner tubas. It is time for at least some preliminary hacking through the jungle.

Sussex 1982   BJ

PRELUDE

On 13 February 1883 Richard Wagner died, from a heart attack, in his room in the Palazzo Vendramin-Calergi, Venice, where he had retired with his wife Cosima after the exhausting demands of producing *Parsifal* at Bayreuth the previous year. Seated in the audience at those first performances of *Parsifal* was Anton Bruckner, whose Third symphony had been dedicated to Wagner on the occasion of a previous visit to Bayreuth in 1877, a visit which had made him the hero of the young blood in Vienna – of whom the youthful Mahler was a passionate Wagnerian – and whose Seventh symphony contains the great Adagio begun in premonition of Wagner's death and brought to completion as a noble elegy for the man and musician Bruckner revered above all others. During that inauguration the humble Bruckner had averted his eyes from the stage, oblivious to all that was being enacted upon it of sacred and profane, his mind and total attention absorbed in the music unfolding in the orchestra pit. It was ever Bruckner's habit so to concentrate at Bayreuth; but with *Parsifal* it was absolute, his simple piety disturbed and distressed by the usurping implications of the stage action. Thus from the outset Wagner's uncompromising and far-ranging dramatic genius was a source of distress and controversy, at times even to his warmest admirers.

Wagner himself, already afflicted with heart trouble, at one time feared that he might not live to complete the score of *Parsifal*. In the event, he summoned sufficient strength to promote the performances of the summer of 1882, suffered a heart attack during the fifth performance, from which he recovered with the words 'another narrow escape', and took over direction of the last from the officiating conductor, Hermann Levi, but surreptitiously so that none knew it until the last curtain had fallen.

One month before Wagner breathed his last, Franz Liszt, old friend, champion from the embattled days of the mid-century, latterly father-in-law, and himself in his declining years, left Venice after spending a few weeks in the company of an ailing Wagner. Before he left, Liszt was inspired by the sight of a funeral procession on the Venetian canals to compose two of his prophetic late piano pieces, *La Lugubre Gondola* 1 & 2, like Bruckner in his Seventh symphony Adagio under a premonition of the approaching death of the master. A short while later Wagner's own body was to be transported by the same means; and Liszt composed another piece to mark the occasion – *R.W. – Venezia*. Liszt wrote four pieces in all relating to Wagner's death, austere, hard-grained, economical music, apparently a world removed from the flamboyant virtuoso adventures with which he had bedazzled, seduced and often befuddled an earlier generation. The sparse textures and predominantly linear technique of Liszt's late music, combined with the harmonic implications and tonal ambiguities of *Tristan und Isolde* and *Parsifal*, were to play a major part in setting modern music on its path, leading to and pointing the way for Debussy on the one hand, Bartók on another, aspects of Schoenberg and his disciples on yet a third, and much else, often by way of Gustav Mahler.[1]

The passing of Richard Wagner reverberated throughout musical Europe. Even Eduard Hanslick, bitter antagonist in criticism of the Wagnerian aesthetic and all it stood for, so far forgot his enmity as to publish a brief laudatory valediction to the man and composer he had rigorously challenged and frequently ridiculed. But neither for Hanslick nor for the world at large would the spirit of Richard Wagner lie quiescent once his bones had been interred at Bayreuth.

All the same, Wagner's death marked the end of one European era and the beginning of another: the end of the rise, the beginning of the decline, though that decline had been long foreseen, not least by Wagner himself whose late music is a seaching examination of it. The hard core, the innermost essence of the nineteenth century, which had begun with high hopes in the wake of the French Revolution and the dawn of the Romantic Revival, was cracked, its mortality exposed. Despite the visions, the high and mighty exultations, the pain and ecstasy of the full-blown Romantic age, its sense of striving for the infinite and the immortal, its formidable challenge to human limitation, it was still in the end obliged to confront mortality, and ultimately to acquiesce, often in bitterness and despair or in arrogance and aggression. The process of internal corruption and decay was after all endemic. For Wagner, too, it began in high-flown heroic assumption. But he was not deceived: he saw that the way out did not lie there, in the gesture of the sword. That at least had to be relinquished.

Thomas Mann put it:

Suffering and great as that nineteenth century whose complete expression he is, the mental image of Richard Wagner stands before my eyes. Scored through and through with all his century's unmistakable traits, surcharged with all its driving forces, so I see his image . . .[2]

2

That is the deep, penetrating truth; but it is still not the whole truth. The nineteenth century was many-sided: no one man, not even Richard Wagner, could totally contain and so sum it up in himself. It took at least two major directions, encompassed in music by the Brahms–Wagner dichotomy or controversy. It was not complete dichotomy, of course; the opposing strands were always interrelated and cross-fertilizing, and the controversy was as often as not simulated, provoked by idle and vicious prattle among camp followers and hangers-on whose snaps and snarls served momentarily to distort the true historical perspectives without either harming or significantly bearing upon the central figures. Yet it did exist; there was a cleavage, and it cannot be ignored or explained away as though it did not matter. It not only mattered, it was and remains crucial to a thorough examination of the roots of the Romantic disaster and its destructive consequences in our own time.

This dichotomy, or 'two-way split', arose out of the nineteenth century's central duality: on the one hand the proud, high-vaulted, ever seeking and questioning, limitlessly gambiting Romanticism of which Wagner was indeed the most complete expression; on the other, the circumspection, the taste for security and solid achievement of a domestically oriented bourgeoisie, that world of which Brahms in one aspect and Schumann in another most eloquently spoke and on behalf of which both testified.

In every age or historical period, however broadly defined, there is the operation of this duality, for just as no single personality is absolutely one thing or another, and no true work of art is categorically definable, once for all, so no age has its single unchallengeable aspect. Broad classification may indicate essentials, determine an overall characteristic; but beyond that the underlying complexities of the social, intellectual and cultural structure lead to ever-increasing areas of cross-fertilization. But the nineteenth century, largely because of the tremendous evolutionary thrust it contained and its accompanying 'knowledge explosion', presented that duality in a particularly emphatic and dramatic form. And it was in this sense that Richard Wagner must be seen as its most complete expression.

The force of Wagner's genius and achievement is not disputed. It may be questioned; it may be resented; but it is not disputed. Even in the days when the star of his popularity and aesthetic appreciation was at its lowest, intellectual fashion with its knife most securely into him, only the ignorant or the hopelessly bigoted sought to deny his specific achievement. And it remained the same in a still later age, when another generation had suffered a similar experience and was asked to believe, without always seeing and understanding for itself, that Wagner was the spokesman for and had helped to corrupt the ear of the principal cause of that suffering and that disgrace. Athough Richard Wagner was, predictably, Adolf Hitler's favourite composer and the unintending inspirer of many of his most cancerous dreams and asphyxiating visions, it can hardly be laid to Wagner's charge that he was in some malignant way the acting titular head of the Nazi party. Though a passionate German patriot in the larger sense, and a devout celebrant of German nationhood and especially of 'Holy German Art', Wagner cast suspicious eyes on the muscular pan-Germanism of Bismarck and was not taken in either by the ascendancy of Prussian militarism or the founding of the German Empire. Bismarck, a political realist of rare practical insight, declared for 'Less Germany' (*Kleindeutschland*) against the expansive concept of 'Great Germany' (*Grössedeutschland*), not from any sense of limited power but simply because the smaller was more manageable and so promised ultimately to be stronger and more secure. It was the reversal of this policy, first under Wilhelm II, then under Hitler, that led to the two outbreaks of bloodletting of the first half of the twentieth century.

But none of this meant anything to Wagner. Such temporal celebrations and political admirations he left to the homely and contentedly enthusiastic Brahms, who worshipped Bismarck and celebrated the victory of Prussian arms in choral music of sturdy conviction and much erudition. For Wagner it was all largely an irrelevance. His vision was set upon farther and less tangible objectives. He would assuredly have spat in the face of the Nazi hierarchy and treated the whole Third Reich with notable contempt, if only because of the way it traduced and corrupted that 'Holy German Art' by which he himself set the highest store (but not only because of that). His entire sensitivity and historical acumen, added to his particular idealism, would have meant that the brutal crudities of the Hitler era must have revolted him. When the Nazis came to power, Arnold Schoenberg was one of those to be dismissed from his post, and in spite of his apparently more 'correct' attitude to the 'Jewish problem', Richard Wagner, too, if he had had the misfortune to be alive at the time, would soon have been observed packing his bags, his position intolerable, his patience more than exhausted. The Nazi period represented a re-emergence of precisely those qualities of coarseness and vulgarity, as well as brutality, that Wagner found so disagreeable in his fellow countrymen and was one of the reasons for his love–hate relationship with Paris and its more refined and civilized life.

The degradation of German art and civilization under the Nazis would not have been tolerated by Wagner for a single week. This is crucial: in order to understand the totality of Wagner as man and artist, the quality as well as the fact of his German patriotic fervour has to be understood. He might for a short time have been deceived, especially in the disintegrative circumstances of the last days of the Weimar Republic, also a disgrace and a degradation; but to suppose that his innate patriotism and national pride was in any normal sense related to or associated with, or would have ever been accepted by, the Hitler Reich is to place the finger of total incomprehension upon the true meaning of his life and work.

All the same, the question cannot be so easily dismissed. There is a connection and association between Wagner and Hitlerism. It is not always what it seems, or is made to seem. It has seldom been understood, or even properly analysed. But it is still there.

The Third Reich and the Nazi aberration was a corrupt and decadent form of that High Romanticism which Wagner himself helped to forge and then epitomized in the most powerful dramatic terms. The abuse of Romanticism reached its nadir in Nazi Germany, but abuse was always inherent in the Romantic movement itself. Romanticism was full of potential danger and fraught with perils that could never have been entirely avoided, indeed were a constituent part of its innermost nature. The worst consequences could have been contained, and would have been had the original vision been followed through instead of being twisted to expose the flaw at the centre. But essentially, the Romantic rebellion, as it has been called, not quite accurately, carried within itself the seeds of its own and so of our own destruction. Wiser politics and saner ethics might have diverted the course, sublimated the more destructive energies, retained firm hold on the rising threat of disintegration. But the peril remained endemic: it could never have been entirely obliterated. A kind of reckless courting of danger and trafficking with the powers of darkness was a concomitant of whole-hogging Romanticism. Nietzsche, though he turned against Wagner and railed against the 'collapse' of the one-time hero, was no less progenitor of the disaster, with his concept of 'living dangerously' and the lauding of the 'superman'. The danger was propounded by Nietzsche; in Wagner it was inherent, and thus more potent.

Yet the central question remains. How far, how deeply, either directly or by implication, was Richard Wagner involved in the Nazi descent into ancient barbarism and the modern distortion of history and evolution? It is a question not easily answered. There are many sides to it, and a number of them continue to be obscure. The nineteenth century dissolves into the twentieth. The transition is nominally abrupt, but the process is in fact not only gradual but slower than has yet been recognized. Until half its course was run, the twentieth century remained a modified continuation of the nineteenth. There were various 'reactions', especially in the wake of the First World War, but these were almost entirely a change of perspective rather than of essence. In music the reaction was principally against Wagner; or rather, against Germanism, against all that the term 'Teutonic' stood for, Richard Wagner himself always at the head, its true and total representative. And yet more and more it can be seen that even where the reaction appears to have been strongest, the by-passing most complete, the shade of Wagner still looms and dominates. Sibelius, Debussy, even aspects of Stravinsky, far from being free from the stain of Wagnerism, of what Erik Satie in France dubbed the 'sauerkraut aesthetic', can now be seen to have been as deep-dyed as any who swore open allegiance. This is by no means a deliberately pejorative statement; it simply demonstrates again the immense force of influence both of Wagner himself and of the historical period which produced him and which he in his turn created. In politics, too, that same influence predominates; and because Nazism was a direct product of the nineteenth century's Romantic nationalism grown overripe and rotten, and came out of that same Germany which produced and was produced by Richard Wagner, he too in a specific sense helped to create it.

The paradox is only apparent. Everything has its obverse; all energy has its positive and negative poles. Thus the Wagnerian world and its life-view, in all its aspects, correlates with what followed it and appears as its existential opposite. Wagner saw himself as the living embodiment of the historic destiny of the German nation. In the same way, Hitler saw himself as cast in a similar role. Indeed, he deliberately fostered that idea, so in a sense Adolf Hitler appears as the distorted mirror-image of Richard Wagner; or, to put it another way, it was a case of the Yeatsian mask and anti-mask, encompassing not the individual only but an entire nation. That the mirror was flawed and became progressively more so is not to be disputed; yet even here certain misconceptions can intrude. It is too easily forgotten that in its beginnings the Nazi upsurge in Germany had its genuinely idealistic aspects; that as many were attracted, especially among the Hitler Youth, by a kind of Rupert Brooke blue-eyed innocence, an unclouded 'now God be thanked Who has matched us with His hour' idealization, as by the crudities and brutalities which made so strong an appeal to other elements in the German psyche. On the other hand, it is as myopic to blame Wagner for the rise of Nazism as it is to blame the aggressive elements in Beethoven's middle-period works for social violence and terrorism. If in one vision of itself the Nazi party attempted, subconsciously rather than overtly, to translate *The Ring* into a practical political system, in another it aspired to recreate in modern terms the German essence of *Die Meistersinger* – and many in its early days actually believed that it could. Though from the beginning it was rotten at the core, it did not appeal only to base motives and barbarous inclinations.

And so Wagner, as the spirit and embodiment of that Romantic burgeoning which arose high and subsequently sank low into the pit of dishonour and disgrace, bore by indirect inference his share of that dishonour and that shame, not so much through his fault as, primarily, and maybe after all paradoxically, through his pre-eminence. The contradictions of history and its persistent ironies throw many perspectives out of focus, the vision clouded, the deductive faculties misled and sidetracked. It is certainly true that the full effect of Wagner's music dramas on Hitler and the Nazis has seldom been properly understood outside Germany; but this is not central to the argument. Wagner's immense artworld and uniquely centralized life-view could always be corrupted and distorted for fundamentally dishonest purposes under the guise of some newly minted 'idealism', precisely because it was so many-sided. And in any case, a deliberate attempt to translate the philosophic and metaphysical content of *The Ring* into any workable political system was bound to produce a chimerical monster. The realities of the imagination are not commensurate with political systems, whatever their directional bias.

When we look into the nineteenth century and observe its arrogance and ignorance as well as its sensitivity, its visionary aspirations and its deep-dyed loyalties and determinations, its leading figures emerge from the backcloth more clearly and in sharpness of perspective. Because we were so near to the nineteenth century for so long, and because for at least the first half of its course the twentieth century was more a continuation of the nineteenth than a period with its own established identity, our own century is more difficult to see in total clarity than ages which lie farther from us in the past. Emotional involvement lingered for at least half a century, and in some way still lingers. Yet precisely because that tremendous century lies so close to us, and because we remain, whether we like it or not, inextricably involved with so much that went into its making and so into its making of us, because it was literally our seedbed and breeding ground – even to the young of our time, born perhaps several decades away from its ending – we have to come to grips with it at many different levels and from constantly shifting viewpoints, to return to the task of understanding it in the light of our continually evolving experience and knowledge. And so its great seminal figures stand behind us like dark forest gods, demanding recognition, making heavy demands upon our understanding and pulling the cords of individual as well as the collective unconscious. Of course, as the years pass and the nineteenth century recedes farther into history, the perspectives alter, the bias changes; yet the central fact remains – because of its pivotal situation between the old and the modern worlds, the nineteenth century still looms over us and requires constant analysis and reanalysis.

Wagner's involvement in and with the nineteenth century, its contradictions and absurdities as much as its great and imperishable achievements, was total. That is the most important objective truth about him. The subjective truth is the force and magnitude of his genius. And the two together, the objective fact of the involvement and the subjective thrust of penetration to the heart of it, carried both the potency and the influence of his work far beyond that age and that century. In so far as most of the great movements in thought and feeling – in science, in art and philosophy and psychology and literature – were born in the nineteenth century, so many of the seminal figures of the modern world came forth with the huge evolutionary thrust forward that took place in the aftermath of the French Revolution and changed the entire concept of human life and potentiality; we are in a particular sense its children and its progeny. Thomas Mann wrote, in the same essay of 1933:

Our attitude to the nineteenth century is that of sons towards a father; critical, as is only fair. We shrug our shoulders alike over its belief – which was a belief in ideas –

and over its unbelief – that is to say, its melancholy relativism. Its attachment to liberal ideas of reason and progress seem to us laughable, its materialism all too crass, it monistic solution of the riddle of the universe full of shallow complacency. And yet its scientific self-sufficiency is atoned for, yes, outweighed, by the pessimism, the musical bond with night and death, which will very likely one day seem its strongest trait.[3]

We may well think, half another century later, that we have at last freed ourselves from the lure of the nineteenth century, or at least have cut the umbilical cord. Yet in the larger sense we probably deceive ourselves. There is nothing new, or strange, in that: epochs of history do not divide themselves at the convenience of the calendar, each century neatly defined and self-contained; and where major thrusts and evolutions are concerned there is still unlikely to be a clear delineation, a precise dividing line between cause and effect.

The roots of modern music, as of modern psychology, philosophy and politics, are to be found in the nineteenth century. It is impossible to say precisely where 'modern music' began, to lay a finger on a particular year or specific work or theory as the undisputed starting point. It did not, of course, actually 'begin' anywhere, as by some sudden stroke of propagation and inspiration, any more than any other of the modern 'movements' had precisely definable beginnings. Béla Bartók once said: 'In art there are only slow or fast developments. Essentially it is a matter of evolution rather than revolution.' If the nineteenth century has to be characterized by a single work or term, it would have to be 'evolutionary'. But if a specific declaration has to be made for the point where modern music began, it might well be the opening bars of *Tristan und Isolde*, with their tonal quicksands and unresolved discords. Even then it would not mean all that much, either historically or aesthetically; all the same, it could still be taken as a viable point of convenience. Though some, like Adele T. Katz in *Challenge to Musical Tradition*[4], have argued that Wagner's invalidating of the older harmonic techniques by a process of overextension was in fact his 'tragedy', and that he was at heart a sound diatonic composer, the truth is that Wagner's extreme exploitation of chromaticism had become inevitable long before *Tristan*, and that his no less inevitable raising of it to a leading principle led in the course of natural musical evolution to atonality and serialism. In the same way, the spiritual disintegration and emotional breakdown of the European tradition across the turn of the nineteenth and twentieth centuries, exposed in musical compositions as varied as Richard Strauss's *Salome* and *Elektra*, Schoenberg's *Pierrot Lunaire*, Stravinsky's *Rite of Spring*, spinning off Mahler's Sixth symphony and *Song of the Earth*, was both inevitable and foreseen, given the fundamental challenge of the new evolutionary situation following the 'knowledge explosion' with which European man found himself confronted.

Wagner himself was aware of the danger, of the slide towards moral collapse and psychological alienation, of the internal tensions building to a point where some kind of cataclysmic disaster became no longer avoidable. That it came most obviously in physical terms, in two world wars and the rise and fall of the Hitler Reich, was due partly to Germany's central position in Europe and partly to the way the inner tensions nearly always find release in physical terms. But Wagner, while he saw the dangers and sought to counter them, was also profoundly aware of the true evolutionary thrust, of the tremendous wave breaking inside the human soul and psyche which during his mature lifetime gathered force and to which his own creative energy was dedicated. In fact, however, that idea, with its corollary of a deep-seated belief in the inevitability of progress, was not in itself an illusion so much as a correct assumption erroneously formulated. The crudity and naïvety came in the misconception that what is 'new' is necessarily 'better', and that in the realm of the arts in particular every major development climbs to fashion and popularity on the back of some superseded and therefore outmoded predecessor. Every true work of art exists in its own right and therefore cannot be judged qualitatively against something different and only superficially related, is autonomous and can never be superseded or supersede anything else, however much it may present itself or may appear as 'revolutionary'. No real artist ever believed otherwise: one has only to read the published writings of Arnold Schoenberg, often facilely thought of as the arch-iconoclast who deliberately rejected all that had gone before him, to see how absurd such an idea is. In Wagner's case the problem is more complex: Wagner's prolix didactic writings may seem at first sight to propagate the notion that the new composite artform he advocated must sweep all before it, reduce all previous operatic and musico-dramatic achievement to a shallow and unimportant form of primitivism. But Wagner never said, or even implied, that. It is an idea that comes from a superficial and inattentive view of what he actually did say and preach. It is a simple case of misrepresentation.

But Wagner was enmeshed in his subjective struggles to define and clarify his visionary conceptions as dictated by his particular genius, in which the creative was energized by the theoretical, the theoretical essential as a preliminary to the full emergence of his creative power. And this need to theorize in advance of creating inevitably led him into byways and ideas that swarmed in the heady air of that teeming age. At the deeper level, Wagner never held or argued that his own work would automatically invalidate that of Bach, Mozart, Beethoven, any of the great composers who had gone before him; indeed, like every true artist, he believed that his work would justify and vindicate the best in the past. If he challenged certain areas of the past, that again was necessary and inevitable; for the specific bias of his genius led him into opposition with certain ideas from the past as it propounded new paths into the future. No one, whoever he or she may be, can accept everything from the past, even what is hallowed by custom and tradition, for that way lies a moribund 'traditionalism' which spells death to art and all creative endeavour. It is always a matter of individual selection. Nor, in the technical aspect of Wagner's dramas, does one thing cancel out another: the juxtaposition of the saturated chromaticism and 'endless melody' of *Tristan* and the broad diatonicism and set pieces of *Meistersinger* at one point in his creative life, and the two techniques brought into a new and subtle relationship in *Parsifal*, shows that Wagner was no narrow-minded pedant tied head and tail to his own theorizing. It reveals instead the breadth and potency of his vision, the innermost vitality of the influence of his theoretical thinking upon his creative work.

Wagner, as I say, scented the danger inherent in Romanticism and in late nineteenth-century art and society. True man of his time, he saw art as salvation and redemption for a sick world, the artist (meaning thereby himself first of all) as high priest. This, as much as practical advantage, even practical necessity, lay behind the creation of the Festival Theatre at Bayreuth, and certainly inspired the injunction that *Parsifal*, the supreme redemptive work, should never be performed except in that holy temple. In this sense, Wagner's life, at one level so obviously, even blatantly, profane, was in its profoundest essence all through a concentration and dedication to the cause of art as a sacred act of redemption and purification. And that too, in one of its major aspects, is nineteenth century all over. The great Wagnerian scheme and concept was in truth cosmic; but then so by the end was the century's view of itself. The two made a good and indissoluble pair, inseparably and eternally linked, embracing the high summer and sunset glow of Romanticism, and leading ultimately to the degradation and perversion of the total Romantic impulse.

In fault and virtue alike they were well matched, Richard Wagner and his century. The Wagnerian sins of magniloquence, bombast, crudity, egotism, exaggerated rhetoric, almost every kind of active engorgement, were also characteristic sins of the century. That the sins were in both cases only one side of the picture and the side that is most likely to be overemphasized and itself exaggerated, only reinforces the point.

Wagner's fecundity as a composer for the musical theatre was more than matched by the prolixity of his prose writings justifying himself and his practice, both artistic and non-artistic. And if we take note of the capacious source material of his music dramas, it is clear that he was also a voracious reader, willing to plough through a virtually unending stream of volumes of history and mythology, often drawing wrong conclusions but digging for gold and finding it as he turned page upon page of old books, transmuting what he found to his taste and his advantage as his fertile imagination prompted. He did everything upon the grandest scale; it wore him out in the end, that and the incessant tussle to have his own way, in worthy and unworthy causes, but it stamped him again with the indelible mark and temper of his times, an all-or-nothing man through and through.

Yet it is damaging illusion to suppose that everything Wagner did that was not immediately related to the creation of his masterworks was irrelevant and a waste of time better spent elsewhere. Some of it was; but that was inevitable. There is waste in every life and it has to come out. If it does not, if it is allowed to remain concealed and suppressed, it may clog the free running of the creative juices. In any case, his involvement in politics, philosophy, psychology, metaphysics, vegetarianism and all the rest of it was a necessary consequence of his cast of temperament, of the kind of man he was. Precisely because he saw art as the salvation of the world and himself as high priest, he had to range beyond the strict confines of that art; because his conceptions were indeed cosmic, he had to confront and tackle everything everywhere. Only by so doing could he fulfil himself and his destiny; become *in toto* Richard Wagner, man of his century and his nation, its foremost spokesman and ultimately its redeemer.

The Wagnerian achievement now belongs to history, to the continuing process that, for better or worse, has brought the world to its present state and condition. Yet, though it grew out of and belongs to a specific context of history, the influence and enrichment of that achievement is permanent and inextinguishable, as the context itself is inescapable and ineradicable in the collective and individual unconscious.

Art as catharsis and purification, let alone as redemption, is not an idea that finds much favour today. The intellectual fashion of the middle years of the twentieth century has long been set resolutely against it. Art today, in many of its contemporary manifestations, has more the aspect of an emetic. Yet the idea itself is neither old nor new; it was simply that the nineteenth century was one of the periods in history when it came to a head in a particular and spectacular form. In that form it was a specifically Romantic attitude and flowering, a facet of the rejection of limitation and the quarrel between mortality and immortality, between the finite and infinite, which was one of the Romantic era's leading characteristics and the essence of the Romantic protest. If today we are more conscious of mortality and limitation, have opted for various forms of determinism and believe that ultimately we are not responsible for our actions, that simply means that we have backed down under the combined pressures of history and scientific theory from the position of those old Romantics who gave the last century its essential force and flavour. That century ended in defeatism, due largely to its failure to answer its own deepset existential questions, and so led inevitably to collapse and disaster and thus to the contemporary predicament.

In order to understand both the disaster and the predicament it is necessary to look continually to the historical roots. We may be wiser and braver, or we may be stupider and more cowardly; we may be wiser and more cowardly or stupider and braver; we may be disillusioned or the victims of even greater illusions: whichever way it is and in whatever combination, we are still caught up in the creative crisis which came to a head in the nineteenth century and produced both its initial optimism and its final pessimism, its 'bond with night and death'. Again, this is nowhere more completely exemplified than in the life and work of Richard Wagner. If it can be argued that Wagner's great edifices, for all their magnificence, contained the seeds of destruction, the potentiality for corruption and perversion, could be seen as the harbingers of disintegration, that may well be because we still do not see Wagner's life and work whole. We ignore the real meaning of *Parsifal* which, significantly, Hitler banned at Bayreuth during the war. The Siegfried image remains both too literal and too crude. The meaning of Siegfried's death, like that of *Parsifal*, is taken too much at face value. The burning of Valhalla should have led to a new era of creativity and genuine progress; instead it turned to bitter ashes and the stench of death and corruption which could only be expurgated by a renewed cycle and in the farthest sense has probably not been expurgated at all, only set upon yet another, if slightly biased, cycle.

We need to know about Wagner and the nineteenth century. Much that we do now know about both they could not have known about themselves. It is part of our superior knowledge, our evolutionary heritage. But it is necessary continually to readjust the focus and the perspectives, or such superior knowledge as we may have will avail us little.

CHAPTER ONE

EARLY YEARS

Wagner was a born man of the theatre; not as stage-struck loon, with feet striving from the cradle for a first tentative hold on the boards; not as actor, however histrionic the nature and temperament, though that too had a small early part to play; but as dyed-in-the-wool dramatic operator with all that implies. His involvement in and with the theatre was as deep and far-reaching as his involvement with his age and his century. If the relationship between music and drama in the nineteenth century took new directions and assumed newly integrated dimensions, it was Wagner's own achievement that made it uniquely so. Yet it was always inherent in the existential currents of the age itself, not something added to or superimposed upon it by the magnitude of one man's genius. After Beethoven, music's expressive powers were predominantly dramatic, and it was inevitable that the dramatic force injected into 'pure' music by Beethoven should mate with the explicitly dramatic nature of the theatre in new and greatly enlarged ways. Wagner's sure instinct led him to discover the key in Beethoven, partly through *Fidelio*, where Beethoven himself had tentatively propounded it, but even more in the Ninth symphony where the implications of combining voices with fully developed symphonic music suggested new dimensions for both.

Wagner's literary and dramatic gifts in fact revealed themselves before his purely musical gifts. And this is to some extent reinforced by the pattern of his childhood. The circumstances of his entry into the world were curious. At his birth, on 22 May 1813, his legal father, Karl Friedrich Wilhelm Wagner, was a police official of the town of Leipzig. Little Richard was the ninth child of Karl Friedrich and his wife Johanna (née Pätz). He did not choose a family of markedly artistic proclivities but an unremarkable *petit-burgeois* establishment of modest, if solid, local standing. To look for an inheritance of artistic gifts directly from either of his legal parents hardly seems at first sight a profitable undertaking. Many musicians have traced their particular gift to their mother; but Richard Wagner certainly did not, and could not. Indeed, his mother, though no doubt an excellent woman in other ways, appears to have been virtually uneducated. The daughter of a mill-owner and married at fourteen, she was culturally ignorant and remained unambitious in that direction all her life, though she appears to have shown considerable strength and resource of character.

However, all this suddenly became at least half irrelevant. Six months to the day after Richard's birth, on 22 November, Karl Friedrich died of typhoid fever, reputedly caught from the corpses left lying about the streets of Leipzig in the wake of Napoleon's invading armies. Enter with less than a year's delay, Ludwig Geyer as stepfather. Geyer was a painter and actor, a man of volatile temperament and some artistic accomplishment. Geyer waited some months before marrying Karl Friedrich's widow only, it seems, in deference to social custom; seven months after the marriage Johanna gave birth to a daughter, Cäcilie. It is clear that Geyer and Johanna had been more than just good friends some while before Karl Friedrich's death. The question therefore resolves itself into: who was Richard Wagner's natural father? Evidence that Geyer and not Karl Friedrich Wagner was the composer's real male parent has come to light and been sifted by scholars and musical historians. It became a hotly disputed point, one controversy among many that have surrounded, and in some instances continue to surround, the figure of Richard Wagner. And as the evidence has been examined, analysed, quarrelled over, the likelihood of Ludwig Geyer's claim to that celebrated parenthood being substantiated have strengthened. It is still not certain; but it seems probable that had the record been straight and the facts admitted openly, the great master of music drama would have come down to us not as Richard Wagner but as Richard Geyer.

If Geyer was indeed Wagner's father, a number of interesting speculations arise. It is perhaps an irrelevance to insist that but for Karl Friedrich living as Johanna's official husband into 1813, we might now be thinking and talking about the Geyer rather than the Wagner music dramas, with the consequent adjectival 'Geyerian' instead of the more rotund and sonorous 'Wagnerian'. A small point; even so, significant in its way. A large one is the fact that the child was pitchforked suddenly into an atmosphere and environment more theatrical and artistic than any he had been born to or could have expected had Karl Friedrich not succumbed to the typhoid. This unquestionably had a positive effect on young Richard's formative years; and if Geyer was indeed his father makes it likely that here was the true source of his artistic inheritance. It might even appear that the sportive gods, having assured him an appropriate name, then rectified their mistake in setting him in the wrong environment by delivering him into the paternal hands of Ludwig Geyer.

And indeed, Geyer himself appears to have taken on Johanna and her seven surviving children as something of an act of penance, as atonement for a perpetrated wrong. That wrong is now generally believed to have been the fathering of Richard Wagner while her husband still lived. What would have happened if Karl Friedrich had not died when he did is another question that invites speculation but can never be answered. The whole business is complicated and contentious; and there will not now be enough evidence forthcoming (unless we are unexpectedly lucky) to end the argument one way or the other. That Wagner did come to regard himself as Geyer's son is indicated at several points, notably in correspondence with Cäcilie in 1870 in which he refers to 'our father Geyer'. This could be simply a form of words, and Wagner in any case was a man who could believe anything he wanted at any particular time to believe. But he had no strong reason for arguing on Geyer's behalf unless he genuinely believed it to be true. He had long suspected it, and in 1870 he came into possession of letters that finally convinced him. He was aware, too, of Geyer's feelings of guilt and desire to atone for a wrong committed. On the surface, it is a thoroughly Wagnerian situation, though in fact there is no direct parallel in any of Wagner's works. There is plenty of guilt and atonement in the operas and music dramas, but none on this familiar plane, an omission which may suggest that for all his lifelong tendency to plunge in at the deep end of any subject that caught his fancy, and in spite of his unquenchable egotism, his true dramatic instinct was more meticulous and more selective, not to be sidetracked by commonplace and obvious autobiographical references of that kind. Autobiographical material there certainly is, but it is invariably on a higher, more totally assimilated level than some mere repetition of a mundane circumstance might prompt. It is for the most part genuinely sublimated.

The argument, sometimes brought forward by those of a doggedly psychoanalytical persuasion, that problems of identity which recur from time to time in the Wagnerian saga indicate that Wagner himself was unsure who by parentage he really was, do not carry much weight. The question of identity was a leading motif of the nineteenth century and of the Romantics in particular. It was all a part of the Romantics' existential quest for liberation from materialism and determinism, and was sharply refocussed by the evolutionary theories of Lamarck, the question that is not of the identity of the individual only but of man himself.[1]

Even so, it does not end there. What if Geyer, as was once widely supposed and as the name suggests, was of Jewish origin? Did Wagner suspect it, resent it, and so make it a factor in his own attitude to Judaism? Again, the question is important, and not only because of Wagner's reputation for anti-Semitism. It is important because Wagner's entire life-work was based upon ideas and theories that ran counter to the basic tenets of Judaism – and that has nothing to do with any form of anti-Semitism. The trouble with Wagner and the 'Jewish question' is simply this: largely because of the horrifying experiences of recent history, it is still virtually impossible to discuss it and related problems in the context of contemporary life in a rational and intelligent manner: one whiff of a criticial analysis on any plane, and charges of 'anti-Semitism', 'racism' or whatever fly around with no thought for precise meanings or accuracy of intention, as slogans instead of genuine ideas, so that a truly prejudice-free attitude, far from being brought nearer, as most today desire and earnestly wish, is driven farther and farther out towards the bounds of practical impossibility.

Geyer's ancestry has been examined and investigated, but with no indisputable conclusions. The census of opinion is that he was not of Jewish origin: his family, like the Wagners, can be traced back into the sixteenth century and appears solidly German. It matters little to us today; but there can be no doubt that in his own view of himself and his artistic mission, it would have been of singular importance to Wagner. It would have been far more important than the later and easily definable circumstances of his 'humiliation' at the hands of the Parisians, among whom Meyerbeer and Halévy, both Jews, reigned supreme. That would only have acted as reinforcement to his feelings about Semitism, and could not have been the fundamental cause of them. In any case, though in a general sense the humiliation was real enough, he received many kindnesses at the hands of Jewish friends, not least from Meyerbeer himself. Certainly Wagner and Minna were driven near to despair, and still nearer to destitution, in Paris; but it was not on account of Meyerbeer or any 'Jewish conspiracy'. Meyerbeer helped and befriended him, as he helped and befriended many others who later attacked him when his power and influence were spent. On the familiar basis that one attacks most virulently those to whom one is under obligation, Wagner may well have found fuel to fire his anti-Semitic ideas in the bitter memories of the Parisian disaster and his personal misfortunes, and in the entirely predicatable course of time and events have used them as props for pseudo-philosophical theorizing.

Although too much scorn has been cast upon Wagner's essays in philosophy and metaphysics, there is no doubt that some of them were the result, in part at least, of the subjective rationalization of prejudices. Yet even at its worst, it can hardly be compared with the way in which Hitler's violent hatred of the Jews can be traced back, as starting point at least, to the time immediately after the First World War when he and two other soldiers shared a Jewish prostitute in Vienna and caught syphilis from her.

It is nearer the truth to see Wagner's so-called 'anti-Semitism', his fundamental thoughts on the Jews and Judaism in general, as existing substantially apart from any personal encounters, disagreeable or otherwise, in Paris or anywhere else. On the other hand, if Wagner, believing Geyer to be his real father, had also believed, rightly or wrongly, that Geyer was of Jewish origin, that might well have signified. In the light of his intellectual as well as his emotional feeling about the Jews, a suspected Jewish parenthood could well have reflected upon his inner development, caused him exasperation, helped to confirm him in his view that the gods were against him and that he was obliged to battle against a kind of providential hostility in order to make his mark on the world, especially since his anti-Semitic leanings were primarily not social and personal, but artistic. Again, though, if it really is the case that the possibility of his 'father Geyer' being a Jew made him uncomfortable and prickly, it was neither overwhelming nor undermining in its effect. Wagner always spoke of Geyer with respect and affection, and in any case his theories and ideas in this, as in most other things, were not the simple result of personal disappointments and retrospective petulances. Only on the transient and totally superficial planes were they ever that, whatever else may be the ultimate truth about them.

Whatever Geyer's, and therefore probably Wagner's own, ancestry may or may not have been, the direct influence of the 'stepfather' was short lived. Ludwig Geyer did not survive Karl Friedrich Wagner by much more than eight years, for on 30 September 1821 he died of a lung complaint. Thus, before he was ten years old Richard Wagner had lost two male 'parents' and his mother two husbands. It was not, from his family aspect, an auspicious beginning.

All the same, Geyer's early influence was considerable – and wholly beneficial. In his autobiographical *Mein Leben*, Wagner referred to Geyer as 'this excellent man who moved my family to Dresden when I was two. . .' In fact, Geyer's presence was materially felt even earlier. Immediately after Richard's birth, Johanna fled with the boy from Leipzig to join Geyer at Teplitz. Exactly why has never been satisfactorily explained. It can hardly have been to escape from the perils of the Napoleonic adventure, which were currently endangering life and property in Leipzig. Teplitz was no more 'safe' than anywhere else. More likely, it was to present Geyer with a first sight of the infant, and this lends additional support to Geyer's claim to the parenthood, although it could have been for some other and more devious reason. It was not until a few months after Karl Friedrich's death that Geyer 'moved my family to Dresden' where he, Geyer, was attached to the Royal Court Players.

Geyer not only took the young Wagner's education in hand – most effectively and considerately by all accounts, including Wagner's own – but actually bestowed on him the name Geyer, so that until he was fifteen and went off to school in Leipzig, Richard Wagner was known to his boyhood friends in Dresden as Richard Geyer. Only after he had gone to Leipzig again did he resume the name of Wagner.

Geyer did not wish the boy to follow him into the theatre as an actor. His first ambition was that young Richard should become a painter. But despite initial instruction to that end, the lad showed little aptitude and the project was dropped. From the outset, however, he revealed a passion for the theatre. His family connections were close and certainly reinforced his own allegiance. One of his brothers and three of his sisters went onto the stage, two of them into the opera. But for young Richard the theatre was infinitely more than a profession and an occupation: it soon claimed his entire life. Small, delicate, abnormally sensitive and with penetrating blue eyes set in an outsize head, his vivid imagination was stirred and animated by anything and everything to do with the theatre. He was taken to see Geyer act, and afterwards would wander around backstage immeasurably excited and stimulated. In particular, Weber's *Der Freischütz*, with its supernatural ambience, produced an overwhelming impression. Terror and delight were inextricably mixed in his reactions; so much so that afterwards inanimate objects in his bedroom would suddenly seem to come to life and he would shriek aloud in fear and horror. There seems to have been something about it of a real-life version of that imaginative recognition which a century later was to lead to the Colette/Ravel miniature masterpiece *L'Enfant et les sortilèges*. Clearly that imaging-forth of the born dramatist was at work in him from the beginning; that sense of created reality which transcends and in its way purifies everyday actuality.

The idea that the dramatist uses his art and craft to escape from the contemporary world by inventing another nearer to the heart's desire is at best suspect, at worst a feeble illusion. It is perhaps true on a superficial plane; but for the true dramatist, the uncompromising creative artist, the opposite is nearer the mark: the art in a profound sense transforms and illuminates the world in which it takes place. Put in its simplest and most self-absorbing form, this is no doubt very much a nineteenth-century view, a Romantic assumption linked to the redemptive conception of art. But in a larger sense it is not confined to any specific time or century. Mozart's greatest music, the least self-conscious art of all, is essentially an idealization of the eighteenth-century aristocratic world with, as in *The Marriage of Figaro*, the revolutionary undertones endemic to the period integrally recognized; Palestrina's music performed a broadly similar function for the Catholic world of the sixteenth century. Only a crude and imitative 'realism' is indelibly tied to the surface aspects of the particular world out of which it emanates, just as only that form of evasive 'entertainment' which ignores all contemporary realities is properly called 'escapist'. As Verdi once perspicaciously remarked: 'It is better to invent reality than to copy it.' Indeed, to copy, to present without invention, is only another form of escapism. 'Realism' is simply another way of hiding from reality. For the artist, of whom Wagner was an outstanding example, invention becomes synonymous with transformation, in the deepest and most penetrating sense, a releasing of the true inner vitality which in the workaday world is overlain by the trivial and the superficially 'contemporary', than which nothing dates or decays more rapidly. And the desire to transform was insistent in Wagner from childhood. In this sense true artistic creation is not an escape from reality but an escape into reality.

His formal education was unremarkable. He was sent first to the village school at Possendorf near Dresden, under Pastor Wetzel, but had to return within a year when Geyer was on his deathbed. In 1822 he entered the Dresden Kreuzschule, where he remained until 1827. The year between Geyer's death and his entry into the Kreuzschule was spent at Eisleben, where his brother Julius was apprenticed to Geyer's brother, a goldsmith. Here Wagner briefly attended another local school, run by one Pastor Alt, but where the actual teaching was in the hands of a capable man called Weiss. The Eisleben interlude was undertaken in an attempt to relieve the strain on his mother at the time of her second bereavement, and also to get him away from the atmosphere of a bereaved household. Thus the natural course of young Wagner's childhood was once again interrupted by family death. It does not appear to have disturbed him unduly.

The real process of his education began when he entered the Dresden Kreuzschule. Yet even here the patterns of the future were not at once revealed. He showed a marked ability and enthusiasm for writing verses; and he was increasingly fascinated by Greek tragedy and mythology. He also discovered a parallel passion for Shakespeare. For the niceties of academic study he had little inclination and less patience, finding the demands of Greek grammar and syntax a particular bore. In this at least there was a pointer to the future: all his life Richard Wagner was determined to go, and have, his own way, and if it upset the conventions of learning, or anything else, that was too bad. At this time, though he was still only fourteen, he deliberately left the school friend's family with whom he had been lodged and set up for himself in a tiny garret, subsisting on 'thin Saxon coffee' and a few other basic necessaries, occupying his spare hours making translations from the Greek as well as trying his embryo hand at vast tragedies on the Shakespearean model. One of these, a variant of the Hamlet theme called *Leubald und Adelaïde*, he sportively recalled as a piece in which he killed off so many characters (forty-two in all) that he was obliged to call them back as ghosts in order to have any kind of denouement, or even to finish it at all. Labouring away in his garret deep into the night, he was slowly finding his line, probing the future, however ineptly, with the kind of dogged determination that was to characterize his entire life and work. 'Freedom above all,' he might have cried, echoing Beethoven. His *métier* for the time being was almost exclusively for the poetic drama. Music, as a major and complementary force in his life, still had to bide its time.

He had taken, as a child, a few piano lessons, learnt enough to find his way around and play what he wanted to play. The seed was planted: it might not yet have taken firm root; but it was already more or less inescapable. And it did not pass unnoticed. The story goes that when Geyer lay dying, the distracted Johanna sent the boy into an adjacent room to play some pieces in order to take his mind off the imminence of death and to alleviate the dying man's final hours; and that Geyer, almost with his parting breath, asked: 'What if he should have a talent for music?'

What, indeed! It was at that time a pertinent, perceptive question. If

Geyer had lived, he would not have been astonished at the development of his progeny. He always had faith in the boy. It was something more than a dying man's moment of insight.

Wagner is often held up as a significant example among the great composers of the late developer and slow starter. This is only a part truth, a misunderstanding of the totality of his full creative gifts. Certainly, he was not musically precocious; he displayed none of the instant aptitude for music, either with an instrument or in composition, of such other 'late developers' as Beethoven and Brahms, and nothing at all of the outright precosity of Mozart and Mendelssohn. He did not really take to music until he was past fifteen – and that, by normal computations, is definitely 'late'. That he was deeply affected by music from his earliest childhood is not in question. Nor is it in any way remarkable: many children who subsequently develop no particular faculty for music are affected in this way. The sounds and vibrations of music frequently touch a child's imagination and nervous system vividly but with no defined or specific implication. It does not necessarily mean anything, one way or another. There is no suggestion that during his earliest years Richard Wagner swam in the waters of music with that unthinking ease and natural spontaneity that mark the childhoods of most accredited musical geniuses, whether in the realm of creation or of execution. In that respect at least he appears to have been an exception to a loosely formulated rule.

Two factors, however, militate against the general assumption about Wagner. First, the specific nature of his genius, working as it did on more than one plane, caused its evolution to be omni- rather than uni-directional; second, when he did come fully to music he at once exhibited those qualities of natural propensity and immediate identification which mark out and clearly define virtually all cases of authentic musical genius. Musicians have tended to stake too exclusive a claim to Richard Wagner; they have been in the habit of playing down his other, perhaps less substantial but no less essential gifts, and so have diverted themselves from seeing him whole and in the round, of insisting upon the fundamentally composite nature of his creative power.

Wagner's genius was of an unusual and exceptional kind. Not necessarily in quality – though it was exceptional in that too, if hardly unique – but in its basic constitution. While his achievements as a musician were the most remarkable and far-reaching, they cannot be disassociated from his achievements as dramatist and master of stage craft. Without these latter the former could not have come to full fruition, at least not in the form we know. This is the central point about Wagner, and the one that most closely links him with his age and his century and his total involvement with it in all its various and contrasting aspects. He cannot be seen from one side alone, even predominantly, as master musician only, the rest unimportant, but must be accepted and judged from that all-embracing standpoint which alone gives full substance and relevance to his life and work. He assuredly was a great musician; but he was not only a great musician, as Beethoven was only a great musician (or a great musician only), as Schubert was, and Brahms likewise; also Bach, Haydn, Bruckner, Mahler, Sibelius, Stravinsky; even Mozart, despite his mastery of opera, and Verdi, whose entire lifework was dedicated to the theatre. Mozart and Verdi, though masters of dramatic music for the stage (Mozart, of course, was master of music in every form), were not themselves dramatists: they set other people's libretti and left the staging to the professionals.

Wagner, by contrast, was not even simply a musician who happened to write his own libretti: he was one for whom the act of creation encompassed the musical and dramatic functions at one and the same time (though not chronologically: the poem invariably came first; but it was always made with the total work in mind, text and music integral in Wagner's mind), the two concurrently fertilizing each other, the interlinking between them so deep-running and so subtle that it is impossible to slip a knife, even the keenest bladed, between the joints and joins. In the event, when Wagner's composite genius was working at full pressure (and it includes staging and production as well) there were no joints and joins. And because he was creating, as he saw it, a new kind of musical drama, he was obliged to attend to everything about it, even its financing, and had ultimately to build a theatre to accommodate it. Farther even than that, because he believed in his work as the artform of the future, the transformation of the world, no less, and so required a transformed world for its total acceptance, the two again working in perpetual interaction, he felt compelled to propound not only the artistic and aesthetic theories necessary to the clarification of his own thoughts on the true relationship between music and drama, but philosophical, political, economic and most other kinds besides. It was all part of a single indivisible process. He may not have succeeded equally in all departments; being human (though he would have admitted that only with reluctance) he could not succeed equally everywhere. But he had to try: his genius had to work itself out in all possible directions (and in a few impossible ones too, in the way of genius) in order that he might pull everything into the net of the completed artwork itself; indeed, so that he might ultimately create in final reality that Holy Art towards the realization of which his life was obstinately directed.

This is not to adopt the hagiology of the old-time Perfect Wagnerite, for whom every work as well as every note was not only Holy Art but Holy Writ. It is simply to define the precise nature and constitution of his creative energies. We are not compelled to agree with everything that Wagner wrote, or did; to take without salt or reservation every page of larded philosophizing at its face value; to set him upon the level of Shakespeare or Goethe or Ibsen in poetic drama, or to class him with Aeschylus, Sophocles and Euripides as tragic poet. But it is necessary to understand what he was doing and what he was trying to do and why he was doing it in every aspect of his work and activity, or there is no possibility of understanding him and it *in toto*. To isolate the music and leave the rest interred in a bygone and superseded age is to diminish the whole, the music along with it, and to introduce an irreversible degradation which effectively prevents a clearing of both the historical and the contemporary perspectives.

Here is the reason why Wagner's early development appears to have been slow and uncertain and without the kind of immediate unconscious thrust forward that marks the growth of less complex, though possibly in some instances higher, manifestations of genius. It was the multiplicity of Wagner's creative faculties that made the initial steps seem hesitant and apparently without a clear focal point.

It was when he went to the Nicholaischule in Leipzig that Wagner's musical faculty was vigorously awakened. Here he disliked the academic routine even more than he had disliked it in Dresden. He was disgusted with the Greek work he was set, had trouble with mathematics which he did not trouble to overcome, and generally came to eschew interest in schoolwork altogether. But he discovered Beethoven.

It was the turning point. He had encountered the occasional Beethoven work before, notably the overture to *Fidelio*. But now it was different. The *Egmont* music, some piano sonatas, above all the Seventh symphony, which he heard at the Gewandhaus and which made a tremendous impact on him. A new world had opened: to his idol Shakespeare he now added the idol Beethoven. He had ecstatic dreams about Beethoven and Shakespeare, 'and talked with them'. Drama and music had come together in his life: they were to remain together as long as he lived.

In Leipzig, too, he consorted much with his Uncle Adolf, brother of the dead Karl Friedrich. Adolf Wagner was a free-thinking scholar with a strong taste for the Greeks, Shakespeare and Dante and the other classic writers, about whom he talked incessantly with the young Richard, who was only too willing to listen. He sent his uncle the gory drama *Leubald und Adelaïde*, at the same time announcing that his schooldays were over and that henceforth he would make his own way in the world, learning only what he wanted to learn. Adolf was obliged to convey this piece of news to the Wagner/Geyer family, who were considerably disquieted and tried to remonstrate. But it was no use: when Richard Wagner, young or old, made up his mind, nothing would or could stop him. He was disappointed that his uncle did not fall in enthusiastically with the plan; but he was already accustomed to disappointment and had learnt to take it in his stride. The stride was not yet so gigantic as it later became; none the less, it sufficed. His attendances at the Nicholaischule, never meticulous, had by now become so irregular that the parting was inevitable.

But the real importance of the decision and the family opposition to it lay elsewhere. In the rebuff, through some mysterious process of compensation, came 'a wonderful secret solace'. No less than this: Wagner came suddenly to the recognition that his dramatic work could only be assessed in conjunction with the music he resolved to write for it. At least, it appeared to be a sudden recognition: more likely it was the bursting forth into conscious recognition of something that had been gestating for some time deep inside him. Either way, he saw how it was and must be for him. 'I intend to start composing immediately,' he wrote.

It was entirely typical of Wagner that although he had no musical training and knew nothing of the techniques of composition, he none the less resolved to get down to the business of providing the necessary music for his plays without further delay; typical of his unquenchable tenacity of purpose and determination to ride roughshod over all difficulties and every obstacle. What had to be done, had to be done; there was never any alternative.

The full significance of this recognition was immense. It was hardly less than the genesis of the entire world and ethos of Wagnerian music drama as it was to evolve over the next half century and more. The understanding that his poetic drama was only one half of a composite whole led Wagner to an immediate and passionate absorption in music for its own sake, but even more importantly to a conception of the fusion of the two, music and drama, that acted like the positive and negative poles of electricity to release new and virtually limitless energy.

To begin with, the study of musical technique was determined but haphazard. He acquired a copy of J. R. Logier's *Méthode des General basses* as his first musical textbook. At the same time, he took lessons from a member of the Leipzig orchestra, a violinist named Müller, in harmony and counterpoint. But again the fiery temperament and imagination of Richard Wagner fell foul of orthodoxy and conventional practice. He found little to inspire him in either the text of Logier or the instructions of Müller: the processes of formal education were still not giving him what he wanted, less on account of their innate inadequacy than because they could never satisfy him, being as they were (and are) designed not for emerging genius but for some common denominator of human intelligence and ambition. Richard Wagner was neither 'average' nor 'normal'; therefore nothing designed for the average and the normal served any useful purpose for him. He was not alone in that: Beethoven before him had experienced much the same thing, even at the hands of the illustrious Haydn.

This is familiar territory; it is basically true for all men and women of challenging genius in the making. Educational methods were not designed for them and cannot assist their inner evolution except incidentally and accidentally. But with Wagner the position was given an additional twist on account of his vision of himself as the unique creator of the artwork of the future, of a transformed and tranforming art, an idea at work in his subconscious long before it was consciously formulated and before he was capable of beginning to translate the dream into reality, or even of understanding its implications except intuitively.

All the same, even a young man of Wagner's anarchistic tendencies and undiminishing self-esteem cannot get by only on short cuts and turnings of the back on the fundamental necessities of learning. He therefore plunged into the study of scores of Hadyn, Mozart and Beethoven. However reckless and self-willed he may have been, young Wagner was never afraid of hard work once he had determined to his own satisfaction exactly what it was he wanted to do. He began to compose instrumental and vocal pieces on lines suggested by those models. He copied out Beethoven's symphonies and made a piano reduction of the Ninth, which he offered to Schott for publication. Schott declined the offer, but found the enterprise sufficiently encouraging to send him a copy of the *Missa solemnis*. And it was a bold enterprise for a young student at that time: in 1829 the Ninth symphony was regarded as almost impossibly 'difficult', all but incomprehensible. But it had totally overwhelmed the young Wagner, even though he had yet to hear an adequate performance of it. With *Fidelio*, however, it was different. Also in 1829 Wagner heard the great dramatic soprano Wilhelmine Schröder-Devrient, who was later to create some of the soprano roles in his own operas (including Senta in *The Flying Dutchman*), in *Fidelio* – and he accounted it, more than thirty years later, among the most powerful experiences of his entire life. It served now to confirm him in both his devotion to Beethoven and his passion for the musical theatre.

In the summer of 1830 Wagner entered the Thomasschule in Leipzig, as preparation for the university. At that time there were revolutionary outbreaks in various European capitals, notably Paris, Brussels and Warsaw. The reverberations were felt throughout Germany and reached Leipzig. Wagner, whose ambition to enter the university was prompted more by a desire to share in student life than to buckle down to academic study, associated himself with the students and was involved in a certain amount of the violence and rowdyism that accompanied the revolutionary fervour. Hints and pointers to the future, to 1848 and beyond, were showing themselves in Leipzig in this as in other ways. Already politics had become important to Wagner. He had not yet formulated in his mind the Art Work of the Future, or seen the direction it must take. But he must have sensed it intuitively and knew already that the world must be changed for its wholehearted reception. It was probably as direct and naïvely simple as that to begin with. Yet it was the necessary starting point: if the structure was as yet vague, tentative and to a large extent amorphous, it was still there in embryo.

At the Thomasschule he was no more apt and obedient a pupil than he had been at the earlier Nicholaischule, and for much the same reason. It was the university he had set his sights on, and that for other than academic purposes. He developed habits of heavy drinking and even heavier gambling, in which he invariably came off worst. He also appears to have been quick to issue and accept challenges to duels. He was only a little fellow; but the fires burned hot inside him, hurling lumps of combustible material in all directions.

He finally entered Leipzig University in February 1833, as a music student, but of the second rank and with limited privileges. Even so, he does not appear to have changed his ways significantly: study remained neglected for the student high life.

Yet even a rogue character like Richard Wagner could not continue to escape indefinitely the consequences of educational indifference. He began to sense that if he was to make his way and achieve his ambitions as composer-dramatist and so release his full creative forces, he must attend to the real matter in hand, pay a certain basic minimum in hard work before he could effectively shake the world and make its teeth rattle. His first experience of public performance of a piece of his music only served to confirm that impression. The piece, one of the orchestral overtures he composed as part of his apprentice work, was given on Christmas Day 1830, at the instigation of his friend Heinrich Dorn, director of Leipzig theatre. Dorn conducted; but the result was a fiasco. Giving rein to his already awakened sense of the mystical and the supernatural, Wagner had written out the score in differently coloured inks for strings, woodwind and brass (a practice adopted in another day and a different context by James Joyce in *Ulysses* and *Finnegan's Wake*), though what exactly was supposed to be mystical or supernatural about that is hard to define. It does, however, seem to have had some minor significance for the aspiring composer.

But it was not this harmlessly eccentric piece of business which caused the trouble: that arose from the way the bass drum thumped out a single loud note at close and almost maniacally regular intervals throughout, a miscalculation that began by arousing the audience's curiosity, continued by causing it annoyance, and ended by unleashing its unbridled hilarity. The disaster bit deep into the mind and consciousness of its perpetrator, who never, throughout his life, took kindly to being ridiculed. Few people do, but Richard Wagner was the last to put even a mildly good face on it.

He tried to redeem himself by offering another, and in his own view better piece. It was turned down. One or two small things met with a limited succes; but overall the experiences with the overture seems to have convinced him that some attention to formal study was after all necessary. Accordingly, he took further lessons in harmony and couterpoint as well as general music theory from Theodore Weinlig, Cantor of the Thomasschule and thus successor in J. S. Bach's old appointment. Now once again Wagner's innate faculty for music showed its colours. He spent only six months studying with Weinlig, but during that time he made such progress and learned so much that by the end of it he had absorbed virtually all he needed and was ready to set seriously upon his course. Weinlig was obviously a musician of tact and learning who had the gift of transmitting both his scholarship and his commitment to music (especially to the old Italian vocal music, his particular subject) to an enthusiastic young pupil thirsting for knowledge and guidance. In addition, Weinlig introduced Wagner to the publishing house of Breitkopf & Härtel, who undertook to issue a couple of small piano pieces.

In so far as he evaded or avoided the requirements of a formal education, Wagner was in most respects self-taught. He forged his own way, however unorthodox. The six months with Weinlig appear as an isolated incident wherein he plunged himself wholeheartedly into study. The reason is not hard to define: he exerted himself with Weinlig precisely because he saw, as he had not seen with his earlier tutors, that the learned Cantor could give him what he needed at the moment he himself recognized that he both wanted and needed it. During those six months his vision was concentrated, his energies clearly directed. Maybe if he had applied himself more assiduously both at Leipzig and at Dresden previously he would have come into his full powers that much earlier and with less trouble to himself. Maybe; on the other hand, that is probably another misreading of his character and the true nature of his genius. Being the man and artist he was, he had to go the way he did.

While at Leipzig University Wagner also attended philosophy lectures by Professor Krug and classes in aesthetic under Weiss. These additional studies were essential to the fulfilment of his most comprehensive abilities. These were beginning to emerge, to work their passage in their own predetermined way and according to the laws of their particular constitution.

They were working out in other directions as well, in ways directly related to the currents of thought and feeling of the times, of the patriotic fervours struggling towards formulation and release in Germany and throughout Europe. Wagner became associated with the proscribed 'Young Germany' party initiated by the poet Heinrich Heine. He formed a friendship with Heinrich Laube, and also with Count Vincenz Tsyzkiewicz, who was involved in the clandestine escape of Polish refugees to France. These and other associations were not simply idle gestures: Wagner believed passionately in the cause of German renaissance and liberty in general, especially intellectual liberty, and by involving himself in these activities he ran risks and put his own liberty in peril. In 1832 he accompanied Count Tyszkiewicz on a trip to Moravia, and afterwards himself went on to Vienna. The political as well as the artistic business of Europe was beginning to claim his close attention, to pull him personally into its complex machinations at various levels. It would all make its firm mark on his life and work, to form and shape the pattern of his inner creative life and at the same time to determine the course of his activities. As he grew older the two tended to fuse together, both with each other and with the emerging pattern of the nineteenth century itself, as well as certain highly significant aspects that were to carry over into the twentieth and react powerfully upon it.

For the time being, he may have been a tyro in his art. But the master is already stirring underneath. There are hitches and hindrances ahead, inevitably; and one of them is poor health. In view of the immense labours Wagner was to set himself, and carry through, his constitution was almost comically inadequate. That he was small is neither here nor there; but his intense nervous sensibility caused him no end of trouble. All his life he suffered from a debilitating form of erysipelas. He also had continual trouble with his eyes which, whether out of vanity or negligence, or both, he seems not to have tried to alleviate by resorting to spectacles. In various ways, therfore, his health was not robust. But whatever its shortcomings, it was obliged to support the heavy burdens he elected to place upon it, even though the erysipelas in particular had a lasting effect on his character and his social and domestic ways of life; it was responsible not only for his insistence on being dressed in and surrounded by the softest of fabrics but also for some of the prickliness of his nature.

CHAPTER TWO

OPERA AND TRANSITION

Even after he had served some apprenticeship and, more important, recognized that he must serve it, Wagner's footsteps were still unsure. As a composer of musical drama, still less as a dedicated reformer of the musical theatre, he did not spring forth fully armed like Minerva from the head of Jupiter, a fearsome battle-cry on his lips. Indeed, in view of his later achievements, by which he appears to musical history as a veritable colossus bestriding his century and its artforms, his beginnings seem remarkably tentative. But this is an impression only, less because his beginnings were in a number of respects tentative, feeble even, than because of the reasons behind them. It was his destiny to shake an entire century to its creative foundations, and to do it deliberately, as an act of positive will. He was therefore unlikely to be able to see that task whole and complete from the outset, or to summon out of himself the necessary resources for it without long preparation and continuously evolving hard work and thought.

During and after six months of study with Weinlig, Wagner continued to compose at an ever-increasing rate, and to find publishers for his work. In this he was aided by his family's theatrical connections and achieved some success. The most important of these early compositions was a symphony in C, publicly performed first in Prague and then in Leipzig. The previous year a couple of independent orchestral overtures, plus another to Raupach's *King Enzio*, had been well received at Leipzig Gewandhaus concerts. All these were firmly based upon impeccable models, the symphony full of echoes of Beethoven with some added melodic inheritances from Weber. It is a lively, competent work with a few pouches of originality in its textures, though still lacking any real show of independent genius. Like many a young composer feeling his way towards an autonomous personal style, Wagner attended carefully to his business and 'wrote over' his chosen models and exemplars, in the largest sense. He did not actually 'compose' a symphony or overture on the exact lines of one by a model, altering only the themes; but he did take a model and follow the example with some diligence. Clara Schumann said that the C major symphony was 'as like as two peas' to Beethoven's Seventh; in fact, as Wagner himself indicated, it is much closer to the Beethoven Second, in D. What is not in doubt is that Beethoven was the acknowledged model. The standards were unashamedly classical, with romantic overtones, mostly from Weber but also an echo here and there from Schubert.

One respect in which Wagner was a genuine slow starter was in the matter of earning his own living. At an age when Brahms had been supporting himself by playing the piano in the Hamburg *Lokale* and teaching a motley collection of paying pupils, and Beethoven had become head of his family, Wagner was still supported entirely by his mother and sisters. He had earned miniscule sums for a composition or two; but any suggestion that he could or would support himself by his own efforts was out of order. And no doubt it left him totally unmoved. Later on, when in full possession of his powers and unflinchingly set upon his difficult course, he not only tended to behave as if the world owed him a living, but actually believed that it did. And from his point of view he was probably right. The benedictions he was bestowing upon the entire world, the all-embracing transformation of human life and art and society that he was in the process of bringing about, made him in his own opinion an immense and invaluable gift to humanity; therefore humanity should reward him by giving him the luxuries as well as the necessities of life that he required. The world did not altogether agree, so Wagner formed the habit of solving the problem by running up massive debts. It came to much the same thing in the end, except that the consequent running battles with creditors became annoying or embarrassing, sometimes acutely alarming. At around his twentieth birthday, he hardly appears to have been concerned about it one way or the other. He was content to subsist on his family's bounty, which he accepted without shame or reluctance.

It was not that he neglected work. He worked hard, according to his own conception of work – which meant doing what he wanted to do and little else. Lazy he never was, at any time of his life (although Berlioz did have occasion to admonish him for a 'kind of intellectual indolence' on account of his overuse of *tremolo* effects in *Rienzi* and *The Flying Dutchman*). All the same, the need to earn, if only to acquire independence, soon began to press. There were two possibilities – composition or an appointment. Since he played no instrument adequately and was not yet master of musical technique, teaching, the accepted standby for impecunious musicians, was out of the question. He would have to rely on compositions that could be sold on a resonably regular basis, or some form of appointment that would pay what he urgently needed. Composition really mattered to him; but an appointment might more easily fill the immediate need, supply a temporary advantage.

He planned an opera. It was to be called *Die Hochzeit* ('The Wedding'); and he wrote his own libretto. That was the most significant thing about it: it established him, once and for all in his first venture for the musical stage, not as a setter of other people's libretti but as creator of the composite artwork, music and drama one and indivisible. Never in his life, not even in his apprentice years, did Richard Wagner set a text for the theatre other than his own.

Another Wagnerian feature was the way in which *Die Hochzeit* was conceived under the influence of a love affair. When Wagner went on his travels with Count Tyszkiewicz in 1832 he visited Prague, and there became entangled with the two daughters of Count Pachta, for one of whom, Jenny, he worked up an ardent passion. It came to nothing, and so in the end did the opera. It is said that his sister Rosalie objected to the crudities of the plot – all about a girl who pushes her too-insistent lover out of a window to his death and collapses at the funeral, so giving the game away – and that is why Wagner abandoned the project after writing only a few numbers. That may have been one reason; it almost certainly was not the only one. It was a false start; simply that. But false starts are not necessarily without value; they can help to illuminate dark corners and concentrate the mind by recognition of shortcomings. Of what was composed of *Die Hochzeit*, including the overture, Weinlig had a word of praise for some vocal qualities and compositional competence.

The 'false start' applied also to the romantic aspirations. Perhaps it was not really a 'start' at all (there had been others – from his extreme youth Richard Wagner was a militant activist of the bed, or certainly imagined himself so); but in this particular context it counts as one. It was the first to be linked directly with a dramatic composition. As Mathilde Wesendonk was to be irrevocably associated with the conception and composition of *Tristan und Isolde*, so Jenny Pachta has her small niche as the immediate instigator of the first operatic project fertilized in the mind of its as yet unheralded composer. And if the music that was composed revealed the hand of a tyro who in the not too distant future would become the master, so the text of *Die Hochzeit* touched, also in embryonic form, those themes of Eros and ethics, the biting contradictions at the heart of things, that were to be the *leitmotiven* of his life and art, the obstinate riddle he had perpetually to question, the hard knot no one can untie and only the keenest blade sever.

Having put aside *Die Hochzeit*, Wagner at once set to work on another opera, *Die Feen* ('The Fairies'). At the same time he undertook his first paid employment. His brother Albert was tenor and stage manager of the little theatre at Würzburg, and he obtained for Richard a post of *répétiteur* there. The salary was not much – ten florins a month (about £1) – but the work was not demanding and, which was more important, provided him with experience of a kind he had not found previously. Taking the post in the first place was something of a bluff, since he was totally unqualified for such work. But Richard Wagner was always a master bluffer, and this one paid off. He had to produce operas of various kinds, including works by Meyerbeer, Marschner and Bellini, and generally undertake the daywork of a provincial opera company. He learnt much, kept his wits about him and made what he could of the limited opportunities. He does not appear to have been notably patient or indulgent towards the inevitable shortcomings of such a situation; but he managed to convince his colleagues that he knew his business, and exert to good effect the personal magnetism and charm that was to endear him to people all his life, even when he behaved badly towards them, bullied them, relieved them of their money, seduced their wives and daughters. (In this last activity, seduction, he was not backward at Würzburg either. Involvement of a scandalous nature with at least two ladies of the chorus are recorded. It caused him a little trouble at the time, though there is no evidence that the ladies in question, Therese Ringelmann and Friederike Galvani, were disappointed in their extra-musical activities.)

At Würzburg, too, his Symphony in C was performed again; and the now familiar Adagio for clarinet and strings, which he wrote for a local player named Rummel, was probably composed. The piece was only published in 1926, and then from an autograph not in Wagner's own hand. Its authenticity has been doubted, and it has more recently been assigned to Bearmann. It is not very important who wrote the Adagio; it remains a pleasant piece about which no issue need be made.

By far the most important activity of the year in Würzburg was the composition of *Die Feen*. The models were Weber and Marschner, the world that of the mild supernatural with the horns of elfland faintly blowing; a work of charm and (again) imitative competence. Parts were performed in Würzburg: they made a good enough impression for Rosalie to be able to obtain a promise of performance in Leipzig. Unfortunately, that did not come off. Though Wagner returned to Leipzig early in 1834, full of high hopes and good intentions, the theatre management, led by Franz Hauser, first vacillated and then refused to proceed. It appears to have been at least in part a matter of politics, of contradictory pulls between the supporters of the 'classics', the old and tried, and the propagandists for the new music, led by Weber and Marschner and avidly followed by Wagner. But whatever the full reason, *Die Feen* was not produced in Leipzig, to its composer's bitter disappointment, for he had staked much on its success, both artistically and financially. In fact, *Die Feen* was never performed anywhere in Wagner's lifetime, and when it was at last staged, five years after his death, in 1888, it predictably made little more impact than that of a mild curiosity. Maybe it would never have swept the boards; all the same, even a *succès d'estime* in Leipzig would have sweetened the path and might have had an effect on his immediate future. It was, after all, his first completed work for the musical stage, and even if it is hardly characteristic by later standards, it contains enough merit to justify its occasional amateur revivals. The overture, heard now and again in concert programmes, has enough Wagnerian fingerprints to justify an unpretentious existence.

The rebuff over *Die Feen* had one rather curious effect. It set Wagner off on a period of extreme frivolity. He turned on his former masters of the new German school of opera, praised instead the Italians and the French for their popular melodiousness, their sophisticated stage techniques and that general spirit of Latin hedonism and sensuality he suddenly found much more attractive than heavy Teutonic pedantry and puritanical rigidity, as he came to see it. Even the beloved Beethoven, mighty Olympian though he was and remained, came under fire as too intellectual, too 'learned', insufficiently appealing to the senses and their rightful indulgence. In his everyday life, too, he ceased to take himself and the world with such solemnity. Instead, he launched into a year's abandon to riotous living and peripatetic bohemianism. It was an ironic situation: that he who is regarded as the epitome of ponderous German long-windedness, full of metaphysical obscurity and earnestness, the mortal enemy of Latin frivolity, especially the French variety, should set his face against the German and uphold the Latin – it was a joke to tickle all the ribs of musical history.

It did not last, of course. It was a passing phase, a part of growing up, much as schoolboys and girls go through phases of incipient homosexuality without any lasting significance. It went on through 1834 with Wagner; it did no harm, perhaps even some good as a kind of blowing of the tubes.

In May of that year, Wagner went with his friend Theodore Apel on a fairly debauched holiday to Bohemia, driving around in a carriage (presumably Apel paid), singing and drinking and arguing with deliberate intent to scandalize. In Teplitz Wagner sang the *Marseillaise* (strictly forbidden) at the top of his voice from his hotel balcony, having first encouraged the other guests to join in the chorus in defiance of the police. It was a harmless enough gesture, but it does serve to indicate the mood Wagner was in that year. He also remade contact with the Pachta girls in Prague, not forgetting that young Jenny had spurned him a year or two earlier. Did he care? He did not care. It was all another splendid joke.

More importantly, because musically, this light-hearted attitude and the alignment with the Italian and French composers led to his next opera – *Das Liebesverbot* ('The Love Ban'), based on parts of Shakespeare's *Measure for Measure*. In contrast to the tortured melodramatics of *Die Hochzeit* or the bottom-of-the-garden business of *Die Feen*, *Das Liebesverbot* is a vivacious celebration of free love, free indulgence and free everything else that engages the senses and satisfies desire by a rejection of all forms of puritanism and hypocrisy as the 'Young Germany' group understood it. *Das Liebesverbot* also languished more or less unheard and unhonoured, except, like *Die Feen*, for the occasional revival of enthusiastic local operatic societies. Again, for Wagner, hopes lavished were to be disappointed, though this time the work did achieve performance within a resonable time of its completion (1835). Anyone coming upon the overture – which is sometimes heard and has been recorded – is in for a sharp shock: it begins with the sound of castanets, tambourine and triangle, which recurs throughout. In a 'blindfold test', few would swear with conviction by the name of Richard Wagner. It has all the flavour of something by Bellini or Donizetti, or some other French or Italian tickler of the public fancy. And indeed, Bellini is a key figure in this transient phase of Wagner's early evolution. One might be tempted, in view of the subject matter, to think of Berlioz's *Beatrice and Benedict*; but that masterpiece was not written until 1862, and in any case the fine grain and sharp wits of the Berlioz is in another world from Wagner's immature effort which, despite his tilting towards the Latin manner, cannot escape altogether a certain Teutonic earnestness, its 'frivolity' somewhat forced.

One reason for Wagner's abrupt embracing of Latin operatic ideals was his friendship with Heinrich Laube, editor of the music magazine *Zeitung für die elegant Welte*, for whom Wagner wrote an article extolling the virtues of the French and Italian composers for the theatre. He was thus already set upon his habit of working out his ideas in print and issuing theorizing prose to justify them. Laube was enthusiastic for the Latin against the 'heavy' German conceptions of opera. But another, and more significant, influence was again the soprano Wilhelmine Schröder-Devrient who had so impressed him in *Fidelio* in 1829, and to whom he had addressed an ardent fan letter at that time. Now he heard her again, in Bellini's *I Montecchi ed i Capuletti*, and was bowled over for a second time. It was her singing of Bellini that convinced Wagner of the validity of that composer's operatic style and revealed to him the full passionate beauty of the Italian vocal line. He thereupon determined to write an opera for the great *diva* in the manner of Bellini, though if he actually thought of *Das Liebesverbot*, which is more in the line of a comic opera in the French style of Auber, somewhat unleavened in parts, as an imitation of Bellini, he deceived himself. On the other hand, it is doubtful if the finished work was ever seen by Wagner as simply a vehicle for a singer, however admired and illustrious. It became more generalized; in the event, identification with the ideals of 'Young Germany' outweighed straightforward adoration of the *prima donna*.

Yet the influence of Bellini was to be far reaching. From the Italian master he learnt the importance of the expressive power of long-breathed melody, saw it in a new light; and that was to become one aspect of both his composing and his theoretical work throughout the rest of his life. Bellini's melodic style also influenced the young Verdi, so its incidence spread through the work of the two major creators of romantic opera in the nineteenth century. In retrospect, Bellini's music appears as classically restrained beside the romantic ardours of early Verdi and Wagner, both in its purity of line and its avoidance of the brash, the vulgar, the grandiose and the rhetorical. But the appearance, at least so far as melody is concerned, is deceptive. Restrained though it is, it is also charged with a kind of passionate romantic melancholy and sensibility – *morbidezza* is the Italian word – and it was this quality that appealed to both Wagner and Verdi. The impassioned melodic outpourings of *Tristan und Isolde* may seem a far cry from Bellini; and indeed it is a far cry. But at a deeper level it is likely, to say no more, that its origins are to be found in the best operas of Bellini, at however distant a remove.[1] The same principle may be discerned in parts of *Die Meistersinger*, and even in *The Ring*. Indeed, many, including Ernest Newman, have from time to time suggested that the application of a little of the Italian *bel canto* style to Wagner's operas would improve their performance no end.

Bellini's genius, however, was almost entirely melodic. His harmonic gift was limited (though it could be effective) and his dramatic sense conventional. This sets him apart from both Wagner and Verdi, each of whom had a vivid sense of the theatre. It was no doubt the limitations of Bellini's style, its dependence on aria and terminal melody, that turned Wagner away from the temporary allegiance. From the beginning the importance of the orchestra was, for him, paramount. Bellini's beautiful melodic arias were supported by comparatively feeble orchestral parts, harmonically uninspired. But for Wagner it had to be different: only through the total and equal partnership of voices and orchestra could the full expressive power of music in all its various aspects be released. The orchestra in mature Wagner frequently carries more of the dramatic burden than the voices and the stage action.[2] Wagner was to work this out fully in his theoretical writings later on, and to translate it into mature practice in his major works. But even at this stage it was implicit.

Returning to Leipzig from his jaunt with Apel, and with the unfinished score of *Das Liebesverbot* in his pocket, Wagner found himself offered a post as musical director at the theatre of Magdeburg, at the instigation of the Leipzig conductor Stegmayer. It was not an inspiring appointment, and when he visited the Magdeburg company at Lauchstädt, the watering place where it was engaged for the summer, he was not impressed. His inclination was to turn the job down and go back to Leipzig. But fate took a hand and played a card that was to alter the course of his life. He lodged overnight in the same house as the leading juvenile actress, one Minna Planer. Wagner was captivated from the outset. In his own words: 'The die was cast'. He accepted the appointment and dashed back to Leipzig for his luggage after agreeing to conduct *Don Giovanni*. It all happened in a flash. The consequences were to be longer lasting.

Minna Planer was a shrewd, cool-headed young woman of twenty-five, four years older than Wagner. She had an illegitimate daughter, Natalie, born in 1826, who she always passed off as her sister; initially the relationship with Wagner appears to have been conducted on her side with much once-bitten caution and circumspection. Whether she actually played hard to get because of that or because it seemed the best way to catch the importunate musician is an open question. Probably an element of both, always supposing she really wanted him in the first place. Wagner himself tended to blow hot and cold in the early stages; but before long he felt that irresistible force of possessiveness at work in him again. She had started by being his good companion, looking after him when he was ill, sharing his disaffection in a daily life that was often boring and in which she seemed the only bright spot. But it did not and probably could not last that way: soon he was pulled in farther, so that when she failed to rebuff other admirers he all but went out of his head with jealousy. Then one evening he went to her house drunk, stayed the night against precedent, and soon after that they became lovers, 'freely and without embarrassment'.

In agreeing to conduct *Don Giovanni*, Wagner was indulging in another piece of bluff. Despite his year in Würzburg he had never conducted a full operatic production, or anything else of importance, out on his own. But he carried the Mozart off with unashamed aplomb, his natural gift for music and his outflowing vital energy making up for what was lacking in practical experience. Despite that, however, and the presence of Minna, life at Magdeburg was not happy. He was still enmeshed in his Franco-Italian enthusiasms, which now included Meyerbeer. Even so, he found the inescapable triviality of his work intolerable. In addition, the theatre manager, Bethmann, was lazy and inept: both the company and Wagner himself were soon in financial deep waters and facing bankruptcy. Wagner was an incurable spendthrift; he went deeper in and nothing seemed able to rectify it.

Musically, though, things were going better. He was gaining experience and authority as a conductor; he composed several useful if unambitious works for the company, including the New Year Cantata, *Beim Antritt des neuen Jahres*, an overture for a play, *Columbus*, by his friend Apel and other pieces. In April 1835 Mme Schröder-Devrient appeared twice in his concerts; she was so impressed with him that she generously agreed to sing at a benefit concert in May, to end the season, by which Wagner hoped to improve his finances. But once again circumstance played him false. Although he exerted himself to ensure a proper reception for his internationally famous guest, the locals made up their minds that it was some form of confidence trick, would not believe that so famous a personage would reappear in their modest provincial midst, and stayed at home. The concert was poorly attended and Wagner's creditors strongly reinforced. The season ended in disaster, and the company finally went bankrupt.

Wagner was obliged to return once more to Leipzig, hopelessly in debt and without employment. His situation was unchanged throughout the summer. Once more he was obliged to rely on the support of his family and friends for subsistence. He was disconsolate and unhappy, for the time being robbed of his customary optimism. Hope of alleviation came when he heard that the Magdeburg company had been revived by its patron, the King of

Prussia, and he could return to his post. This he accordingly did, in September 1835. At the same time he could rejoin Minna Planer. It seemed that his fortunes were on the turn, not spectacularly but at least moving in the right direction.

He was deceived again. Although he put all of himself into improving the quality of the resuscitated company, even so far as to go on tour, at his own expense, to find new singers, little success came his way. He worked hard completing *Das Liebesverbot*, intending to produce it the following March as another means of restoring his financial affairs. It was his contemporary lodestar: by following it everything would come right. But everything did not go right. The company went bankrupt again and the season ended before time. Though the singers agreed, out of loyalty to him and in gratitude for the work he had put in on their behalf, to stay on for the benefit production, it was no use. The opera was too long and too complex for the time available for its preparation. In spite of all his personal efforts the first performance, the proceeds of which were intended to cover the costs of production, was a shambles. And the second, from which Wagner would draw his personal benefit, never took place. Violent quarrels broke out among the cast, whose internecine rivalries and jealousies effectively aborted the enterprise.

Wagner's position was now desperate. The Magdeburg engagement was irreversibly concluded. He had no prospects and his creditors moved in, issuing writs. In addition to the *Das Liebesverbot* fiasco, Minna herself had some time earlier become so embroiled in the rivalries and jealousies that she had departed for Berlin; and although Wagner carried on so effectively that she was recalled and reinstated, relations cannot have been all that congenial. Minna had agreed to marry him on her return; but neither can have found the general atmosphere much to their liking.

In May 1836 Wagner set off for Berlin, hoping to have *Das Liebesverbot*, still his bright star and bright hope, accepted and produced there. Minna went off to fulfil an engagement in Königsberg. So they were parted yet again, which caused him renewed anguish. Never a man to take kindly to being thwarted, Wagner fumed inwardly – and sometimes outwardly – at the newly enforced separation, made all the worse because, partly from past experience and partly because of his own possessive nature, he never really trusted Minna. Nor can matters have been improved by his reception in Berlin. *Das Liebesverbot* was turned down and there was no appointment open. The situation was, however, partly retrieved by Minna, who obtained a job for him at her Königsberg theatre. But even this misfired: the temporary conductor, Schubert, from Riga, who should have returned to his permanent post, dallied and delayed because of his infatuation with the local *prima donna*. Thus Wagner was left hanging around in a subservient position with no real work to do. He was promised the conductorship when Schubert departed – and on that slender hope he and Minna were married in November.

Despite all the passionate preliminaries, it was not a propitious match. The wild, starry-eyed, financially irresponsible Wagner and the cautiously calculating Minna were fundamentally incompatible. They quarrelled before the marriage, they quarrelled at the time of it, and they went on quarrelling afterwards. Already deep in debt, Wagner plunged still deeper into the red setting up home with his bride. Creditors pursued him, brought him to court, threatened ruin from all sides. And then, to repeat the Magdeburg dosage, the Königsberg company wobbled into bankruptcy. Nothing, it seemed, would go right for him.

Yet artistically the currents were running in a mysterious way towards his self-realization. Waiting impatiently for his appointment to materialize, he made a libretto for a light opera deliberately designed to tickle the public fancy and so replenish the empty coffers, a frivolous thing to be called *Die gluckliche Barenfamilie*. He composed part of the music; then something snapped and he gave it up as not worth the trouble. It was a kind of turning point: whether he knew it or not at the time, his period of loose-minded hedonism with its attendant appeal of Latin frivolity in opera was over. He was recalled to the serious business of art, as the succession of unhappy events in his private life had enjoined upon him the 'seriousness' of life in general.

That, however, is to take a somewhat superficial view. It is doubtful whether Richard Wagner ever took either life or art anything but seriously. It was simply a matter of bias and emphasis; during these years he saw the 'seriousness' of both from a different and, as it turned out, temporary angle. This was in fact young Wagner's 'Shelley period'. It is a phase through which all young people of a romantic disposition are likely to go. Shelley is essentially the poet of adolescence — which is in no sense a pejorative statement: adolescence is an honourable estate, and Shelley, far from being Matthew Arnold's 'ineffectual angel', was a man of decisive intellect who at one time seriously considered whether he should devote his life to poetry or to metaphysics. Shelley's combination of moral earnestness, extreme egotism, and determination to set the world to rights whether it liked it or not, made him at once attractive to women and an overbearing companion. It is also characteristic of adolescence — and it was certainly applicable in one form or another to the young Wagner. The trouble is of course that Shelley himself, by contriving to be drowned in a sailing accident before he was thirty, never had time to outgrow his own 'Shelley period'. Wagner did, and it became transmuted in him into a kind of higher degree of existential intemperance, that discomfiting extension and exaggeration by which great deeds are performed and great goals pursued more or less in defiance of the equanimity of the world and its more judicious inhabitants. Wagner, as he had to, shed the hedonism and increased the egotism and earnestness. Both were substantially without that ingrained sense of humour which alleviates certain other and more amenable persons. But if Richard Wagner had possessed a sense of humour, would Bayreuth ever have come into being or *Tristan*, *The Ring* and *Parsifal* ever been composed? And *Meistersinger* in this context does not constitute an exception. It is a particularly German characteristic; and Shelley's philosophical bias was, like that of Coleridge, strongly rooted in the German tradition.

Wagner was now swinging onto his proper and predestined course. But before this could come about, fully and decisively, his domestic affairs were to cause him further trouble. His marriage solved nothing. If he had entered into it, in the true Romantic fashion, as redemption through the love of Woman, he was to be disappointed. Within a year, Minna, driven to distraction by his mounting debts as well as by emotional incompatibility, left him and took off with a rich Königsberg merchant by the name of Dietrich. Wagner, discovering the unpleasant truth one day upon returning to his home and finding it deserted, was thrown into a paroxysm of rage and despair. Somehow scraping together the cost of the fare, he followed her. He found her wretched and disconsolate. He had been negotiating for a post in the Baltic town of Riga; and largely on the stength of that he managed to persuade her to try again for conjugal bliss. But it still wouldn't work, and after a short time Minna again took flight, again with Dietrich.

The exact nature of the relationship between Minna and Dietrich remains somewhat obscure. But one thing is clear: whatever views Wagner may have held and propagated on free love and hedonistic indulgence of the senses, they did not extend to the conduct of his wife. Like many a man in such a situation, he preached one thing but demanded something entirely different in his own domestic arrangements. (The resemblance to Shelley comes up again here.) He felt slighted by Minna's double defection, his renowned, as he saw it, sexual prowess brought into public question. There is no doubt that Minna had been guilty of infidelity. It drove him nearly mad with jealousy and frustration. It may have been in order for him to stray from the path of domestic rectitude – that was one thing, his inalienable right as an artist and bold apostle of total freedom in thought and action. But for Minna, his wife, it would not do at all. That was quite different.

Yet by another quirk of circumstance, the defection of Minna, temporary though it proved to be, was once again the instrument of advancing his artistic fulfilment. When she left him for the second time, Wagner returned again to the sanctuary of his family. Unlike some great composers, Brahms and Beethoven for example, Wagner did not come from a social environment of near-poverty and deprivation. There was always a comforting, and comfortable, cultured bourgeois background to lean on, a family ready and able, if not always too willing, to bale him out from the worst consequences of his recklessness. This time he took refuge with his sister Ottilie and her husband, Hermann Brockhaus, in Dresden. And it was while staying with them that he read Bulwer Lytton's *Rienzi: The Last of the Tribunes*, a long and involved historical romance of fourteenth-century

Rome and sundry intrigues and betrayals leading to the hero's death at the hands of his former loyal supporters. He not only saw in the 'heroic' figure of Rienzi someone with whom he could identify, the strong man cast down and traduced by the petty and the insignificant, but more importantly discerned a potential plot for a grand opera of the kind he had been vaguely contemplating ever since he had heard Spontini's *Fernand Cortez* in Berlin a few months before. He had already made one or two abortive starts; but nothing had yet germinated. Now *Rienzi* took root: slowly in his mind ambition and aspiration expanded. Meyerbeer, it seemed to him, held the key: Meyerbeer and Paris. In Paris Meyerbeer was rich and famous; his immense spectacular operas had made him the most celebrated as well as the most prosperous composer in Europe. Therefore, if he was to succeed, Wagner believed he must conquer Paris by writing an opera that would challenge the supremacy of Meyerbeer; no less. It was not at this time a simple question of direct challenge, of outright rivalry; it was more a case of using the example, and if possible the personal influence, of Meyerbeer to further his own ends. Another case, it might reasonably be said, of jumping on the likeliest bandwagon.

He went to Riga in September 1837. It was again no great shakes as an appointment. The orchestra was small and feeble, the opportunities meagre. But none of that counted in the end: it was the conception and partial composition of *Rienzi* that gives the Riga episode its true significance, and gave Wagner himself a rare feeling of happiness and hopefulness. *Rienzi*, large and far more ambitious than anything he had so far turned his hand to, would finally scatter the groundlings, rebuff the unbelievers, and set his star once and for all in the ascendant. In addition, Minna, now penitent and recognizing at last that she must take Wagner as he was and not try to 'reform' him and his wayward character, rejoined him following confessions of guilt and promises to mend her ways, which Wagner, who had been at one time determined to divorce her, accepted. She was as good as her word: they appear to have come to an understanding that life was going to be a tough struggle anyway and they had better pull together.

One thing had not changed. The perennial problem was still with them: their lives were at the permanent mercy of clamouring creditors, who were by no means penitent and whose demands grew ever more pressing. So much so that early in 1838 the unscrupulous manager Holtei, who also had designs on Minna, used the pressure of creditors to deprive Wagner of his living. In March he was peremptorily dismissed, to be succeeded by his old friend and one-time benefactor, Heinrich Dorn, on the plausible excuse that his financial situation made his continued presence in the town undesirable and his liberty precarious. Yet once again, however, ill fortune played into his hands. He had already made up his mind to shake himself free of Riga and its restricting provincial atmosphere, where the more serious the work the less acceptable it was to the public. Now he was given another push of the kind that often alters the course of a life, or at least bends it in the direction it has to go. And that was, geographically at any rate, towards Paris, and *Rienzi* was his musical entrance ticket.

Paris, though, was not the immediate objective or the initial destination. The prime necessity was to get out of Riga. Plagued by creditors, deprived of their passports because of their debts, Richard and Minna had to contrive a devious means of flight and escape. This was accomplished with the help of a loyal Königsberg friend, Abraham Möller, and accompanied by an even more faithful Newfoundland dog, Robber, their constant companion who unfailingly distinguished himself during the escape by keeping his mouth shut and padding silently behind his master and mistress, unobtrusive and unobserved.

There were hazards in plenty. The Cossack patrols at the frontier had orders to shoot on sight anyone trying to cross, so that the escape had to be timed to coincide with the changing of the guard, aided by a small amount of bribery. The final dash for safety was both exciting and perilous; but it was safely made. Even so, the whole adventure was harsh and distressing, especially for Minna; so much so that Wagner, usually the total egoist who believed that everyone else should suffer with him and for him without complaint, was moved to write later that he could find no words to 'convey my regret to my poor, exhausted wife'.

Their destination was, for the moment, London, where Wagner hoped to make himself known to certain influential people, Sir George Smart and Bulwer Lytton among them. But before they arrived there were further perils to be surmounted. They boarded, at Pillau, a small merchant vessel, the *Thetis*, of under one hundred tons, perfectly adequate for a summer crossing taking around a week. But this summer proved itself treacherous. After a period becalmed they encountered fierce storms which obliged the captain to seek shelter in a Norwegian fjord. An abortive resailing led them into even more violent storms on the open sea. The Wagners were not the only ones on board to think their lives were about to come to an abrupt end. The crew became suspicious of the strangers in their midst, believing them to be escaped criminals and the cause of their misfortunes by laying a curse on the ship. Minna, in the true Romantic heroine mould, wished to be tied to Wagner's side so that they might die together.

They did not die, and eventually they reached London on 13 August. The voyage had taken nearly three weeks rather than one. But yet again – it had almost become a *leitmotif* in Wagner's life – dangers and discomforts and the perils of a journey proved to be of considerable value. He had already read the legend of the Flying Dutchman, and it had implanted a seed in the oyster of his mind. Now he heard the story confirmed by the sailors. He heard the sailors' songs and they filled him with joy and exhilaration. He saw the massive cliffs of the Norwegian coastline, and they too made a deep impression on him. Best of all, he experienced the full fury and violence of storms at sea at first hand. If that voyage from Pillau to London had been calm and uneventful, would we have had the magnificent 'sea music' of *The Flying Dutchman*, the chorus of sailors and the steerman's song in the same vivid and authentic form he came to give them? Also, perhaps, the subtle background of the sea and seasong in *Tristan and Isolde* even, the implications of the water motif as much Freudian as physical. Possibly; but there is no doubt that this fraught crossing activated Wagner's creative impetus in a way that gave his opera its unmistakable imprint of the sea.

Although both George Smart and Bulwer Lytton were out of town and so could not be visited, Richard and Minna spent an agreeable week in London, their lodging place the King's Arms in Old Compton Street. Wagner, pursuing Bulwer Lytton, was able to attend a debate in the House of Lords. He was much impressed. Shortage of money served, as usual, to undermine total enjoyment (it is reported that a bleak English Sunday produced an even worse and more depressive effect). All the same, it was a thoroughly pleasant, if from the business point of view slightly disappointing, interlude.

Their ultimate destination remained Paris. The next move was across the Channel to Boulogne. Again fortune smiled. The crossing itself was uneventful, sea and weather compliant. But on the boat he passed the time of day in conversation with two Jewish ladies, Mrs Manson and her daughter who, marvellous to discover, were not only friends of Meyerbeer but were able to tell him that the great man was at that very time spending a holiday in Boulogne. This was a gift from the gods indeed, the more so since he was there and then given a letter of introduction. Some time earlier, from Könisberg, Wagner had written to Meyerbeer, a letter full of apology for troubling so celebrated a person, but full of characteristic insistence and adulation. He confessed that at the beginning he had been impelled by a passion for Beethoven which made his first efforts 'incredibly one-sided', and went on to make some shrewd observations on the current state of opera in Germany. He received no reply; but that was not likely to daunt Richard Wagner. He had also at the same time tried to raise the interest of Eugène Scribe, the Parisian librettist and man of the theatre, through sister Cäcilie's fiancé, Eduard Avnarius, the agent of Brockhaus the publishers.

Now, through the chance meeting with Mrs and Miss Manson, he was on surer ground. Accordingly, on arrival in Boulogne, he lost no time in calling on Meyerbeer, who received him with formal cordiality. Whereas previously Wagner had staked his future on *Das Liebesverbot*, the text of which he had sent to Scribe, now everything depended on *Rienzi*. He read Meyerbeer the libretto of the first three Acts. Meyerbeer was impressed, asked to keep it for further study, offered to look at the music when it was finished. This was decidedly encouraging. But Meyerbeer went further. He gave Wagner letters of introduction to persons of consequence and influence in the musical world in Paris, including the manager and conductor of the

Opéra, and the publisher Schlesinger. Altogether, Meyerbeer showed himself a man of patience and generosity. For several years afterwards he continued to help Wagner: it did not save him from virulent attacks later on, the all but inescapable fate of all those reckless enough to incur Wagner's indebtedness to them. But at the time his support was welcome and welcomed.

So Wagner set off for Paris after a fruitful month in Boulogne, full of high and apparently justified hopes. He really believed that the letters of introduction in his pocket would prove to be the keys to the kingdom of Paris, and after that to the whole of Europe. The combination of his own genius and his influential introductions must surely bring about a real change in his fortunes.

It was not to be. The two and a half years – 16 September 1839 to 7 April 1842 – he spent in Paris were to be the bitterest of his life. He suffered constant rebuffs and humiliations; he and Minna sank ever deeper into poverty and debt. His letters proved far less effective than he anticipated. Duponchel, the manager of the Opéra, was simply not interested; Habeneck, the conductor, was more helpful but still did not make a material difference to the declining fortunes of the disappointed composer. And always the wolf of privation was snarling at the door.

Partly it was his own fault, the result of an ingrained impetuosity. He had meant to conquer Paris with *Rienzi*, a work well suited to that purpose, with its spectacular pageantry, its massive dramatic effects and its rewarding parts for star singers, all in the best Meyerbeer vein and openly designed for a Meyerbeer-like success. But he confronted Paris not only before *Rienzi* had been accepted, but before it was even finished. If he had waited until *Rienzi* had been taken up by the Opéra, as Minna had tentatively urged before they left Riga (only to be overruled), it might have been a different matter. But Richard Wagner was never a patient man in his dealings with the world, however patient he may have been in the dedication to his art, and he decided to assault the French capital without the necessary means to prove his point and establish beyond doubt his claim to its attention.

As it was, he found himself reduced to all manner of desperate expedients in order to survive at all. Early on, it became necessary to pawn most of their meagre possessions – wedding presents, pieces of silver, the small quantity of theatrical costumery Minna had saved from her previous career. Wagner wrote a few French songs; no leading singer would take them up. He did hack work for Schlesinger, for which he at least received prompt payment. Some of this work was bizarre: he was asked for a treatise or 'method' for the *cornet-à-piston*, then all the rage. When Wagner told Schlesinger he had not the least idea how to go about it, the publisher sent him five existing treatises and told him to 'gut' them to make a sixth. But in the meantime the sixth appeared independently from another publisher and Wagner was told to forget about it. Instead, he was asked to write fourteen suites for the *cornet* based on popular tunes from operas. Other hardly less incongruous tasks fell to his hand, in addition to writing articles for Schlesinger's *La Gazette musicale*. One bright spot was the acceptance of *Das Liebesverbot* by the Théâtre de la Renaissance. But yet again a theatre connected with Wagner went bankrupt and the hope was extinguished. On the strength of the acceptance Wagner and Minna had moved into better lodgings and acquired a little furniture of their own. It all fell suddenly apart and left them in still deeper waters.

Threatened with imprisonment for debt, Wagner had to seek help from someone. His family had by now given him up as a vainglorious adventurer: they would no longer come to his rescue. So he wrote a pathetic letter to his old friend Theodore Apel. Receiving no immediate answer, he had Minna write again, intimating that Richard was actually in gaol. There has always been some uncertainty about whether he was actually sent to prison; on the whole, it seems that he was not, though it was a close-run thing. The passage in Minna's letter had been inserted at Wagner's own prompting, to emphasize the urgency of the situation.

It worked. Apel sent money and the day was saved, temporarily. Another time they were saved by Schlesinger, who out of the blue commissioned Wagner to make a series of arrangements of various kinds from Donizetti's *La Favorita*. Schlesinger offered a total of 1100 francs, with an immediate down payment of 500. The Wagners breathed again.

Yet all this was getting him nowhere. It was a sheer battle for survival. Such a hand-to-mouth existence would have broken the nerve and destroyed the spirit of many men. It did not break or destroy Richard Wagner; but it did sink deep into the texture of his consciousness, bit into his soul and left a permanent legacy. Its effects were to reverberate through the rest of his life.

Yet another pill, bitter to the taste and hard to swallow at the time, though in the long run it did him no harm, was in the matter of the preliminary scenario for *The Flying Dutchman*. This was accepted by the Director of the Opéra, but composition of the music was entrusted to someone else, to Pierre Dietsch, who made a conventionally sorry mess of it. Wagner was obliged to let the text alone go for 500 francs, because as usual he needed the money and could not keep to his original decision to refuse the deal. In the end, though, this was another blessing in disguise: the money enabled him to settle to work on his own *Flying Dutchman* score, greatly expanded and elaborated from the first scenario. The encouragement to begin work came from the acceptance, at last, of *Rienzi*, though in Dresden not Paris. In this at least his confidence in himself appeared justified.

Paris was never Wagner's lucky city. When he returned, two decades later, to present the revised version of his *Tannhäuser*, he again suffered insult and humiliation, though he was then in a stronger position to deal with it. Paris, in short, was always two-faced as far as Wagner was concerned, holding out hope and promise to begin with, but deceiving in the end. Even now, in this first Parisian encounter, all was not sourness and deception. There were good friends, and through them some good times. One such occurred on a New Year's Eve when his friends (all impoverished like himself), Anders of the Bibliothèque Royale, Samuel Lehrs the classical scholar, the painters Pecht and Leitz, arrived at his dwelling bearing food and drink – for all the world a living likeness of the impoverished quartet in Puccini's *La Bohème*. And it was appropriate, for this was to be the end of Wagner's bohemian period. Henceforth, with growing confidence through increasing recognition (though not increasing financial security), his outlook and attitude would be different. The acceptance of *Rienzi* and the immersion in work on *The Flying Dutchman* set him firmly upon the course his destiny had mapped out for him long ago, but which he had been obliged to discover for himself through years of trial and error, of hardship and frustration during which even his monumental self-confidence and often arrogant self-esteem were put under severe strain and at times severely dented. It was not over yet; but it was the end of the initiation.

And it left its mark, the hard road he had to follow. At one time in his life Wagner said: 'We two, the world and I, are two stubborn fellows at loggerheads, and naturally whichever has the thinner skull will get it broken.' It was well said; yet perhaps it was not so much a case of skulls as skins. Wagner was born with the thinnest of skins; but he soon developed, under duress and to the outward impression at least, the toughest of hides, so that it and its contact with the world's hard skin was nothing if not abrasive. It began generally during his Paris residence during 1839–42. It taught him many harsh lessons, and some think it resulted in a permanent warping of his character. Perhaps in the bias of his attitude to France and the French it did; otherwise it was probably more or less incidental. No doubt he was never the easiest of men; but the young Wagner, self-indulgent hedonist though he was, appeared hopefully irresponsible rather than malicious. The hard case came later, after he had to learn many lessons from first-hand experience of the harsher realities through rough contact with the world and its ingrained habits of either outright hostility or plain indifference, or frequently both; and he learnt, too, that in order to do his great work he would have to adopt stances of total obduracy for much of the time. If he often brought misfortune upon himself, that didn't alter the situation. He had a mission, a great ideal: he had to get it out, project it into the world, make the dream reality. And to do that, to succeed against the odds, he had to develop that essential streak of ruthlessness, of iron in the soul, without which no great deeds are done, no significant goals reached. After the first Paris confrontation Wagner's life and career followed a course that effectively reversed a popular commonplace: from now on it was for him a case of if you can't join them, beat them.

And that is precisely what, after the tempering in the fires of Paris, he set out to do – and did.

CHAPTER THREE

A SOLITARY VOYAGE

When Wagner sold the scenario of the one-act 'curtain-raiser' version of *The Flying Dutchman* to Pillet, he parted with his text reluctantly but pocketed the 500 francs with relief. Even before he had seen the colour of the money his mind was reaching out towards the full and extended version of the story that he had originally intended and always wanted to develop. Encouraged by the acceptance of *Rienzi* and temporarily free of financial worry, he was immediately spurred into a fresh bout of creative activity. The least workshy of men, whatever else may be said about him, he now drove himself relentlessly, burst the threatening bonds of inhibition that had begun to enmesh him in the face of increasing difficulties and misfortunes and completed his own *Dutchman* opera in seven weeks, composing the overture, the most immediately original part, last. Themes and dramatic evolutions had already become fixed in his mind: some had come to him on the perilous crossing of the *Thetis*; others had been brewing in his subconscious, ready to surface at the right time.

The extent of Wagner's subconscious immersion in the entire legend and project of *The Flying Dutchman* is revealed in the close relationship of themes and motifs. He himself relates how he suddenly realized when the work was well advanced that he had not only forgotten to write out the Steersman's Song but could not remember having composed it. He set it down there and then, and 'it greatly pleased me'. Having finished that, he then realized that the same thing applied to the Spinning Chorus. His mind must, he admits, have been playing tricks, for when he had composed both words and music, there were, he saw, clear internal linkages springing apparently spontaneously from the deep recesses of his creative mind.

Ironically, while *The Flying Dutchman* marked the turning point in Wagner's career, the old scenario, re-emerging as *Le Vaiseau fantôme*, was a complete flop. There was no joy in that for anyone, and Wagner himself was probably too preoccupied even to notice. Yet there is a lesson of a kind in it:

45

an idea for an operatic production is never enough in itself; what is required is a comprehensive insight into the full dramatic significance and the creative form of its essential elements, plus the sheer capacity of talent to translate it into something new and original. This is where Wagner broke ground and set German musical drama onto its proper course. Weber, original genius that he unquestionably was, still could not take complete hold of all the implications of his forward-looking work and grasp the uncompromising purpose necessary to its ultimate fulfilment. Congenital ill-health resulting in early death, adverse circumstances in the operatic theatre of the day which he could not effectively challenge, and a perhaps too easy-going temperament combined to frustrate the full realization of Weber's great gifts. His achievements were considerable; but they should have been still more so. The composer who could reach the magical heights of the best of *Oberon* but let them become hamstrung by the chaotic hotch-potch of the rest was no heir of Gluck in the reform of opera and no true immediate precursor of Wagner in the evolution of German Romantic music drama. And it is no use to argue that Weber, like Handel, was trapped by the operatic and theatrical conventions of his day and his age: men of strong will and tough fibre create the conditions necessary to the emergence of their work; they do not succumb to existing bad habits and moribund traditions.

And so it was left to the tough-minded, dedicated, utterly ruthless Richard Wagner to erect the immovable monument to the German Romantic musical theatre, against all odds and often in circumstances that would have defeated a less determined, more easily corrupted man.

If Wagner had been less strong-willed and ruthlessly motivated by a destiny that in the end showed as little pity to him as it did to Beethoven, he might have gone down in musical history as a brilliant entertainer, a kind of superior Rossini or Meyerbeer (which is not intended as a slight on either), producing marvellously effective stage spectacles of splendour and ebullience. But an ingrained Teutonic seriousness of purpose and puritanical devotion to his art prevented his resting content with an emergence of that kind, or with any such dalliance on a lasting basis with the ideas and ideals of his hedonistic period. No doubt from today's perspective nothing could seem more unlikely than a permanently free-wheeling Wagner; but to the contemporary idea of the 1830s it would not have seemed preposterous at all, especially on the evidence of *Das Liebesverbot*, upon which during that time he staked his reputation and his future and which he sent round to anyone likely to show a spark of interest.

In *The Flying Dutchman* Wagner at last came into his own. There had been more than one pointer to the direction he was about to take in the score of *Rienzi*. But the stylistic dichotomy was largely unsolved in that grand spectacle, the compass bearing, so to say, still uncertain. The overture, which is characteristic (like that to the *Dutchman*) and has ensured itself a healthy independent survival, defines both sides of the picture, the merits and the still active limitations. The first part, the slow music encompassing the theme of Rienzi's Prayer with its Wagner 'turn' in the melodic line, anticipating a leading feature of his mature style, *Tristan* and *The Ring* included, is full of the true Wagnerian tone and thrust. But much of the rest, the quick sections, is little more than brash, noisy Paris Opéra music *c.*1840. It was to take Wagner some time yet to expurgate this vulgar element from his work, although it was largely bypassed in the *Dutchman*. Most commentaries on Wagner take the *Dutchman* as the starting point; but *Rienzi* still retains a place on the European opera stage at least.

What indelibly hallmarks *The Flying Dutchman* and sets it apart not only from anything Wagner himself had so far written but also from virtually everything else in the contemporary music theatre is that despite its obvious shortcomings, its continuing lack of stylistic unity, its reliance upon many conventions of the operatic stage, its leanings on the Italian melodic line and the formal set piece, deep down it vibrates with the inescapable force of personal genius, Wagner's genius, uninhibited and fully unleashed. It is easy to pinpoint shortcomings in construction and execution; impossible to mistake the individual surge and vibration. If the engine is still not running smoothly and at full efficiency in all its parts, the power of thrust is not to be misconstrued. There are clumsy passages; others that might have come out of early Verdi, notably the passage in which Senta questions Darland about the Dutchman at the end of Act II (Scene 2 in the original version); but it doesn't matter. The thrust is true and potent; the torque incontestable.

There were several reasons for this. Partly, it was a comparatively straightforward matter of natural evolution, a predestined point reached as Wagner's composite creative faculty clarified and defined itself. But it was also due to something else, something at least as potent and meaningful, both in itself and in the larger context of German Romantic life and art. This lay embedded in the subject of the 'doomed' sea captain under the Devil's curse, obliged to sail the seas until he should find a woman whose love and fidelity would at last redeem him, allowed to set foot on land once every seven years for that hope and purpose. Here was a theme which accorded very well with the Romantic temperament in general, and with the German Romantic temperament in particular. The figure of the doomed man, the self-conscious and defiant ousider, standing against the elements and the amoral gods, flinging back the challenge, shaking a fist at any deity, actual or potential, who would impose limitation on man, is a familiar one in Romantic art and literature (though not ónly there). The Faust or Manfred figure stands at the centre of one aspect of the Romantic experience, the existential conflict, that is, between the finite and the infinite.

There is something decidedly Faustian about the Flying Dutchman, an ancient legend; and the idea of redemption through the pure love of a pure woman was another, linked idea dear to the Romantic heart and imagination. At this precise time in Wagner's development, these two strands came together and infused a passionate if imperfect artwork for the musical theatre.

It is significant that immediately before coming to grips with *The Flying Dutchman*, Wagner had written an extended orchestral overture on the theme of Faust. *A Faust Overture* is a necessary link in the chain. During his miserable first winter in Paris (1839–40), one bright spot had been a performance of Beethoven's Ninth symphony by the excellent orchestra of the Conservatoire under François Habeneck, the conductor to whom Wagner had been directed by Meyerbeer with a letter of introduction and who had received him with some kindness. This was a revelation. Although Wagner had fallen under the spell of Beethoven in his musical youth, his ardour had cooled during the heady days of his bohemian hedonism. But he had never until then heard a competent performance of the Ninth symphony. The one he had heard in 1834 appears to have been of the sort which reinforced the idea and general opinion in Germany that the symphony was the work of a once great mind that had regrettably become unhinged. Habeneck and the Conservatoire orchestra changed all that for Wagner, changed it for ever in a single evening. Now, in Wagner's mind, that superlative old performance of *Fidelio* in which Mme Schröder-Devrient had so thrilled and overwhelmed him was linked to this new revelationary experience; and Beethoven stood once again at the centre of his artistic vision.

One immediate result was the composition of *A Faust Overture*, a purely orchestral work in which Wagner sought, not too successfully, to parallel Beethoven's dramatic use of sonata form as a medium of musical expression. It was originally intended for the 'first section of a grand Faust-Symphony', but the rest was never undertaken. The *Faust Overture* was considerably revised fifteen years later, in 1855, when Wagner was engaged in the composition of *Das Rheingold*, to its considerable advantage. This is the version invariably heard today; but the original, with all its defects and immaturities, was of value and importance to its growing composer in 1840. As with Brahms's B major piano trio, also substantially rewritten by the mature composer, the revision may be more satisfactory, but the original illuminates and should not be cast out peremptorily.

For Wagner, a more significant result of the Beethoven–Habeneck concert was the confirmation of certain tentative ideas on the relationship between voices and orchestra in dramatic music that he had already partly formed and had even begun to work out in print. His theories were not formulated in full until later; but it is clear that they existed and to some extent operated, if half-consciously, on the composition of the *Dutchman*. There is a basic 'tone' in *The Flying Dutchman* in its best and most original parts which relates musically to the Beethoven Ninth in a way that inaugurated a new era in German opera. This emerges even more clearly in the retrospect of both the nineteenth century and of Wagner's own subsequent work.

Although Wagner took his immediate cue from the Ninth symphony, the example of *Fidelio* was in fact the more decisive. He thought that in the Ninth symphony Beethoven had recognized that a musical structure could not become wholly articulate and totally realized without the assistance of the poet. It was an argument on Wagner's side promulgated to sustain a larger general theory and not in itself perfectly valid. Certainly there have been some, the late Hermann Scherchen among them, who have believed that the finale of the Choral symphony ought to be 'operatically' produced and presented, possibly with a dramatic parting, if not actual rending, of the curtain at the entry of the human voice. A more pertinent assessment is that Beethoven, having sought for and finally found a 'vocal' melody, decided on purely musical grounds that it made sense to introduce voices with words to sing it. Add the known fact that since early in his life Beethoven had cherished an ambition to set Schiller's verses to music, attracted both by their sentiments and by their dithyrambic rhythmic impulse, and we have the most likely explanation of that contentious finale which many still regard as a 'mistake', if a noble one. For Wagner, working towards a different solution of another problem of dramatic music, the Beethoven Ninth became a focal point.

He believed that his own mature compositions carried on broadly from where Beethoven in his last symphony left off; that his 'symphonic' evolutions as well as his particular combining of voice and orchestra, word and tone, were a logical continuation of Beethoven's work, not only of the Ninth symphony, but also of the *Missa solemnis* (obviously) and from the formal standpoint the late piano sonatas and string quartets. It was to a considerable extent true: Wagner, though given to exaggeration here as elsewhere, was not merely shouting odds. And inevitably, the more mature he grew and the more autonomous his genius became, the farther did he leave the direct Beethoven contact behind.

But Wagner did not work out his own ideas in full until he came to write *Opera and Drama* after the completion of *Lohengrin* in 1848.

A more penetrating musical analysis, however, will show that what he was really talking about and working towards at this time was more relevant to *Fidelio* than to the Ninth symphony. That it appeared to Wagner as though the symphony was the key work, and may still appear so to some, lies in the nature and musical structure of *Fidelio*, a work by no means easy to sum up and assess accurately.

The main problem with *Fidelio* is not that it is too 'symphonic', as has frequently been argued, but that it is not symphonic enough. Beethoven's creative mind moved naturally in symphonic terms activated by an intense sense of the dramatic. Thus the finest parts of *Fidelio* are those where his natural tendency to make a symphonic structure and move in its specific terms predominate. If Beethoven had been primarily instead of incidentally a composer for the musical theatre, he might have developed opera, or music drama, along organic lines of growth that would have made much of

Wagner's groundwork unnecessary, if not redundant. But Beethoven's creative processes worked in terms of the inner-directed drama of sonata form, in symphony, piano sonata, string quartet, rather than in the more exteriorized and histrionic forms of the theatre. It was not that Beethoven's dramatic force was more subjective than Wagner's – in fact Wagner's was in many ways more subjective than Beethoven's – it was simply that the subjective force took different forms, because of its different constitution and because the creative and cultural environment in which, in each case, it worked reflected the ambience of two different though consecutive periods of the evolution of the expressive powers of music.

Fidelio is basically a German *Singspiel*, spoken dialogue separating the main musical numbers. The operatic influences, like Wagner's early on, were French and Italian, as well as German.[1] It was thus a hybrid; inevitably, no doubt, at a time when German opera was still perched somewhat precariously between Mozart and Weber, still struggling to find its autonomous tone and voice, the transition from *Singspiel* to fully developed music drama as yet only partially seen and understood. Steering clear of those elements of the supernatural which Mozart sometimes exploited and Weber wholeheartedly embraced but Beethoven disliked, *Fidelio* advanced the cause of German opera in its ethical and philosophical aspects on the one hand and in its organic evolutions on the other. But *Fidelio*, partly because Beethoven was not a born operatic composer, still had its conventional elements and remained trapped between *Singspiel* and organic music drama. This can easily be seen by following the various versions of *Leonora–Fidelio*, which caused Beethoven more trouble than any other of his major works, with the possible exception of the *Missa solemnis* (but that was a totally different matter), and most of all by the way the real dramatic essence is distilled into the *Leonora* overtures, especially No.3 which is the real parallel in Beethoven of Wagner's *A Faust Overture*. While *Leonora No.3* is in every respect essential Beethoven, *A Faust Overture*, though in its revised form a fine piece, is incidental Wagner.

Wagner took the ethical–philosophical tone and organic development of the symphonic parts of *Fidelio* from Beethoven, together with a prophetic way of combining voices and orchestra in the Ninth symphony, and from Weber the imaginative infusion of the supernatural. Early in his life he had become passionately addicted to the writings of E. T. A. Hoffmann, whose *Bergwerke von Falun* he had turned into an opera libretto to earn another much needed 200 francs during his last months in Paris. And he had been no less deeply affected by Weber's *Der Freischütz* as a boy. The ingredients were therefore varied and various. The line of evolution of German opera runs roughly from Mozart's *Magic Flute* through *Fidelio* to Wagner's mature music dramas via *Der Freischütz* and, to a lesser extent, *Euryanthe*.

The growth and maturing of German opera is in this context a term with a twofold significance. It applies to the development of German opera itself from *Singspiel* to music drama; and it applies to Wagner's own contribution to that development. But it applies no less to the growth of the German national consciousness, to which Wagner also contributed exceptionally as it contributed to his maturing. Nationalism is a facet of Romanticism, the search for identity, the gathering in to the centre of the variegated strands of communal and popular sentiment and feeling so that elements from the collective unconscious become transferred and emerge as the collective conscious. Although the unification of Germany under Bismarck did not take place until 1871, German nationalism, as an essential constituent of German Romanticism, had been gathering force for at least half a century, and afterwards grew and consolidated until it reached its peak in the decade before 1914. Wagner's part in the rise of German natonalism and therefore of all that came after cannot be diminished, let alone ignored, by sweet thoughts or evasive words. And the aberration, as it became, of German nationalism was an essential part of the Romantic disaster out of which the two major holocausts of the twentieth century were bred. It was not a wholly German phenomenon; but in its specific manifestations its kernel was in Germany.

Fidelio, as I have said, tends to come apart at the seams not because it is too symphonic but because, overall, it is not symphonic enough. The organic growth and inner continuity of Beethoven's typical dramatic sonata form in orchestral and instrumental music could not, at the time of *Fidelio* and in view of Beethoven's inexperience as a composer of opera, function effectively in that context. However pregnant the main sections, the episodic structure of the whole in the end aborted true symphonic growth except in self-contained scenes. But symphonic growth, if it is to be more than a passing gesture, must apply to complete entities, not to isolated parts. What Beethoven had not mastered, and from his particular standpoint in time probably could not master, certainly not in a single opera, was that art of transition which Wagner erected as a leading principle and by which he set such store that he tended to declare it to be the true essence of the art of music.

And it took Wagner himself a long time to master it. In *The Flying Dutchman* he made a beginning; but only a tentative one. Indeed, it is doubtful if at that time he consciously recognized the full necessity for it. In so far as he did achieve some beginnings in that work he did so virtually by instinct alone. He had not yet rationalized and defined his operative theories. And so in its basic structure and organization, the *Dutchman* stands closer to *Fidelio* than to Wagner's mature music dramas or to Beethoven's own symphonies and sonatas. He did make something nearer a continuous musical structure by cutting out the spoken dialogue of the *Singspiel* style of *Fidelio* and *Der Freischütz*; but nothing in the *Dutchman* strikes so profound or searching a note as the best parts of *Fidelio*, or reaches the imaginative fancy and romantic *innig* of the best of *Der*

51

Freischütz. All the same, *The Flying Dutchman* struck a new note, and in a sense an ominous one, in German opera. The deep-dyed subjective Romanticism had nothing in it of Weber's easy-going fantasies, which even at their darkest do not really trouble the deeps and never have the threatening quality of Wagner's first authentic music drama.

This is most readily heard in the two overtures. Wagner's is clearly, indeed overtly, based upon Weber's so far as general principles of construction are concerned. And both, in their ways, are magnificent 'nature' pieces, Wagner's dealing with the sea, Weber's with the mysterious forests. Both are built out of themes from their respective operas, summing up in orchestral terms the essence of the drama to follow (though not annihilating it as Beethoven's *Leonora 2* and *3* do with *Fidelio*, Gustav Mahler notwithstanding). And each was written, perhaps inevitably, after the stage works themselves were completed. Yet there is in Wagner's a sombre, brooding quality, a fatefulness which points not only to the character of the legend but even more to the direction Wagner's creative mind was by now resolutely set upon. The powerful theme of the Dutch sea-captain, the all-pervading theme of Senta's Ballad, the superb storm music and the motif of the sailors' songs (both drawn indirectly from Wagner's own experience on the voyage of the *Thetis*) – it is all there in the overture, richly woven into a living fabric of sound that throughout strikes the unmistakable note of authenticity.

Despite its inconsistencies of style and its conventional elements, *The Flying Dutchman* still achieved a degree of musical and stylistic homogeneity surpassing that of both *Fidelio* and *Der Frieschütz*. This is even more clearly revealed in the single-act continuous version in three scenes Wagner originally intended and later produced at Bayreuth. Wagner made the three-act version to suit the convenience of the contemporary German theatre; but he always saw the other as the correct version and it is the one always given today at Bayreuth, even though the three-act affair is still commonplace practice elsewhere. The differences are significant, for although the musical alterations involved in making one act three, or three acts one, are not in themselves important and consist largely of scissors-and-paste work at the joints, dramatically they make a real difference and give a clearer indication of the way Wagner's mind was working than their actual substance suggests.

The legend of the Flying Dutchman appealed to the depths of Wagner's creative imagination. Where, and when, the story originated is not precisely known. It appears to be a later variant of the older tale of *The Wandering Jew*. It was certainly around and more or less common currency at the onset of the nineteenth century, when it attracted several authors to treat it in their own ways.[2] Wagner seems to have been at least aware of it from his early youth, though he probably read it in detail for the first time in Heine's *Memoirs of Herr von Schnabelewopski*, published in 1834, which contains a chapter devoted to the subject.[3] Unquestionably, when he sailed from Pilau in the *Thetis* it was 'continually in my mind', confirmed rather than initiated for him in conversation with the little ship's crew. Indeed, so deeply immersed in it was he as early as 1839 that the actual fishing port where they took refuge from the storm, Sandwike, the great granite cliffs of the fjord, the shanty-type songs sung by the sailors, all appeared literally and by name or direct quotation in the opera.

Whenever Wagner set himself to a major project he took great pains to find out everything about the particular subject and to read as much as he could lay his hands on pertaining to it. Thus, although Heine appears to have given him the leading facts and some of the details, he almost certainly went to various other sources before addressing himself to the actual undertaking. And having explored in depth and breadth, he made his own adaptations for his specific dramatic purposes. The story of the Flying Dutchman, filtered through many different minds, went into the making of the poem Wagner wrote in May 1841. It had seized hold of his imagination, 'unlocked it' in Ernest Newman's apt term. It was hardly surprising: here was the kind of legendary romantic yarn most likely to inflame the creative faculty of Richard Wagner in the maturing years of his career. (It was also from the libretto of *The Flying Dutchman* that Wagner saw himself, in his own view as a dramatic poet rather than a mere librettist.[4])

Although Wagner's restructuring of the story places the central emphasis on the motif of Redemption, thus anticipating a leading theme of his entire life work, there is no doubt that he identified himself with the lonely figure of the Dutchman. The central drama therefore becomes forcibly turned inwards towards the existential centre. The solitary voyager, destined to battle for ever against fate and the elements unless redeemed by the love of a good woman, greatly appealed to Wagner and in a general sense accorded with his conception of himself as set against the hostility of the world (especially after his Paris experiences) and under fateful sentence to triumph or go down. It was also very much in accord with the sentiments of the Romantic movement as a whole in the nineteenth century. In his extreme youth Wagner had composed some pieces to words from Goethe's *Faust*; and immediately before setting to work on the music for *Lohengrin*, in 1846, he inserted passages from Goethe's masterpiece into his own programme notes for a performance of the Beethoven Ninth, which he was currently rehearsing with a combination of impassioned vehemence and patient dedication. Thus the subject of Faust was deeply ingrained into his consciousness, as it was ingrained in the consciousness of the age, though its contemporary relevance was different, as it had to be, from that of the seventeenth century on the one hand, when Christopher Marlowe wrote his *The Tragical History of Dr Faustus*, or on the other of Thomas Mann's great novel, *Doktor Faustus*, in our own time. And in Goethe's *Faust* Love is exalted as the all-redeeming power, exemplified in perfect form in Woman and 'of Divine origin'. The theme runs all through Romantic art and literature: Liszt ended his own *Faust Symphony* (1854) with a setting of Goethe's 'Chorus Mysticus' which insists upon that very point. For Wagner it became a crux of his life- and world-view, and so of his art.

The precise origins of Wagner's version of the Flying Dutchman legend have always been in some doubt. He himself left contradictory accounts of it at various times. In particular, did he inject the redemption-by-woman motif more or less on his own account, and because it accorded so well with his own feelings, or did he find it at least intimated in some prior source with which he had become familiar? It is suggested by Heine, and although he later tended to play down the Heine influence, there is little doubt that, on his own admission. Heine was a major source.[5] All the same, he may well have encountered some other version or versions, including a stage play produced in Amsterdam that he had seen or heard about, in which the redemption motif had prominence. It is an intriguing matter; but it does not significantly bear upon the emergence of Wagner's first true masterwork.

The redemption through perfect woman, in Wagner's own words, the completely 'womanly Woman', the *Woman of the Future*, was inextricably woven into the Romantic conception of woman in general. According to this, which may be expanded to embrace the Victorian–Romantic idea, or ideal, woman tended to be either angel or whore – sometimes a whore with a heart of gold. This uneasy dichotomy, which is an over simplification of a complex subject that will have to be returned to in a later discussion of Wagner's mature work and thought, notably in *Tristan und Isolde*, had some disconcerting results. The typical Romantic heroine, the 'good woman', was likely to be beautiful but frail, on the surface anyway, and therefore somewhat insubstantial – which is no doubt why the 'bad' woman, the viper of seduction and lascivious temptress always trying to lead simple-minded and honest-hearted men to their destruction, is often more interesting and more convincing. The principal figures of the era seemed more or less evenly divided in their view of the matter. To Brahms most women were whores at heart (with the exception of Clara Schumann, definitely an angel); for Tennyson they were, or should be, predominantly angels, and even when they were not deserved a kind of paternalistic compassion. Wagner, especially in his earlier years, was temperamentally on the side of the angels, though susceptible to the wiles of the Kundry–Venus description. Though given strong music to sing, Wagner's early heroines still do not escape from the Romantic cliché so far as coming out on their own and attaining decisive character is concerned. They have musical identities, but otherwise tend to remain ciphers; that is to say, their existence is determined by their music but they do not achieve real dramatic independence or establish autonomous personality.

Wagner was at pains to insist that Senta in *The Flying Dutchman* should not be presented as a soft-fibred sentimentalist of the conventional theatre kind but a sturdy Northern maiden bred out of the rugged environment of sea and storm. Yet despite the central importance, both dramatically and musically, of her Ballad, the figure of Senta still lacks active personality. She is a medium rather than a person in her own right. Her obsession with the Dutchman and his legend may be indicative of strength rather than weakness; all the same, that strength is general rather than particular, more reflected than direct – it derives from the object (the doomed Vanderdecken) instead of from the subject (Senta herself). Senta is the medium of the Dutchman's redemption, but not the active cause of it. Wagner was right to insist that the part of Senta must be given strength and determination; but that in itself does not make her a figure of freely realized personality. Yet a medium in the truest sense is still a figure of strength, and nothing more enfeebles Wagner's opera than a portrayal of Senta as a drooping, sickly milksop. Nothing in the score or the poem can justify that.

The problem of Wagner's, and indeed the whole Romantic movement's conception or misconception of the real nature of woman is important to his development and to his relationship to his age. In *Opera and Drama* he wrote:

The nature of woman is love: but this love is a receiving, and in the receiving an unreservedly surrendering, love. Woman first finds her full individuality in the moment of surrender. She is the Undine who glides soulless through the waves of her native element, until she receives her soul through the love of a man . . . A woman who loves without this pride of surrender, truly does not love at all.

There is the nub: autonomous existence of women is virtually denied, the self-realization of the personality refuted by an imposed dependence, so far as women are concerned. And this is one area in which the Romantic world- and life-view diverges sharply from our own; a fundamental area. We do not have to go to the farthest extremes of Women's Liberation (which has the opposite but no less inimical effect of making women dependent on their own independence) and its shock tactics to understand that the Romantic attitude banished women to a position of unbreakable subservience. The idea that a woman's full individuality, her full emergence into personality, to be more accurate, is gained only in a moment of surrender to a man, will not be accepted for one moment by a woman of today; it is in fact precisely the attitude that has led to the extremes of rebellion, with their equally disastrous consequences, since it implies the kind of emotional dependence, bondage even, that would continue to exist even when material dependence is abolished. It is fundamentally a metaphysical rather than a physical or economic problem, and one which has still not been squarely faced.

There is of course at least one sense in which all this is very much a matter of appearances. Women have seldom been quite so subservient as men would like to believe. Woman's 'surrender' has always, as much in the Romantic legend of the nineteenth century as in any other, been a matter of diplomacy as well a straightforward fact. Women in history, whatever the legal and practical situation may have been at any one time, have invariably contrived to exert a considerable influence on events and on male personages by the simple expedient of allowing men to think themselves uniquely dominant while all the time 'bending' things to their way. And that is true even of the most oppressively paternalistic societies, such as Victorian England (an admirable if also ironic example because of the powerful influence exerted on that society by a woman at its head, Queen Victoria). Aristophanes was certainly not the first to see this more subtle truth and to expose it in a highly effective serious comedy. All the same, the general current of historical philosophy and sociology has been on the side of the subservience of women. Wagner's idea coincided accurately with that of his time and epoch; and in a corrupted form that idea degenerated into the idea of women as breeding machines at the service of and in the interests of a ruthless political dictatorship.

Paradoxically, Senta's 'surrender' is in one sense self-willed, an act of free volition. Or so it appears. It is certainly symbolic. Yet it is at the deeper level still predetermined, dependent upon the Dutchman and his fate. Without that existence and that fate, Senta must remain, however restlessly, one of the spinning girls, her troth given to the ardent if puzzled Erik. Senta is not, after all, a freely active agent. She is set upon saving the forlorn seaman, is obsessed by the desire to be the means of his redemption, to lift the curse off him. More than that, she is convinced in the depths of her being that such is her true destiny. Yet because she ultimately has no free choice, cannot reject him even if she wants to, she is without autonomous personality and is thus subservient to a kind of predestined destiny. Not until Isolde did Wagner create a heroine of undisputed personal autonomy, a woman who, despite the Love Potion and the fatal compulsion, still both retained her identity and realized her unique personality, and whose 'surrender' was therefore a genuine act of free will arising out of total personal independence, and thus became an act of true tragic significance and depth. In Isolde and her Liebestod 'surrender' has become liberated into ultimate metaphysical meaning.

In Wagner death is never an end but a beginning. It is always a transformation. The union becomes mystical. After Senta has plunged from the cliffs into the stormy seas, the Dutchman's ship sinks and the two figures, redeemed and redeemer, man and woman finally united, are seen slowly ascending towards the heavens. Isolde's Liebestod is not well named. Originally that term was to apply to the Prelude. The Liebestod is not really concerned with death at all, not in any normal and humanistic sense: it is a true transforming, a literal transubstantiation. It is not a flight from reality but an escape into it. The raising by fire of Valhalla denotes not the end of the world but a new beginning; not final ruin and destruction but rebirth. That was the intention in Wagner's mind, even if it did not, and perhaps could not from the initial premises, work out in practice. But there is no doubt that in Wagner's vision the burning of Valhalla and Brünnhilde's Immolation was to be seen as a purification leading to new life, as transformation on the social and communal plane rather than the individual It amounted in the end to the same thing. Far more than the rather obvious 'Transformation Scene' in *Parsifal*, virtually all Wagner's music dramas (with the exception of *Meistersinger*) end in some kind of transformation. Each denouement is a declaration on behalf of a higher form of existence via some, in a sense, apocalyptic heightening and intensifying of reality. In one way or another this is the function of all art; yet because Wagner was Wagner and the Romantic era what it was, with all that implied, it took the particular form it did, and had to take.

It is always a transformation. That is why the habit of accompanying images of the disasters of war with passages from *Götterdämmerung* is so ludicrous, such a total solecism. Wotan's willing act of self-destruction, of Valhalla and all it stood for, himself included, has, again, true tragic implication. It has nothing to do with the crude and commonplace plunge into death and disaster of the conventional military and political mind. It is always a transformation; a bid for new and higher life forms.

This Wagnerian-Romantic idea of death as transformation may at first sight appear as a kind of corollary of the Christian concept of death as the road to ultimate union with God. In fact it is much nearer the Buddhist conception of Nirvana, an intimation that is conformed by reference to *Parsifal*, though, in retrospect at least, it underlines nearly all his work from *The Flying Dutchman* onwards, again with the partial exception of *Die Meistersinger*.

Although this idea of transformation or transubstantiation through death is commendable for the romantically biased individual temperament, a legitimate aspiration towards a final escape from the constrictions of the ego, in social and communal terms it can be, and has been, highly dangerous. It can all too easily lead to the idea of death in battle as 'honourable' – that is, to a falsely mystical identification of the national consciousness with some unexpurgated ideal as manifested in the person of a national leader or dictator. In contemporary terms this might be equated with Hitler on one side and Stalin on the other (although perhaps Lenin would be a more potent source figure), as two sides of the same distorted coin. The idea of national Nirvana, or a corrupted idea of the doom of contemporary gods, is a direct legacy of the Romantic idea of transformation and redemption through death; and as such it was a legacy of the work of Richard Wagner. Creatively valid, often noble, in its time, it played its part in leading towards one of history's most outrageous aberrations.

Wagner himself believed that, 'We must learn to *die*, and to die in the fullest sense of the word' – that is to say, we have to accept death in and for itself, not try to evade it by seeking recompense in some belief in a form of afterlife, as a release from the burden of living. But that in itself is a form of transformation, of a radical restructuring of consciousness, a vindication of the true essence of tragedy as 'joy to the man who dies'. Learning to die thus becomes a primary source of life. All deaths in Wagner are directed towards that end. In this sense, as in several others, *The Flying Dutchman* touches the core of the Wagnerian ethos. If it had been written at the end instead of at the beginning of his solitary voyage, when he was in full rather than embryonic command of his material, it would have appeared in sharper, more clearly defined perspective.

In Wagner's mind the musical and dramatic structure of *The Flying Dutchman* expanded from the central point of Senta's Ballad, which follows the Spinning Chorus. The contrast between the girls at their wheels and their uncomplicated 'work song', and the withdrawn, obsessed figure of Senta is dramatically decisive. Senta's Ballad in fact 'spreads' through the entire opera as the spiritual and emotional penetration of her mind. It is a potent individual conception, worthy to carry the load placed upon it (more so than the 'Prize Song' in *Meistersinger*). But Wagner had not yet evolved the technical mastery to make an opera grow as an organism from a central germ. He could not dispense with the operatic trappings, though he did make a start.[6] The gulf between Wagner's and Dietsch's setting of the story is immense and unbridgeable, and it is in part the gulf between the conventional opera of the day (though not a remarkable example of it) and the new music drama which Wagner was in the process of launching.

Wagner's execution in *The Flying Dutchman* was both bold and tentative – bold because he was already gripped by a determination to create a new type of musical drama and did not flinch from its implications; tentative because he still lacked the experience and certainty of touch to carry it through without hesitation or inhibition (primarily because he still had not formulated and so resolved the basic problem in his own mind). He was obliged to rely to some extent upon set arias, duets, ensembles and traditional theatrical 'effects', in part for practical reasons but more because he had not yet learnt how else to put a musical drama together. But at the same time he was able to infuse the main musical and dramatic points with a new and individual creative power. It was characteristic of his ability at this time that the evocative music of the sea, the ships, the sailors, as well as Senta's Ballad and the Dutchman's motif, are successful and original, while the 'love' scenes and the link passages are largely unremarkable.

The 'pendant' characters, Darland, Erik and Mary, are competently handled in a not particularly striking manner. Wagner did, however, have decided ideas on how these too should be presented. The acquisitive, slightly devious Darland, a shrewd and brave mariner ready to sell his daughter for the Dutchman's proffered treasure, was intended neither as parody nor as comic relief. Though there is a strain of vulgarity in Darland, and in his music, there is nothing preposterous, certainly nothing disreputable. Darland's conduct is perfectly straightforward and perfectly commendable, according to his own lights. He is neither subtle nor

58

sophisticated; like Rocco in *Fidelio* he is eager for riches and not one to disdain an easy buck. But unlike Rocco he does not find the price too high. After all, the price of gold for Rocco is murder; for Darland it is simply the hand of his daughter to a fellow seafarer. In any case, marrying a daughter off to a rich man is still considered no unforgivable crime: it is usually thought of just as a 'good match'. Wagner himself would have seen nothing wrong in a man advancing his cause by such an arrangement.

Erik is different again: another straightforward character caught up in strange matters he cannot properly understand, his cause is lost from the start. Senta's obsession with the legend of the Flying Dutchman and the portrait that hangs on the wall of the spinning room leaves him no room for manoeuvre. But although he has no chance, and recognizes it, he faces up to it with honest, manly fortitude. And he too must be played, at Wagner's insistence, with strength and character, not as some feeble, whining, disappointed swain. He is in the context of the drama what Henry James used to call, after the French term, a *ficelle* – that is, a character who belongs less to the subject itself than to the manner of relating it. Despite his misfortunes, Erik is not a tragic character, only a sorrowful one.

But the Dutchman himself is another matter. This Wagner–Vanderdecken figure is the positive pole of the dramatic and psychological centre of the drama, as Senta is the negative pole. If the redemptive essence lies in Senta and her Ballad, the Dutchman is the activating principle of everything. He is a true figure of tragedy, recalling in his presence and situation Lady Gregory's words to W. B. Yeats that 'tragedy must be a joy to the man who dies'. Without that joy in death, and through it a transcendence of the merely mortal, there is no tragedy, only pity for the self, nihilism, negation. The active creative principle is present in the person of the Flying Dutchman, as it was present, indeed even omnipotent, in Wagner himself. A powerful evolutionary thrust, though in its early stages so far as Wagner's work is consciously concerned, is evident in *The Flying Dutchman*; and that, despite the shortcomings and conventionalities, is what gives the opera, and the drama upon which it is based, its symbolic force and vibrant individual note of authenticity.

And here, too, is another leading Wagnerian motif. The Dutchman's joy in death looks forward to the ecstatic last moments of Tristan and Isolde. If ever there was a case of death being a joy to those who die, it is in *Tristan*, which is therefore (but not only therefore) one of the world's supreme tragic masterpieces. But the joint deaths of Senta and the at last redeemed Vanderdecken are full of joy too, a joy both holy and unholy, and this is also genuine tragedy. Wagner was a true tragic artist, his work full of the joy not only in creation but also in the consummation in death that is the hallmark of all great tragic art, which is never morbid, never full of either pity or contempt for the self, always positive, never a futile negation. It has nothing whatever to do with that perverted glee in destruction or spite that seeks to bring everything down with it if it cannot get its own way, which distinguishes a certain type of political and military mind; nothing of that greed for desolation that characterized the last years of the Nazi party, in its decadent post-Romanticism.

We have lost, temporarily no doubt, the art and meaning of tragedy because we have lost that supreme sense of fulfilment on the final denouement that takes death out of the commonplace area of decay and regret and elevates it into a true active principle.[7]

In *The Flying Dutchman* Wagner made a real start on his life's work, set forth upon that solitary voyage which would end with *Parsifal*, a renunciation in which the element of joy in death was almost but not quite exchanged for a species of transtemporal serenity, and would lead him, like his own doomed sea-captain, through all manner of storms, tempests and tribulations. Vanderdecken had sworn that he would round Cape Horn even if it took him until the Day of Judgement. The Devil therefore laid a curse upon him that he should sail the seas forever, or until he should find a woman faithful literally unto death, whose unflinching love would redeem him. Wagner set out upon a similar voyage, swearing that he would transform the world and everything in it through his art; and sometimes he too felt that the curse was upon him, seeing in his ceaseless pursuit of his art, from which he could not escape, a parallel with the Dutchman's perpetual tossing upon the angry sea. Whether he actually saw it that way and in those precise terms at the time is neither here nor there. It amounted to the same thing in the end, as he was soon to find out for himself. And if *The Flying Dutchman* was only a beginning, and a successful one only in part, it was none the less a remarkable achievement for a young man still in his twenties. He knew it: looking back on this first opera in which he promulgated his ideas in practice and found his authentic voice, the first in which he unmistakably 'spoke out', and which he always held in high affection even though he did not spare it his critical asperity, Wagner recognized that he had taken the first momentous step along his path. He wrote in some justifiable pride and self-admiration that he did not know of any other case where an artist had made so total a transformation as he had between *Reinzi* and *The Flying Dutchman*. (The motif of transformation again.)

A new form of German opera had been born, and with it a new man and artist under the skin of Richard Wagner. It can hardly be said that 'modern music' had been also born. But it is unquestionable that the full Romantic impulse had been given new and ominous articulation, and that with it a new aspect of the human psyche had been opened, with its powerful implications for the future. The conductor Franz Lachner, who said that every time he opened the score of *The Flying Dutchman* 'the wind blew out of it wherever you looked', spoke truer than he suspected. The wind blew not only out of that score; it blew through the mind of Richard Wagner, the tempest internal as well as external, and out of it again and thence across the mid-nineteenth century itself, determining much that was to come afterwards. It has continued to blow well into our own century and our own times.

CHAPTER FOUR

TOWARDS THE VORTEX

He longed to return to Germany. All his efforts now became directed to that end. Germany, he was sure, would restore his fortunes. He was not without cause for that optimism: *Rienzi* had been accepted in Dresden; *The Flying Dutchman*, on Meyerbeer's recommendation, had found favour in Berlin. Everywhere he looked, Germany called. On both personal and professional levels it was time to turn his back on Paris.

Again he was to suffer disillusionment and the dashing of his hopes. 'Just as I had been undeceived in Paris,' he wrote, 'so I was doomed to disappointment in Germany.[1] It was not a case of simple patriotism, either way. Ironically, political France appealed to him rather more than political Germany, with its conservative stuffiness and provincial lack of vision. It was, he said, 'the feeling of utter homelessness in Paris that aroused my yearning for my homeland,' though he did not deceive himself that the real Germany corresponded in any sense or degree with the Germany of his dreams. That, the Germany of his dreams, the homeland of his vision, he knew he had to create out of his own effort, through his own creative force, much as the Flying Dutchman, Vanderdecken, had not only to find but in some deeper and more symbolic sense himself create the perfect Woman who would at last redeem and so liberate him from the Devil's curse, and as the imagination of Wagner had in fact 'created' Senta.

The acceptance first of *Rienzi* in Dresden and then of *The Flying Dutchman* in Berlin confirmed Wagner in his vocation but still did not provide him with a living. Optimistic as always, he hoped that it would; but although *Rienzi* achieved immediate success when it was eventually staged, the *Dutchman* was thought by comparison to be altogether too dark-toned, gloomy, morbid almost. Operatic taste in Germany, as in Paris, remained steadfastly and obstinately addicted to the full-blown, the splendiferous, not to say the overtly gaudy.

61

So the matter of earning his living and barring the door to wolves of various kinds continued to press hard upon the person and character of Richard Wagner.

Before leaving Paris he had done more hack work to support himself and Minna and to put a little aside for the journey home. He made arrangements of Halévy's operas, wrote articles and three short stories embodying his current ideas on the artist's life and fate, made a libretto to a commission from the Czech Jewish composer Josef Dessauer out of Hoffmann's *Bergwerke von Falun*. At the same time, because of the signs of a certain advancing success in his work, largely due to the acceptance of *Rienzi*, he began to receive renewed support from his family, who were apparently ready to give him the benefit of still more doubts and believe that he really was taking life and living seriously at last.

All the same, he was obliged to borrow the money for the homeward journey.

The journey itself was uneventful but uncomfortable. It took five days and lodged in Wagner's memory as another unpleasant experience. Yet, as with the voyage on the *Thetis*, it provided nourishment and stimulation to his imagination. For the first time he set eyes on the Rhine, and the sight stirred his deepest feelings for Germany, the true and essential Germany, not the political and social one that he despised. Then, too, he saw the Castle of Wartburg near Eisenbach, and that in its turn set creative vibrations in motion, summoning visions of the Minnesingers, the Contest of Song, Venus and the Venusberg. He had already made contact with the folk legend of 'the noble Tannhäuser', and his mind was working towards a new opera on that subject. The impact of this journey was to be less direct, less immediate, than that of the storms and maritime matters on the *Thetis*, which had led to the great sea music of *The Flying Dutchman*. But it sank deep none the less.

Though a Saxon himself, Wagner tended to dislike Saxony and the Saxons when he finally reached Dresden, finding them crude, boorish and lazy. No doubt, though he might not have admitted it, Paris had rubbed some of the coarser German edges off him, exercised its subtle civilizing influences. But Dresden was prepared to stage his work as Paris had not been; and that made the difference.

He threw himself wholeheartedly into preparations for the production of *Rienzi*, taking the most active part in everything pertaining thereto, as usual sparing himself nothing in the pursuit of the highest standards possible. Even so, it did not go smoothly or straightforwardly. For one thing, Wilhelmine Schröder-Devrient, his old flame and heroine, was to take the female lead but insisted on singing a Bellini opera before *Reinzi*, so there was inevitably delay to play upon the nerves and patience of the irate Wagner.

Meanwhile (in fact somewhat earlier) he had, out of homesickness for

Germany, sketched an idea for another grand opera in the *Rienzi* line and succession. It was to be based upon a historical incident revolving round the exploits of one Manfred, son of Friedrich II, in Arabia, and to be called *The Saracen Woman*. The project, which came to nothing, has little importance except for two features. Firstly, he went to an incident from the distant past (the Hohenstaufian in this case) for his operatic subjects, the contemporary German scene apparently no attraction for him. But this could be a misinterpretation: the particular constitution of Wagner's mind and imagination virtually drove him to the past and to ancient legend. It was part of his status as a myth-maker that the lure of historicism was unusually strong in him. Although his work was consciously dedicated to the creation of a new world and a new order of freedom and creativity, he sought the necessary symbolism and mythology in the past. So far as the present was concerned, he contented himself with pamphleteering and with getting himself involved in revolutionary activities which had nothing whatever to do with the real essence and value of his work but was probably essential to a man of his nature and temperament.

Secondly, in *Die Sarazenin* he again created a female character, 'wove an imaginary female figure' into the historical plot, as he put it. This parallels his manner in *The Flying Dutchman* where Senta, if not entirely his unique creation, was worked out according to his own idea and conception, and confirms his predilection for centralizing his dramas on one or other form of Woman (*Das Weib*), perfect and idealized. Significantly, Mme Schröder-Devrient objected to the concept of the Priestess in this *Sarazenin* text, if only because 'the *Prophetess* can never more become a *woman*', as Wagner himself phrased it. Apparently the great diva was herself at the time enmeshed in an *affaire* that had thrown her temporarily off balance and even caused her to turn temporarily on Wagner and demand the repayment of money she had earlier lent to him.

And as usual it was money that lay at the root of his troubles. *Rienzi* was finally produced in Dresden on 20 October 1842. It was a tremendous and immediate success. Wagner had feared during that première that the extreme length (a foretaste of the future) would provoke jeers and catcalls. In fact, the entire work greatly pleased its audience and earned him the first real accolades and the first full-hearted popular applause of his career. He became instantly famous, achieved star status virtually overnight, as Byron had with *Childe Harold's Pilgrimage*, an earlier and distinguished example of the High Romantic impulse.

But even success could still turn sour, or rather it did not alleviate his difficulties. News of *Reinzi's* triumph soon spread throughout Germany and beyond. Having wind of it, Wagner's creditors reawoke and began to move in once more. They came from far and wide, from Magdeburg, Riga, almost anywhere he had been in previous years, learning nothing, forgetting – elephantine – nothing. They moved in with demands backed by threats. His past, like a tin can tied to a dog's tail, followed him wherever he went, whatever he did. The world had not yet learnt the lesson he required it to learn, that it owed him a living and should therefore cancel all past indebtedness and overlook present and future ones.

But all was by no means on the debit side. The quick success of *Rienzi* had two positive and beneficial results. It encouraged the Dresden theatre management to negotiate the release of *The Flying Dutchman* with the Berlin theatre, which had not yet produced it and was quite ready to oblige; and it led to his being offered an appointment, for life and with a regular salary, as joint Kapellmeister at the Dresden Royal Theatre, a post he accepted with reservations and only after hard bargaining. Before accepting he had rejected a more menial position; the timely death of the man he was appointed to succeed opened the way for him. He was thus at last, and for the first time in his life, not only a famous composer but a man in stable employment with an assured income. It did not help repel his creditors, but it did delay the pressure of new ones.

The Flying Dutchman was produced in Dresden, having been unconditionally released by Berlin, in January 1843. Unlike *Rienzi* it was not a success. The reasons for this appear to have been various. In the first place, the rendition of the name part was far from adequate, and despite the presence of the great Schröeder-Devrient as Senta the whole production seems to have fallen short. But a more profound reason lay within the drama itself. The dark, sombre tone, the introspective nature of much of it, the relatively complex psychological implications, above all the unspectacular nature of much of the music, these could not be offset to the audience's satisfaction by the brilliance of the sea music and the melodic attraction of numbers like the Spinning Chorus. Expecting a repetition of the coloured splendours of *Rienzi*, in the form and style to which it was accustomed, the audience was substantially nonplussed by the starkly ominous and original tone of the *Dutchman*. It lasted through only four performances, then was taken off, and did not reappear in Dresden until 1865.

After the success of *Rienzi* and the failure of *The Flying Dutchman* Wagner could have been forgiven for returning to the style of the conventional Grand Opera. Indeed, his idea for *Die Sarazenin* was precisely that, as well as (once again) a vehicle for Wilhelmine Schröder-Devrient. He might therefore have continued with that, or something like it. But he had already given up any such idea, in either of its aspects. He did not write another Grand Opera and he did not compose for any star singer, however admired and cherished. Instead, as might have been foreseen, he followed his own line of evolution and produced a new opera which would give further practical demonstration of his developing ideas on musical drama. His duties at the Court Theatre entailed a good deal of journey work and presented a number of administrative difficulties due to long-established and moribund 'traditions'[2], both on the production side and in the personnel department; but he coped with it all with his familiar mixture of indulgence and impatience, occasionally flying into a temper but for the most part containing himself and sorting out problems with reasonable tact. He was appointed conductor of the Dresden Choral Society and composed a number of 'official' pieces for it. Life was busy and lucrative.

But it was the gestation of the new opera that made all else irrelevant. He had first made acquaintance with the Tannhäuser legend in his youth through the narrative of Ludwig Tieck. Then, in Paris, he had come upon a German *Volksbuch*, a somewhat mysterious volume which has never been traced and in which he found not only the outline of the Tannhäuser story but also a hint of the connection between Tannhäuser and the Contest of Song. It fired his imagination and revived old memories, linked his own mind back into German folk mythology and the collective unconscious underlying it. He returned to Tieck and saw, from the two together, the subject of his next opera. He developed this by combining the *Tannhäuserlied* with the old story of the Minnesingers and the Wartburg Contest of Song, which he probably took in its final form from E. T. A. Hoffmann's *The Serapion Brethren*, a collection of stories from medieval romance and folk legend. It has sometimes been stated that the combination of the Tannhäuser legend with the Contest of Song was Wagner's own invention. In fact, as he himself says, it was first suggested to him in his *Volksbuch*. But the precise form it took and the manner of its presentation (especially in relation to the Court of Venus) as it emerged in the opera was his own, no doubt partly as a result of his seeing the Castle of Wartburg on the journey from Paris to Dresden, which must still at that time have been sharp in his memory.

He set to work on the preliminary draft during a brief holiday in Teplitz in the summer of 1842. The poem itself was written the following April. Work on the score progressed through the latter part of 1843, continued through 1844 and was finished in the spring of 1845. The première took place in Dresden on 19 October 1845, with Wagner's old friend Josef Tichatscheck, the creator of Rienzi, as Tannhäuser, his niece Johanna as Elisabeth, and the ubiquitous Mme Schröder-Devrient as Venus.

As usual, Wagner banked his future and his solvency on his new work; and as usual he was disappointed. There was no quick triumph for him this time. Things persisted in going wrong. Despite care taken in rehearsal, the first performance gave the impression of being poorly prepared. It was a flop. Subsequent ones went better and the production was tightened up; but *Tannhäuser*, although it went into the standard repertory, never repeated the success of *Rienzi*.

Perhaps it was inevitable. In *Tannhäuser* Wagner set himself to rid his stage work of the conventional operatic elements that still persisted in *The*

Flying Dutchman: the set pieces, the Italianate arias and duets, the separation of parts to the detriment of the whole. But although his intentions were impeccable, his execution of them was still not assured. In fact, *Tannhäuser* is the weakest of all Wagner's musical dramas. It has, either in embryo or *in toto*, virtually all his most heinous failings, all those elements which feed the anti-Wagnerites with invaluable ammunition. It is noisy; it is sentimental; it contains passages of exhausting longeur; it displays in various forms that propensity, which is not specifically Wagnerian but overall German, for incessantly explaining and haranguing; it tends to mix a kind of fake mysticism with bombast in a manner calculated to induce aural indigestion, especially in the interminable Act II. And ironically, where it did succeed in catching the public ear, and retaining it, was precisely at those points where it most resembled conventional opera – in the set pieces and individual arias. Indeed, were it not for their incurable philistinism and stupidity, one might have a certain reluctant sympathy with the chinless wonders of the Jockey Club who effectively wrecked the Paris presentation of the revised version in 1861. True, these loud-voiced and bird-brained creatures were only protesting against the lack of their accustomed ballet sequences in Act II when they could drool over their pet ballerinas. But if they had possessed the wit and sense to recognize it, they could have found ample cause for censure in the opera itself, which undoubtedly seemed coarse and crude to the more refined Parisian taste. That is probably a side issue; but the fact remains that *Tannhäuser*, for a number of reasons, tends to be 'Wagnerate' in the bad sense. It did, and does, his reputation little good.

And yet it did some good in its time. This is understandable, for precisely the reasons he himself foresaw. It dipped into German history and thus made a direct appeal to the contemporary garnering of national aspirations towards German unity and fulfilled indentity. It referred back to the medieval German world, which appealed no less to the German Romantic imagination. It dealt with those closely related subjects of sacred and profane love and redemption through renunciation, which also made a strong appeal to that imagination. In the central figure of Tannhäuser it had a genuine protagonist, 'the spirit of the whole Ghibelline race for every age', and the representative of 'a poor artist athirst for life'. In addition, the decisive combining of the Tannhäuser legend with the Contest of Song gave the whole a richness and complexity neither would have produced independently, and was a further tribute to Wagner's intensity of vision and insight.

Thus *Tannhäuser*, in the tally of Wagner's dramatic works, has its twofold aspect, its double-sidedness. Its faults as well as its virtues derive in part from the flaws and potencies of Wagner's own creative constitution at the time, and in part from the nature and constitution of the German Romantic movement itself. This is nowhere better illustrated than in the character of Elisabeth. Here is one of Wagner's and the Romantic age's 'wet' heroines; in herself a 'character' without character; a cypher at once feebler and more endemic than Senta in *The Flying Dutchman*. Senta at least has her strength of purpose, even if it is not entirely her own, a manifestation of an actively realized personality, a genuine force of character, which is personality in action. But Elisabeth, Saint Elisabeth, is represented as a kind of pure angelic figure who mediates on behalf of the sinful and lustful male hellbent on perdition, and ultimately expires in the attempt, whether 'successful' or not. It is a familiar device, and it never convinces. Bernard Shaw's stinging remark that 'gentle Jesus meek and mild is a snivelling modern innovation with no warrant in the Gospels' should be applied not only to Jesus but to the saints and angels who are victims of the same delusion. Yet it is, in the present context, a particularly Romantic solecism.[3]

The juxtaposition of the saintly Elisabeth and the 'wicked' Venus is a clear case of the Romantic conception of Woman as either angel or whore, with the luckless (or lucky) male trapped in between. It depends on which way you come to it; from which side of the equation.

It is of course easy to scoff at such an idea from the perspectives of today. Yet there was in the Romantic hypothesis of the dual nature of Woman contesting for the soul of Man, himself torn between the desires of the flesh and awareness of the world of the spirit, something not only fundamental, but in a curious way still a good deal more laudable than the twentieth century's greedy materialism, whether it is the economic materialism of America or the ruthless political materialism of the Soviet Union. Paradoxically, both capitalism and Marxism also originated in the nineteenth century and in the true historical sense still belong inescapably to it. But the nineteenth century at least tried to work out the dichotomy, was genuinely aware of the distinction between sacred and profane, and brought it to crisis though not to resolution in a way that the twentieth has, temporarily no doubt, abrogated.

Tannhäuser as a work of art falls below the level of *The Flying Dutchman*, in large part for the simple reason that it attempts more. The *Dutchman*, for all its conventional elements, is more concentrated, more inner directed from the musical point of view, especially in its proper one-act form. Its construction is, for German Romantic opera, reasonably taut, its tone powerfully concentrated. It avoids, as *Tannhäuser* does not, the prolixity that is one of Wagner's most irritating faults. The coarseness of the scoring, the longueurs, most noticeable in the second act, the passages of bombast and outright vulgarity – these are all the faults and impositions that anti-Wagnerians resent. That they are counterbalanced by a genuine originality of conception, many felicities of execution, considerable stretches of finely wrought and undeniably powerful music and drama, does not alter the basic proposition.

It was necessary for Wagner at this time to work through the faults and aberrations of *Tannhäuser*. Some of them are endemic and can never be eradicated, even if they can to some extent be tamed; but others had to be purged out of his system before the higher art of the subsequent masterpieces could be reached and confirmed. That they had to come out and could not be altogether suppressed is shown by the manner in which they persist, though to some degree modified, in the revision for Paris a decade and a half later. By that time Wagner, with the experience of composing *Tristan* and half *The Ring* already behind him, was another, infinitely more mature man and musician. Yet the same characteristics remain: they could not be expurgated.

At the time of the composition of *Tannhäuser* Wagner resembled the Germany at some two decades later, when Bismarck had shrewdly remarked: 'Let us get to work. Let us heave Germany into the saddle. She will soon learn to ride.'[4] A kind of immature self-assurance underlay all the strong, outgoing effort in the man as well as the country. *Tannhäuser* pitched Wagner into the saddle. *The Flying Dutchman* had taught him much and released his unique creative energies. Even so, seen in retrospect it was still technically and aesthetically linked to the conventional idea of opera, and owed allegiance to the past and to his own *Rienzi*. But in *Tannhäuser* he consciously set out to explore new ground, to extend the frontiers of musical drama. He heaved himself into the saddle; but he still had to learn to ride in the new style. The coarseness and crudity that he observed, to his displeasure, in his native Saxony and among the Saxons, was still an active part of his own nature and character: the civilizing processes had not yet completed their work. In one sense they never would; a man's essential self does not change with changing times and circumstance. Richard Wagner remained German to the end, as Germany itself remained what it was and in the perspectives of history had to be. Wagner at this time, like Germany a few decades later, was not free of the character of the *parvenu*, partly because of his accruing wealth and newly acquired position, partly because of the cultural ascendancy of Austria for at least the previous century. It is a complex question; but perhaps it can in part be defined by Goethe's remark to Eckermann, in 1827: 'We Germans are of yesterday. We have indeed been properly cultivated for a century; but a few more centuries must still elapse before so much mind and elevated culture will become universal among our people that they will appreciate beauty like the Greeks, that they will be inspired by a beautiful song, and that it will be said of them, "it is long since they were barbarians".'

Wagner, like Nietzsche, in fact like most of the leading Romantics, was strongly attracted to the Greeks and the Hellenic ideals of art and beauty, saw there the perfect realization in primary form of his own conception of the relationship between drama and music. Indeed, when he came to formulate his own ideas on the creation in modern terms of the total composite artform, it was the Greeks' classical combining of music, drama and dance that he took as his starting point. Appreciation, if not complete understanding, of the ancient Greeks and their world was a leading motif of the nineteenth century and its arts.

Despite its particular admixture of faults and virtues – and whatever one may say about it, it does represent in its best part a genuine advance in Wagner's art – *Tannhäuser* has its extra-musical peculiarities, its Romantic attitudes at the centre which hardly support an objective scrutiny, let alone an ontological one. It is difficult, even from the standpoint of mid-nineteenth century Romanticism, to take the dominant idea seriously – that some dalliance on the Venusberg with the luxuriant Venus is a sin so venal that only a miracle can expiate it. Certainly Tannhäuser himself, intoxicated by the experience, is determined to uphold and praise the admirable qualities of Venus and her Court, much to the displeasure of the Landgrave and the assembled nobles and to the discomfiture of the 'pure' Elisabeth. Even so, that his 'sin' should cause him to be damned to eternal perdition unless the staff in the Pope's hand shall put forth green shoots, that he therefore be summarily dismissed from the Pope's presence when he had gone to Rome to seek pardon, is an idea so curious, even if it is intended as symbolic, that only a wild exaggeration of the dichotomy between love sacred and profane could be held to account for it. It would hardly have occurred to the eighteenth century; and it would appeal a good deal less to ours. Indeed, it did not appeal to many in its own time. An unpardonable sin, to be expiated only by a miracle, this enjoyment of the sensual pleasures? And of course the miracle does take place – after the death of the saintly Elisabeth, apparently of a broken heart. No wonder some charged it with being barely concealed Catholic propaganda.

Wagner, of course, was unrepentant. He had made progress in his art, and knew it. And if he saw the progress more clearly than the still active anomalies and miscalculations, that was only to be expected.

His practical life was still in a parlous state. As usual, he was in desperate need of money. He had come to the conclusion that if he was to prosper through his compositions, he must both have them published and see them performed in more propitious venues than Dresden and the other provincial German cities. He had accordingly arranged for publication at his own expense with the Dresden music dealer, C. F. Meser. He borrowed money, took credit as and where he could, put himself further into hock. His bill with Meser climbed ever higher, joining others he had already contracted through his habit of living in determined luxury well beyond his means. In pursuance of seeing his dramas performed in the capital, he went to Berlin to sound out possibilities of having *Tannhäuser* produced there; but was turned down. He returned to Dresden in some apprehension. And with cause.

Suddenly the bottom seemed to fall out of his world. He was back in the kind of straits he had hoped to leave behind him in Paris. He and Minna had to leave their apartment and move into humbler quarters; their good name as well as their effects were threatened with forfeiture. They were obliged to sell furniture to meet the most pressing debts. Everyone who had lent him money, even old friends including Mme Schröder-Devrient, demanded repayment or the immediate settling of accounts. There seemed nowhere to turn; and indeed there would have been nowhere if it had not been for the Dresden Theatre fund which helped him out with a grant of funds, though it was handed over with reluctance and with petulant scoldings in respect of his extravagant ways and moralizing reminders of his good fortune in being employed at all.

It bore heavily upon him, not as a matter of conscience but purely as one of inconvenience. He could not live as he wished to live, as he considered an artist had a right to live. He was immersed in thoughts for new dramatic works, but lack of money with its attendant worry continued to distract him.

His thoughts for new work were running two ways. During his years in Paris he had come upon the subject of Lohengrin. It fascinated him, but did not for the moment take firm root. Now, during a 'cure' taken in Marienbad, his favourite watering place, he found that subject jostling in his mind with another, the Mastersingers of Nuremberg, which he had recently come across by reading Gervinus's *History of German Literature*. He had been advised by his doctor not to work during his 'cure'; but to tell Richard Wagner not to work was like telling Casonova to keep away from women or Napoleon to abjure military campaigns. It simply was not in his constitution to let time slip idly by, unused and broken.

But he did try to keep off *Lohengrin*, which was beginning to haunt him, as much because he could not for the time being see the proper form the story should take as on account of the subject itself.

So he turned to the Mastersingers, ostensibly as a means of entertaining himself by fashioning a piece of rough comedy but also as counterpart to the 'serious' business of *Tannhäuser*, much as the Greeks liked to set a Satyr-play beside a Tragedy in the interests of balance and proportion. He was particularly taken with the idea of 'the Marker', with whom he saw the opportunity to poke some malicious fun at his enemies and at official dunderheads in general, of whom there were plenty in provincial Germany.

But he was not yet ready for *Die Meistersinger*, much though the subject attracted him. *Meistersinger* would have to bide its time. His particular mood of the moment was not to be assuaged by comedy of any sort. He returned to *Lohengrin* – or rather, *Lohengrin* returned to him, and with such intensity that he forsook all else for it, neglected his 'cure', leapt out of the Marienbad baths before his time in order to write down all that had come into his mind, and was soon abandoned by his doctors as an unsuitable case for treatment.

Of course, the real treatment lay, as always, in the work. He had gone to Marienbad in the first place out of exhaustion at the end of a hectic season with the Dresden Court Theatre. And from labour of that kind he certainly did need rest and relief. But not from his own creative work. That was the meat of his life, the wine of his bloodstream; that was not 'work' in any normal or accepted sense, even though in its own way it exhausted him even more. Yet his outgoing energy in the direction of original composition was essentially self-renewing; the other took energy out without putting a nearly equivalent amount back.

So *Lohengrin* progressed. He returned to Dresden from Marienbad with the Prose Sketch in his pocket. He immediately began work on the poem, and then to 'feel' the corresponding music forming within and alongside it. And as always, once he had plunged into creative work, he became obsessed and possessed by it, transformed and taken out of his everyday, egotistical, often arrogant self. It became more real to him than the outside world, which he was again feeling alien and hostile to everything his artistic being strove for, himself a kind of heroic loner in an inimical enviroment. And that environment still had to play its part and make its inescapable claims – inescapable because it continued to provide a tithe at least of the ever-needed financial resource. He was not popular with his colleagues at the Court Theatre, however, largely because he was determined on a course of reform and improvement, of eradicating lazy habits and bad traditions, of pulling the entire organization together and aiming at higher standards all round – all activities and ambitions sure to make him resented by entrenched officials and employees and others anxious to draw pay without putting in really demanding effort. Richard Wagner may have been many things, by no means all of them admirable – but he was never in his life one of that description. All the same, diligence in those departments also preoccupied him, to the interruption if not the exclusion of *Lohengrin*, his true work and labour, here as always *primus inter alia*.

He continued to compose occasional pieces; but the most illuminating aspects of this work, which was by no means all a matter of time wasted, was his preparation and eventual establishment of Beethoven's Ninth symphony as a regular feature of the annual Palm Sunday concerts, and his revival and rigorous editing of Gluck's *Iphigénie en Aulide*. His ideas on the latter may raise an eyebrow today when the search for 'authenticity' is all and scholarly editions proliferate even where the original has obvious shortcomings or elements dependent upon contemporary inadequacies of performance or production or moribund convention. But it should be remembered that when Wagner made his version of *Iphigénie en Aulide*[5] it had become encrusted with all manner of bad habits and careless 'traditions' from the immediately preceding age, and what Wagner did was to bring it into line with current taste and practice. It may not be our current taste and practice; but at least it did show a genuine attempt to understand and present Gluck's drama. Work on *Iphigénie* undoubtedly helped to clear his own mind on the entire subject of drama and music, ideas which he was only able finally to clarify to himself when he came to write *Opera and Drama* after the completion of *Lohengrin*.

The subject of *Lohengrin* is again sacred and profane love – but this time with a different bias. Whereas in both *Tannhäuser* and *The Flying Dutchman* it was the sinner, the too worldly man, who sought redemption and salvation through renunciation via the love of perfect Woman, in *Lohengrin* the position seems at first sight to be reversed – it is 'pure' man seeking release, or at least surcease, from his unworldliness in the love of mortal woman. Wagner himself explained that, just as the central idea of *The Flying Dutchman* related to the Homeric legend of Odysseus, so now the central theme, grafted onto the old Lohengrin romance he had found from reading ancient German poetry, was suggested to him by the Greek story of Zeus and Semele, the god who assumes human form for love of a mortal woman but can only reveal his identity on pain of death for them both. This too, this question of unrevealed identity, is central to *Lohengrin* as Wagner conceived it: it became the energizing force of the drama, the focal point of the conflict between the two kinds of love.

The story of the opera is therefore not quite as simple as it may seem. It is easy (and this has often been done) to represent it as an unconvincing tale about a rather stupid young man who makes a mystery of who he really is and an equally silly girl who gives her persecutor, the wicked Telramund, every opportunity to chide her for agreeing to marry a man who will not even tell her his name. And so on the surface it appears; perhaps there is a little more to it, but not all that much. Even if it did rest there the cause would not be entirely lost: operas have been made and will probably go on being made out of material as unpromising and improbable as this. It is, as the semi-Wagnerites are always telling us, the music that counts. That too is not to be disputed. Wagner's greatness does lie primarily in his music, even if it does not, as is too facilely assumed, lie only there. In every Wagner work, though the music remains paramount, the essential matter is many-faceted and does not lie in one element alone. The drama carries the burden, is the skeleton which supports the flesh and blood of the music, enables by a kind of parallel evolutionary process the music itself to expand and extend a skeletal structure of its own which becomes progressively more complex and in the end achieves that supremacy for which it was always destined.

In *Tannhäuser* the tension between the sensual pleasure of the Venusberg and the 'pure' love of the saintly Elisabeth was comparatively straightforward. In most respects it accurately anticipates Freud's contention that natural desires are in perpetual conflict with higher aspirations and the demands of civilized society: it is a more or less direct analogy of the prostitute/wife situation which Freud accurately discerned and defined.[6] In *Lohengrin* the entire business tended to become sublimated, and as usually happens in such cases sublimation involves both substitution and a large measure of reversal. On this plane, straight sensual pleasure, or to be more specific, debauchery, does not come into it directly, though it still does by implication. (It did not come directly into *The Flying Dutchman* either; but there Vanderdecken's making a pact with the Devil brings him firmly into the 'profane' category by an only slightly different route.)

Inevitably, such exercises, especially when they are cloaked in Romantic symbolism, are neither naturalistic nor realistic. There is always what the novelist John Braine refers to as 'the point of improbability'. And in Wagner, as in all Romantic opera,[7] it is invariably a fairly substantial one. The Wagnerian improbabilities are, like everything about him, on the largest scale. Nothing, on the face of it, could be more improbable than the unheralded arrival of a young man in a boat towed by a swan to champion a maiden in distress at precisely the right moment, and then marrying her without revealing his identity and finally leaving her stranded because she asks him to reveal it. Add the fact that the swan turns out to be the maiden's brother, taken for dead and the cause of all the trouble in the first place, who is now restored to her as compensation for the loss of her husband, and the improbabilities are endless and require such suspension of disbelief that it is a wonder there is time to attend to the music at all.

But that, as I have said, is not the nub of the matter. It is partly a case of symbolism, partly a recreation of a medieval legend in modern psychological terms, partly a matter of national mythology, all of it deep-rooted in the collective unconscious, beyond and outside the rational. It is no wonder that *Lohengrin* was Adolf Hitler's favourite opera. In part consciously, but for the most part unconsciously, Hitler saw himself as a knight in shining armour sent to rescue a maiden (Germany) in distress. Much of Wagner, but *Lohengrin* in particular, fed his fantasies, encouraged him to trust in his intuition, helped him to believe in the power of the irrational, in that anti-logic and anti-rationalism that lay at the bottom end of full-blown Romanticism, turned it from the full-blown into the flyblown. The entire Hitler/Nazi eruption does not belong in the field of politics and economics and can never be understood there. It is a matter of mythology. Politically and economically, it was unremarkable, for the most part a fairly commonplace variant of conventional socialism turned inwards instead of outwards. It is only on the plane of mythology that it begins to relate to what actually happened. Hitler, like Wagner, was essentially a myth-maker; and therein lay his strength and his extraordinary appeal on the one hand and a no less violent antagonism on the other. Hitler's political, economic and military acumen was incidental: it was not what enabled him to rebuild Germany and not what constituted his hold over the German people. That hold was rooted in the first place in the appeal in and by myth; the political, economic and military rejuvenation that gradually gathered force from 1933 to its climax in 1940 was the result of the myth, not the cause of it. It was the practical outcome of the deep-seated national energies that the myth released. If Hitler had been merely a clever politician who manipulated his own and his country's affairs to their mutual advantage and then blundered into a destructive war and consequent defeat through megalomania or miscalculation, or both, he and his world would soon have passed into the darker pages of history and within a generation or two become a more or less anonymous historical character. Who remembers the Kaiser today – or even remembered during the latter years of his life? There was no mythology. It is the same with most of the characters in history who once seized power, started wars, lost them or won them, then sank back into the obscurity from which they emerged, of interest only to historians and students. Nor is it just the enormity of Hitler's crimes which keep his memory and his hold alive: it is the mythology.[8] He thought of himself as a 'political somnambulist': he understood the truth about his own power. Wagner too was in a certain sense a somnambulist, in composition. He would often be in a kind of dream state while composing. This is not of course particularly rare, especially in artists of a strongly Romantic disposition.[9] D. H. Lawrence would often write several pages by a kind of unconscious motivation, not knowing what he had written until he read them over. Nearly all Hitler's major moves were in the nature of inspired improvisations. Ironically, the only one which he took deliberately and from reasoned determination over a long period, the invasion of Russia, was the one that finally brought about his downfall.

Hitler was an astute politician; but he was not only that. He was not even primarily that. He was a myth-maker and he saw himself in Wagnerian terms. He saw himself originally as a kind of Lohengrin, and so he appeared to the majority of the German people once he had begun the work of reconstruction and had shown his power in operation – a kind of folk hero. But he soon revealed himself as a somewhat rarer phenomenon, a folk-demon, a hobgoblin of the collective unconscious projected into the material world. That the world and the order he tried to create was in virtually every respect the antithesis of what Wagner foresaw and dreamed of for the future of the world and mankind is, in this context, neither here nor there. What matters is that both relied upon myth; and myth with a strong ingredient of nationalistic identity.

In fact, of course, all national leaders rely to a greater or lesser extent upon the power of myth. Alexander the Great did; Genghis Khan did; Napoleon did; Mussolini did. The appeal to the British by Winston Churchill in 1940 was also in its way an appeal to myth, not just a simple exhortation to buck up and pull a bit harder on the rope. In a sense, every national leader of this kind not only uses but in himself creates a myth, becomes as the cant phrase has it 'a legend in his lifetime'.[10] Abraham Lincoln both embodied and created the American myth, or dream, or legend. But Hitler, partly through circumstances, partly because of his own instinctive genius and psychological insights, and partly because of the deep-seated emotional susceptibility of the Germans, exaggerated as it was by the calamity of defeat and the breakdown of the social and economic order in the early 1930s, was able to create a new myth out of the German psyche and German history which was more hypnotic and more far-reaching than almost any other, certainly in modern times.

W. B. Yeats held that mankind had taken a wrong turning in about the seventeenth century by opting for science and rationalism in place of magic and intuition. It is not as simple as that; the dichotomy is again complex, a kind of perpetual balancing act, and as science and technology have advanced the act has become more precarious. By a strange paradox, that very advance in science and technology has opened the way for a new revelation of magic and intuition – as the recent idea had it, perception rather than conception. All Romanticism is a gesture on the side of magic and intuition, as its primary constituent part; but it has also to be backed by the intellect or it will fall into ruin and chaos, as has happened many times and may still happen again. Kant's 'perceptions without conceptions are blind', is a dictum which needs constant redefinition.

All the same, Yeats's contention still holds. That is why for Yeats and his Irish colleagues the eighteenth century, the age of reason and enlightenment, was abhorrent, the 'hated century'. Yeats was Irish to the bone, and of all Western peoples the Celts have the deepest sense of magic and the most potent awareness of myth and legend of the kind especially associated with magic, with the irrational, including a strong element of the supernatural. It is also strong in the Nordic races in a different form, and in the Germans with a mixture of both. Thomas Mann speaks, somewhat apprehensively, in *Doktor Faustus* of 'the grim deposit of saga in the soul of the nation', meaning Germany. It was this deposit that both Wagner and Hitler invoked, though in the case of Wagner it was not entirely 'grim' or 'crudely legendary'. It is Romanticism, German Romanticism especially, the high peak in one, the lowest depths, ultimately, in the other, that links the famous composer and the infamous dictator. The rise and the fall: if it had not been for that common link, that fatal denominator, there would be no connection. But it is there; and it signifies.

Nineteenth-century Romanticism, especially German Romanticism, made a powerful bid to return to the reality of magic and intuition. There is a strong dualistic character to the nineteenth century. On the one hand it was, especially in its later decades, the great era of scientific expansion and application; on the other, it was remarkable for its belief in myth and symbol, its profound sense of the inner conflict between the finite and the infinite, the rational and the irrational, the existential quarrel between the mortality of limitation and immortal aspiration, limitless potentiality, of the deep-rooted relationship between the conscious and the unconscious as defined by Sigmund Freud but understood intuitively long before. It was from this dualism – order, reason, prudence, circumspection, bourgeois domesticity on the one side; valued ambition, trafficking with the powers of darkness to find the light, whole-hogging, hell-or-nothing recklessness on the other – that what I have elsewhere called the two-way split in music and art (to reduce it to its central personalities, the Wagner–Brahms controversy) originated.

Richard Wagner was the nineteenth century's great myth-maker; and in *Lohengrin* he took the first decisive steps towards bringing the myth completely under his control. In *The Flying Dutchman* he had made his preliminary contact with folk-myth; in *Tannhäuser* he had tried, not too successfully, to work towards a new form of musical drama; in *Lohengrin* he found that he had reached a point beyond which he could not go without a total revision of the whole idea and conception of music drama. It would be easy to say that musically *Lohengrin* strikes a new note from its first bar. So it does, but the appearance is deceptive. It was in fact the third act, the most obvious and conventionally lyrical, that was written first. He progressed backwards, so to say. As was his frequent practice, at least before his full maturity and even after that in certain respects, Wagner learnt as he went along. The finest, most original parts, the Prelude and the whole of Act II, came later and less easily, much as the overture to *The Flying Dutchman*, in many ways the section of the opera surest of touch, was composed last.

The differences may be seen in microcosm in the two *Lohengrin* Preludes, to Acts I and III. The latter is colourful, energetic, but conventional; the former is one of the most beautific and original pieces Wagner had yet composed for the orchestra: here indeed a new note was struck. Unlike the familiar type of opera overture, like those to *The Flying Dutchman* and *Tannhäuser*, both derived from Weber, and both containing a kind of integrated pot-pourri of leading themes and implications, that to *Lohengrin* is a virtually self-contained tone poem in its own right. It has its thematic links with the opera, and so on practical, commonplace grounds justifies its existence and its position. But it is in no sense a showcase or evocation for what is to follow nor intended simply to fix the main musical themes in the audience's heads. Wagner was to use this latter type again in *Meistersinger*, and in a still more richly developed form; but here, for *Lohengrin*, he created the first of those inward-looking, mood-evoking preludes that are related to what comes after in a newly subtle way, leading to similar, and still more advanced procedures in *Tristan* and *Parsifal*. This magnificent and extraordinarily beautiful depiction of the descent of the Holy Grail, and the revelation of its glowing spiritual splendour, touches for the first time the true Wagner note of penetrative imagination.

According to Wagner himself, *Lohengrin* is 'no mere outcome of Christian meditation, but one of man's earliest poetic ideals'. Elsa is 'the Unconscious, the Undeliberate into which Lohengrin's conscious, deliberate being yearns to be redeemed'. If Elsa appears as yet another of Wagner's (and Romanticism's) 'wet' heroines, that is something again deeply rooted in the whole Romantic consciousness, the attempt to 'spiritualize' the feminine virtually out of mortal existence. Properly to understand *Lohengrin*, and indeed Wagner's entire conception of Woman, it is necessary to strip the character as represented of its more febrile implications and its inherent soft-centredness and relate it directly to its opposite: not as may first appear, to Lohengrin, but to Ortrud, just as the innermost meaning of Elisabeth in *Tannhäuser* is only understood in its complementary relationship to Venus. It is probable that Wagner himself did not, and could not, see it that way at the time. Arguing as he did that Woman only fulfils herself through the act of surrender to a man, both Elisabeth and Elsa appear to achieve self-realization only on those terms, as in a slightly modified form does Senta in the *Dutchman*. But Senta stands alone, and to that extent is the stronger character. Both Elisabeth and Elsa nominally stand, in relation to Tannhäuser and Lohengrin respectively, in much the same way, but in fact only realize themselves or can realize themselves as the opposing poles of Venus and Ortrud. This is the inner psychology of both operas; the mask and anti-mask only reveal themselves in relation to their real opposites before they can relate directly, and with full meaning, to their male counterparts.

In *Lohengrin* Wagner made a number of further advances towards artistic maturity from his own standpoint. He began to rationalize and subtlize the use of *leitmotiven*. He did not yet have the skill to work out an entire system of leading motifs; indeed, he did not yet understand the full implications of what he was doing. His later, fully developed use of the technique was evolved slowly and alongside his total revaluation of the true relationship between music and drama. The use of the 'leading motif' has been exaggerated as the primary element in his musical style and because of it wrongly seen as his singular contribution to musical form and technique. And in its elemental form, as the associating of specific characters or situations in opera with specific themes, it was certainly not his own invention. It is, and always has been, a perfectly normal, almost conventional, device. It was Wagner's greatly extended and interlocked use of it that gave it special prominence in his works.[11] In *Lohengrin*, although he gave his 'leading themes' positive identity and linked them to personages and situations in the drama, he still made a comparatively tentative start. He had yet to learn how to fragment his leading themes and motifs to coincide with the fragmentation of a situation, or with particular aspects or facets of a character, rather than the whole of one relating to the whole of the other. His technique in *Lohengrin* was still one of 'block' reference.

All the same, *Lohengrin* not only prepares the way for much that is to come; it also stands foursquare on its own legs (some might say too foursquare rhythmically). But it is an end rather than a beginning. Wagner reached it from *The Flying Dutchman* via *Tannhäuser*. The motif of redemption takes on a contrary aspect; but it remains the nodal point of his thought. Lohengrin's reluctance to reveal his identity has its origins in the deepest recesses of mythology and folk culture. It represents on the one hand the ancient fear of the unknown percolating through into the Middle Ages, and on the other the essential mystery through which the gods maintain power and influence. To know too much is to diminish inner as well as outer power. Secrecy is the basic principle of governments, especially autocratic governments, and the military, as it is of the gods. Those who would know too much, who would ask the unanswerable question, like Socrates, who would penetrate the light as well as the dark, are doomed and shall be deprived. All the great Romantic heroes asked questions that should not be asked, and suffered for it. Faust, Manfred, Vanderdecken, Tannhäuser, all of Promethean independence and obstinacy . . . In *Lohengrin* the roles are reversed and it is perfect Woman who is brought down by this determination. But it amounts to the same thing in the end. More than the same thing: redemption through renunciation; and it is Woman as much as Man who is called upon to renounce. It is a two-way process, a dual pact.

Late in his life Wagner saw the sin of Tannhäuser as passing through Tristan to Amfortas. It appears thus to bypass Lohengrin. But Lohengrin is the son of Parsifal and a knight of the Holy Grail, which is why he may not reveal his identity. And Parsifal was the instrument sent to redeem the sin of Amfortas who, like Tannhäuser, had been guilty of trafficking with the powers of darkness, dallying with Kundry in the magic garden of Klingsor, and had likewise been stained with the sin of worldliness and sensuality. Thus *Lohengrin* also plays its essential part in the total sequence. Both musically and spiritually *Lohengrin* was a vital part of Wagner's innermost evolution as man and artist. In more senses than one *Lohengrin* throws a rainbow bridge across the years to *Parsifal*.

CHAPTER FIVE

THE RING AND THE EVOLUTIONARY THRUST

Lohengrin marked the end of German Romantic opera for Wagner. He could go no farther on that line. A fresh start, though rooted in what had gone before, was required of him. It was a turning point, not only for Wagner himself but for the entirety of German, in fact of European thought and feeling in and through music. But much, and not all of it directly musical or even theoretically dramatic, was to supervene before the next significant move could be made.

Revolution was in the air; and Wagner was more than susceptible to its call and influence. It began in Paris in January 1848, then soon percolated through into Germany and Austria. Also in that January Wagner's mother died. He and his mother had not been close during the latter years of her life: he maintained his affection for her and did his filial duty at the funeral; but he does not appear to have reacted particularly to the event. All the same, it was another link with the past gone, another mark upon the newly turning page of his necessary evolution.

He finished *Lohengrin*; but there was no immediate likelihood of production. More and more his hopes resided in social revolution, if only as a stepping stone to the creation of a new world order that was essential for the proper reception and recognition of himself and his works. Things now appeared to be moving his way. Plans for the unification of Germany and a new administration in Saxony encouraged him to draw up an ambitious project for the founding of a German National Theatre in Dresden, in which composers and dramatists would replace Court officials in charge of artistic affairs. Once again he was to be disappointed. After initial encouragement, he was turned down. Despite an apparent fresh spirit abroad in the wake of the revolutionary upsurge, entrenched forces of obstruction and indifference to the arts continued to prevail. Realization of his ideals, both for the theatre and for society as a whole, seemed as far off as ever, himself confirmed as a solitary voyager. It was hardly surprising: entrenched officialdom is never willing to relinquish its hold on the rewards of power and position.

He knew that the future for him had to be two-pronged; that the only possible hope for the full reception and understanding of his art depended on the creation of a fresh and revitalized political and social environment. But not only that: he was no less aware that his own art, which would play an essential part in the creation of the New Order, still needed clarification and, so to say, codification. *Lohengrin* had taught him that. *Lohengrin* had sounded the death knell of German Romantic opera in the line of Weber and Marschner, though perhaps none but Wagner yet recognized it. All the same, the true way ahead was still not clear. He had come to the end of one road, but he had yet to clarify in his own mind precisely where (or how) the next move would have to be made or where it would lead him. That is why after *Lohengrin* he did not set himself at once to the business of writing another opera or musical drama, but instead launched into the dual activities of political and theoretical matters.

At first he turned again to the past and away from the immediate contemporary reality, from the disillusioning present. He started to draft a piece on the subject of Frederick Barbarossa, to be called *Friedrich der Rotbart*; but that soon proved abortive. The failure was inevitable. Richard Wagner was never a 'historical' dramatist, at least not in any recognizable sense. He needed for the fulfilment of his artistic aims and ideals not historical actuality but subjects rooted in myth and legend. History was too exact, too analysed, too demanding in recorded detail. The full realization of his ideals required not the particularities of history but the generalities of legend. And this, combined with his increasingly parlous situation in Dresden – the usual mounting debts added to a growing disenchantment with the political climate – remorselessly pushed him away from both the impositions of history and the hollow ring of the present.

He found himself increasingly at odds with the social and political developments in Saxony and increasingly disillusioned with his belief that the radical changes he desired and saw as absolutely necessary for the reception of his art, and an essential part of it, would (or could) come from the top – that is, from a form of enlightened establishment. Encouraged by a change of government ministry following the institution of the Frankfurt Parliament with the aim of drawing up plans for a unified Germany, he prepared his *Plan for the Organization of a German National Theatre for the Kingdom of Saxony* and presented it to the Minister of the Interior. He initially received a sympathetic hearing; but it soon foundered on the indifference and obstinacy of the general authority. He was forced to recognize that no hope lay in that direction. And worse even than that, he soon found himself virtually *persona non grata* in Dresden, his works as well as his ideas either evaded or actively suppressed.

Seeing that established authority, despite an apparently more liberal régime, was neither willing nor able to accept his ideas, and never would be, he gave up all attempts to alter the situation and instead turned to his deeper conviction that any meaningful change must come from below, from the people, from the 'Folk' or *Volk*. It was not so much a change of attitude as the confirmation of an already deeply entrenched one. He risked dismissal from his post at the Dresden Court Theatre by a speech he delivered to a political union in which he demanded a genuine lead from the monarchy freed from hidebound convention and moribund institutionalism. Such reckless behaviour further undermined his position and imperilled his already disastrous finances. Revolution was still very much in the air; but it had been successfully resisted in Berlin and Vienna, and the Saxon Court took the hint and engaged in its own forms of reaction and obstruction.

Richard Wagner, however, was never one to be put off by such inconveniences. There was nothing for it now. He openly espoused the insurgent cause. When revolution broke out in Dresden in the spring of 1849, Wagner was actively involved, standing briefly at the barricades with the leading Russian anarchist and nihilist, Mikhail Bakunin. The frightened Saxon government, driven to still more obdurate reaction, summoned Prussian troops to its aid. The revolution failed; Wagner was driven into exile, a price on his head.

He had kept half his wits about him. He sent his wife to safety with his sister and brother-in-law at Chemnitz. He had supported the revolution more for the sake of his dream of a revived and glorified theatre than from direct political motives. But either way Minna could not go along with him. It seemed to her, a practical and long-suffering woman, that he had wilfully thrown away a modest, though still precarious, position for some vague and insubstantial dream of future glories. To her it was all of a piece, a typical gamble on the part of one who was determined to follow his own path, seek the fulfilment of his own dream and vision no matter what the cost (especially to other people, but to himself also). This time she jibbed: she helped him to escape, obtained him the means to slip off to Switzerland, initially on the way to Paris, but would not go with him. His ambitions were totally incomprehensible to her.

A New Order, total and all-embracing – that was the ultimate ideal, art the key and cornerstone. He was by no means the only one to have seen art as the revitalizing force in a rejuvenated society. It is a persistently recurring motif in history, at least from Plato's philosopher kings. Yet it by no means always appeared in Wagner's precise terms. More often art has been (and is) 'used' as an instrument of political manipulation, obliged to promote or conform to some political theory, made the tool of authoritarianism and subservient to political dictation and thus itself devitalized. That is why all dictatorships, whether of the Communist or the Nazi/Fascist, military or civilian description, demand of the artist not his proper function of freedom to question, probe and elucidate – to act, to put it bluntly, as the perpetual opposition – but as servant of the State, obliged to say 'acceptable things', providing a kind of opiate of the people. Wagner reversed that process, established the primacy of art in a society that it created itself. He saw that in the conventional, traditional type of society, the artist is always guilty of sedition. For Wagner the primacy of art, as he himself understood and created it, was the condition of the evolution of the new society. Conventional political systems, whether of the Right or the Left – and the two more often than not coincide at the salient points – tolerate rather than actively promote art in its most fundamental aspects and implications; and the more they tend towards authoritarianism the more they tend only to tolerate it in so far as it can be manipulated to their own ends. Again, Wagner reversed the process in the context of his own vision of a New Order or rejuvenated society, albeit not always from entirely altruistic motives.

It would be foolish to pretend that Wagner did not propose a New Order of society on a self-advancing basis; that he did not seek to recreate the world in his own image. But to a greater or lesser extent that is true of all great reformers, and has to be true. Without some great force of inner subjectivity, of self-centredness, no truly potent vision of the future is possible. Probably only God can see the world with total objectivity. This does not mean that the vision must inevitably be selfish or egotistical in the narrow sense; still less that it must necessarily be inimical towards either majorities or minorities. It is, at its most potent and creative, substantially free from malice, hostility or envy. The subjective impulse is not itself narrowly self-centred or inimical, for as Kierkegaard asserted, 'Truth is subjectivity'[1]; even before it can fully reveal and justify itself it has to be transcended.

Richard Wagner was at his best a supreme subjectivist, at his worst the supreme egoist. Except in a few rare beings in whom the subjective and the objective are perfectly balanced, the two are inextricably related. Even the saints are often pitiless and intensely self-centred in their pursuit of oneness with God: and Wagner was no saint. He saw himself at loggerheads with the world; but his life's work was essentially dedicated to the creation of a world with which he would no longer need to be at loggerheads. When he described his Siegfried as one who 'never ceases to love', he may have deceived himself; but the ideal remained valid.

Lohengrin was finished in 1848, but, largely because Wagner had fallen out of favour in Dresden, it was not produced until 1850, and then by Liszt in Weimar with poor singers and an inadequate orchestra. Wagner himself did not hear it performed until 1861, when it was given in Vienna, although there had been excerpts from it in the Zürich concerts of 1853.

After completing *Lohengrin* Wagner did not compose again for several years. He became otherwise occupied. In part this was due to his personal situation – in exile, in debt, in and out of love, full as usual of grandiose dreams. But it was really due more to a deeper necessity within him, a necessity directly related to his art and its proper elucidation. He had for the time being to devote himself more and more to the theoretical aspects of what he was trying to do. The years 1849 to 1851 were to produce his most important theoretical writings, culminating in *Opera and Drama* (*Oper und Drama*). All his life he wrote with undiminished prolixity, upon any and every subject that invaded his fertile brain; pamphlets, books, articles of any and every kind. But the works following the completion of *Lohengrin* provide the central exposition of his thinking on his art and all it embraced and entailed.

He did not at once see how to reach ahead. Partly this was because of the twin disturbances of the aftermath of the revolutionary failures in Dresden and the resulting quarrel with Minna. He eventually made his temporary peace with Minna and settled with her in Zürich, with the help of Franz Liszt. But his mind would not be quieted: he was obsessed with ideas for the total reformation, transformation, redemption of the world, with himself as the active agent. His head was buzzing with ideas for new dramatic works. But it was only buzzing, not deeply involved or committed. He had his eye fixed on Paris as the place to find new success. Paris again called to him. In all his life no city so fascinated, seduced and ultimately deceived Richard Wagner. Yet he was always ready to go back, anxious to believe that his personal salvation lay there. It took Ludwig II and Bayreuth to cure him of that delusion; and even then it was only a partial cure.

He wrote a libretto, *Wayland the Smith*, and took it to Paris, out of loyalty to Liszt whose exertions on his behalf had directed him there, but also in the old delusion of Parisian triumph. It was not forthcoming: it could not be forthcoming. Parisian musical, social and artistic fashion had not changed: it was still entirely hostile to everything Wagner stood for and wanted to stand for. (It is a neat question how far the German fascination with Paris–Hitler had it too – has been a result of some sense of cultural inferiority; something analogous to what Goethe hinted at to Eckermann in the extract I have already quoted.) He took *Wayland* to Paris at the beginning of 1850. It was an abortive trip in every way. He got nowhere; achieved nothing except further depths of depression and still larger debts.

Or so it seemed. But the devil's luck which often appeared to brush him when he was plunging to the lower depths and needed it most now came forward again, in the familiar guise of woman – in fact two women, Julie Ritter and Jessie Laussot, both from Dresden.

Frau Ritter was an elderly and wealthy widow, friend of Theodore Uhlig, a Saxon violinist and composer who was the recipient of Wagner's confidences. She was the mother of Wagner's young friend Karl Ritter, who was to be involved in Wagner's initial association with Cosima. Julie Ritter, though an active benefactor, remained for the time being in the background. But Jessie Laussot was another matter: a young Englishwoman, née Taylor, who had studied music in Dresden, had met Wagner, and was unhappily married to Eugène Laussot, a French businessman from Bordeaux. Either from artistic principle of from pure altruism the two ladies decided that Wagner must be helped, and arranged for him to receive an annual income. Salvation had come; and only just in time. The shoe had begun to pinch in a way even Wagner found intolerable.

Of course the inevitable happened. He was invited to visit the Laussots at Bordeaux, went – and immediately fell in love with Jessie, and she with him. He assumed his familiar mantle of martyred and misunderstood artistic hero, she the role of sympathetic comforter and listener. It was a situation altogether Wagnerian.

Understandably, Minna did not like it at all, Wagnerian or not. She objected, largely on the grounds of pride, to being the recipient of charity even before she had sniffed a suspicion of some more passionate involvement. She demanded Wagner's immediate return to Paris; he took offence and informed her that their marriage was at an end and that henceforth he intended to travel in the Near and Middle East, although he omitted to mention to her that he proposed to have Jessie as his companion.

And so he did propose. But it misfired. He went to Montmorency, near Paris, to wait for Jessie to arrive with the wherewithal for the forthcoming expeditions. Minna set out from Zurich in pursuit; Wagner went to Geneva to avoid her, still expecting Jessie to join him. She did not. The *affaire* had come out and Laussot threatened violent retribution. Wagner went from Geneva to Bordeaux, found the birds had flown, and returned to Geneva where (for the first time) he met Frau Julie Ritter face to face.

Jessie had given in under pressure. The matter was nipped off, letters were intercepted, the dust kicked up. Wagner was roundly condemned as a bounder and an adventurer. Tidings reached Minna. But instead of widening the breach between them, it closed it for the time being. Wagner was full of remorse, realized that he needed Minna and that she cared for him rather more than nominally, beyond pride, in the face of betrayal and humiliation. She had taken and furnished a small house beside the lake at Zürich, hoping he would return to her in time. On 27 July he did.

It was not, could never be, a satisfactory reconciliation. Wagner and Minna were never well matched. From the beginning they had been obliged to make the best of each other; and it was never all that much. Now it was even less. Neither was wholly to blame. No doubt Wagner was often, if not invariably, selfish, self-centred, egotistical in his daily life. Minna was shrewd, practical, down-to-earth, the typical middle-aged bourgeois *hausfrau*, and was never able to understand his ideals or see deeply into his heart. They were largely incompatible, and remained so until the end. Yet he certainly did need her, and in a curiously Wagnerish way loved her for a number of years.

All the same, he remained sunk in depression. He wrote to Liszt that he felt suddenly old and was 'living an indescribably useless existence'. Part of the trouble was due to his health, which continued to plague him. Erysipelas and constipation often made his life a misery. He tried another cure; but it only made his depression worse.

Yet all was not gloom and despondency. Concerts of his music were given and his fame was growing. He still could not return to Germany for fear of being arrested by the police; but Germany was beginning to listen. More than that, despite the time of apparently 'useless existence', much was going on beneath the surface. He had drafted the poem of *Siegfried's Death* (later to become *Götterdämmerung*) and the entire Norse saga of the Nibelung had implanted itself in his mind as the subject of his next major work, though the exact form it would take was not yet revealed to him. Before that could happen, it was necessary for him to work his way through a number of expositional works, outwardly to convince a recalcitrant world of the righteousness of his cause and his ideals, but in reality to clarify them to himself. The most important of these writings were *Art and Revolution* (1849), *The Art Work of the Future* (1849), and *Opera and Drama* (1851), plus the smaller *Art and Climate* (1850) and the notorious *Judaism in Music* (1850). No understanding of the totality of Wagner's thought, not only on art but on society in general, is possible without concentrated attention on these central writings. He continued to issue verbal salvoes to the end of his days, expanding, elucidating, sometimes confusing, his ideals and intentions; but it is these central works of the years 1848–51 that cleared the way for him and set him upon his true course.

At the end of *A Communication to My Friends* Wagner had made a direct declaration of his primary concern and foresaw the entire plan of *The Ring* cycle in embryo. 'I shall,' he asserted, 'never write an opera again', but instead what he chose to call, for want of arguing about a precise title, 'dramas'. He had already seen his attempt to compose *Siegfried's Death* and have it immediately produced on the stage as 'aimless and impossible', ostensibly because he doubted both contemporary opera singers' ability to do justice to the kind of music he wished to compose and the contemporary public's ability to comprehend it; but at the deeper level because he had not yet brought the immense project into clear focus. He recognized that *Siegfried's Death* could not stand alone. Accordingly, he conceived, at the instigation of Liszt, a preliminary drama, *Young Siegfried*, 'the Winner of the Hoard and Waker of Brünnhilde'. But the central difficulty remained, the kernel of the nut uncracked. Even with two dramas the great plan 'had not as yet entirely passed over into the sensible reality of Drama'. Many internal 'connections' and elucidations required further development of the kind that could not be 'relegated to the reflective and co-ordinating power of the beholder' but needed to be proclaimed 'in actual physical situations'. Once he had realized that, the entire grand design became clear to him. It was to take the form of three complete dramas preceded by a 'lengthy

Prelude', each a self-contained whole but the whole to be presented 'in the course of three days and a fore-evening' at 'a specially appointed Festival' at some future time (a direct anticipation of Bayreuth).

Thus the entire conception of *The Ring* was revealed to him in all its essential parts by 1850. But although the idea of the whole had become clear, the full means of its realization had not. He had already written and published *Art and Revolution* and *The Art Work of the Future*, in which many of his ideas for a true musical drama had been formulated, notably that, derived from the ancient Greeks, of combining all the Muses into one single and comprehensive Art Work in which each would be freed, in that combining, from separateness and limitation. But it needed the major clarification of *Opera and Drama* before he was ready to commence work on the realization of *The Ring* cycle with the kind of absolute self-confidence such a project demanded.

Even so, the completed poem of *The Ring*, beginning with *Siegfried's Death* in 1848, was not ready until 1853. He then had fifty luxurious copies printed and distributed – at his own expense and with his usual 'damn the cost' attitude – to as many influential people as he could hope might be interested in furthering the mighty project, including Franz Liszt, Hans von Bülow and the philosopher Arthur Schopenhauer. Inevitably, most of them were nonplussed, even dumbfounded. This was not only far from the conventional idea of opera libretti; it was totally alien to it. The structure of the verse was enigmatic, full of assonance and alliteration, entirely different from the standard versifying of the day; a mixture, in fact, of the old German manner and the individual quirks of Wagner's entirely nineteenth century mind. Inevitably, too, the finished version as presented to these distinguished persons differed in many respects from Wagner's original ideas, especially those adumbrated in *Siegfried's Death*. In the meantime, he had refined his approach to the Norse sagas, altered the bias of the relationships, individualized much that had originally been generalized.[2] It was also clear from the outset, though it may have been so at first only to Wagner himself, and then only to a limited extent, that the musical corollary was latent in the verse. Those who argue that Wagner's dramatic verse will not stand up on its own forget that it was never intended so to do, that it was always but one half of a much larger equation. The form of the poetry is an integral part of that whole. But still only a part.

There have been many and lengthy expositions and critiques of *Opera and Drama*. They need not be recapitulated here. Ultimately nothing but the text itself will suffice if a total unfolding of Wagner's thought processes as he approached the composition of *The Ring* is required. It has been called an apologia for *The Ring*, and that is to some extent true. But more importantly it was a deliberate act of self-analysis, which enabled *The Ring* to be written in the first place. On the one hand he continued with his analogy of the true contemporary art-work with the artistic ideals of the Greeks; on the other he went to considerable pains, after demolishing conventional ideas of opera and operatic practice,[3] to elucidate his own ideas of the right kind of poetry for musical drama, a new type of 'word-tone-speech' arrived at by a new relationship between primitive man's 'tone-speech', with its emphasis on tonal semantics or 'vocalized tone'[4], and civilized man's 'word speech', the one largely elemental and emotional, the other predominantly intellectual or critical, together with a freshly evolved type of melodic structure derived from it. There is of course a good deal more to *Opera and Drama*, a verbose and often confusing document, like most of Wagner's prose expositions; but for present purposes only these two points demand scrutiny.

Wagner's reference back to the world of the ancient Greeks was to a fair degree based upon an illusion, the familiar Romantic illusion of the ancient Greek world as a kind of earthly paradise, a lost Eden of human aspiration, untarnished and uncorrupted compared with the totally corrupt and tarnished contemporary world. It was a dream, like Romanticism itself, which faded. This illusion was an obverse of that other Romantic fancy, the delusion of the 'noble savage'. But the Greek world was by no means all sunlight and communal joy, as evidenced in Greek classical tragedy. There was a dark strain of pessimism in the Greek life- and world-view, a sense of mortality, of the transience of the world and its inhabitants, at times of ultimate futility almost paralleling the late Romantic sense of disillusionment and world-weariness. Out of it grew Nietzsche's concept of 'tragic optimism' and the 'conquest of pessimism through art'. To a certain extent Wagner himself shared these views, though sometimes more by inference than directly, even if he was also highly susceptible to the Romantic illusion in his more idealistic moments. Yet it was Wagner's insistence in the end on a form of 'tragic pessimism', within his concept of redemption through renunciation, that led to the final break with Nietzsche, whose ethic of life-affirmation through 'tragic optimism' came in the end into fatal conflict with Wagner's Schopenhauerean pessimism and life-denial. On the other hand, Wagner's conception of Greek classical drama as genuinely popular composite art, embracing all aspects of artistic activity, rooted in the communal consciousness, was largely correct. At least it was correct enough for him to take it as the starting point for his own dramatic theories and eventual practice. Greek drama was a genuinely communal art-form; it did rest upon widespread public comprehension, and it derived its subject matter from myths deeply rooted in the popular psyche.

But Wagner's attitude to and drawing upon the dramatic art of the Greeks is illuminating from another angle, that of the nineteenth century as a whole and its difference from the twentieth. The nineteenth century, with its strong belief in 'progress', in general went back to the past in order that it might go forward from it; the twentieth tends to go to the more distant past as an escape from the recent, at least from the too near past. An exaggeration, of course; and perhaps 'escape' is the wrong term anyway. But the distinction is valid even if the basic premise may be questioned. One finds, for example, in the Greek evocations of Carl Orff, *Antigone* in particular, an attempt to recreate the Greek tragic theatre with 'modern' techniques but in a simplistic spirit that in fact belies the 'modernity' of the sound. Stravinsky's returns to the past, whether overtly as in *Persephone* or *The Fairy's Kiss*, or by inference in *Les Noces* or even *The Rite of Spring* as examples of a kind of contemporary primitivism with a highly sophisticated technique, display an ambiguous attitude to the past which is characteristically twentieth century. Wagner, by contrast, evoked the spirit of the past, not only of ancient Greece but even more specifically of the German national past, in a manner that was particularly 'modern', nineteenth century that is, in his own day and time.

Like most nineteenth-century musicians, Wagner was no enthusiast for 'authenticity' in the older artforms. In *Art and Revolution* he spoke out vigorously against 'slavish Restoration'. Referring again to the Greeks and Greek tragic drama, he wrote: 'We have thus quite different work before us than to tinker at the resuscitation of the old Greeks. Indeed, the foolish restoration of a sham Greek mode of art has been attempted already . . . But nothing better than an inane patchwork could come of it . . . No, we do not wish to revert to Greekdom; for what the Greeks did not know, and not knowing came by their own downfall, we do know.'[5] That is, of course, a typically nineteenth-century attitude; that 'knowing better', which was the result of the belief in progress, sometimes shallow and naïve, but at its best genuinely evolutionary. It does not mean that the nineteenth century was 'wrong' and that we are 'right' – or vice versa; it simply postulates a different historical bias of direction which may not at the deeper level be either contradictory or incompatible.

On the surface, nothing could appear farther from Greek tragedy than Wagnerian music drama at its most highly developed. But that is to miss the point, to overlook the essentials. Taking the elements, the fundamentals of Greek tragic drama, Wagner created a composite artform which, to put it bluntly, honoured that tradition without aping it. It was a case of converting the past into the currency, psychological as well as technical, of the present.

Like all the great Romantics Wagner appears to be an apostle of the irrational. He is always going on about emotional as opposed to critical (i.e. intellectual) understanding. And this, in his own terms of reference, derives from the music. To this extent those who insist upon the primacy of the music in Wagner's works would seem to be justified. He himself insisted that the proper function of the artist was to bring the unconscious elements in the human psyche into the area of consciousness; that is, to make the unconscious articulate. All artistic activity has in it some element of tapping the unconscious. It is not a unique contribution of the Romantic generations, specifically defined. Classical Greek drama was charged with it, so much so that it has given names to certain aspects and conditions in later psychological analysis. The plays of Shakespeare are full of unconscious articulations. In Beethoven there are frequent intimations of the slow uncovering of the unconscious, notably in the Adagio introduction to the Fourth symphony, parts of the Fifth and certain movements in the *Rasoumovsky* quartets. There are innumerable undercurrents in the works of Mozart that suggest even if they do not directly expose motivations from the unconscious. But none before Wagner had so decisively and so deliberately opened and exploited the layers of the psyche in large-scale artforms overtly dedicated to that end; had, so to say, peeled off the layers of the onion of the unconscious down to its centre. In resorting to myth and legend, not only in *The Ring* but in virtually all his musical dramas, which represent the unarticulated communal or collective unconscious, Wagner sought to give his works a specific universality consciously intended to evoke a response in his auditors beyond direct intellectual comprehension. In this too he was by no means unique, though his particular exposition of it may have been. Much of the appreciation of all works of art depends, to a greater or lesser extent, on intuitive reaction at least as much, and frequently more than, intellectual penetration. Bernard van Dieren's dictum that 'emotional intimacy not analysis supplies the final understanding' is more than superficially true. It touches profoundly upon the appreciation as well as the creation of all art.

Not only in the music itself, with its rejection of terminal melody in favour of what he called 'unending *melos*' (the use of the Greek term was both intentional and significant), but in the structure of the dramatic poems with their devices drawn from German medieval poetry known as *Bar* and *Stollen*, Wagner made another appeal to the Folk, more specifically to the German *Volk*. It was in the *Volk* that he rested his hopes for the future of the world and the final justification of his works, however much he may at one time or another have exploited, often cynically, existing official establishments and persons for the practical furtherance of his plans.

Yet the primacy of the irrational in Richard Wagner can be deceptive. Only a man of formidable and continually active intellect could have carried through the vast structures of his dramas, kept an iron control over all the diverse elements, all the musical and dramatic internal relationships and multifarious cross-references, or have held with such exceptional determination to his course in the face of all difficulties and obstructions. Paradoxically, he needed to rationalize his approaches, expound what he was about to do before he could give intuition its head and finally do it. He once claimed that his prose theorizings represented a poison he had to get out of his system before he could immerse himself in the creative work itself. He spoke truly, from several points of view, though he might have expressed himself better. His prose writings were by no means all 'poison'; but their purpose was a kind of flushing of the system, a clearing out of the waste matter that inevitably surrounds the preliminary chartings of any major ground-breaking undertaking. Although he was a prophet of the irrational in the act of creation, he also had many of the attributes of the theoretical man, with a thoroughly German propensity for arguing, dogmatizing and explaining which may at first sight seem merely wilful but at the deeper level was an inescapable part of the way his total genius worked. The emotional appeal, the intuitive contact with the audience, the magic spell cast by Wagner's music, even over those who are sometimes initially resistant to it, grew from the creative soil prepared and cleared by the prose writings.

There is no doubt that Wagner's music does weave spells and create an aura of magic, which is the ancient term for what cannot be explained. And it is not accidental, certainly not incidental. Both words and music are directed to that end, in various forms and from different angles, taking the music dramas as a whole. The total appeal, though it must excite the critical understanding and engage the mental faculties, as it did Wagner's own, is primarily to the emotions and the deepest layers of the psyche. It can be rationalized; but only after the event. I have never understood Thomas Mann's claim that he began to make the Wagnerian enchantment his own when he came 'to penetrate it with my understanding'. It is certainly necessary to penetrate the Wagnerian artworld with the understanding, but only after it has first reached into the depths of the psyche and animated the unconscious. The intuitive response must precede the intellectual penetration. That, indeed, is one reason why it may offend the fastidious, trouble the too rational auditor and erect a barrier between itself and minds dedicated to the force of reason and suspicious of all unreason, intense emotion and unresolved passion, minds that are hostile to the primacy of intuition. Such a mind, confronted by the Wagnerian enchantment, may find itself seduced, even overwhelmed in spite of itself, its defences penetrated; and may as a result find itself not enchanted at all. And therein lies the origin of much anti-Wagnerism, the kind of hostility always likely to arise when entrenched reason confronts something for which it cannot properly account and over which it senses that it cannot exercise rational control.

And here we touch upon another parallel with the phenomenon of Adolf Hitler, especially with Hitler as orator. Hitler's power to raise the emotional temperature of a huge audience, a profoundly mesmeric power, was noticed by all who attended the Nuremberg rallies in the 1930s. Of course, any political demagogue can rouse the rabble by an appeal to fears and angers, envies and jealousies. There is nothing remarkable in it; it is indeed the usual way of such cynical manipulators of the popular psyche. But there is little doubt that the Nazi rallies upon which Hitler played with such devastating effect were by no means of the straightforward demagogic kind. They were demagogic, inevitably, but they were also a great deal more than that. For one thing, they were as carefully and deliberately stage managed as any theatrical spectacle, each consciously organized as a kind of religious festival, a mystic communion between State and People through the voice and person of the Führer. The parallel with the Wagnerian music drama as sacred Festival observance, another kind of communion, can hardly be mistaken or misconstrued.Hitler as political orator and crowd manipulator cannot be set beside or in the same class as the composer/dramatist Richard Wagner. All the same, it is not difficult to discern the inner relationship or to understand how the one could, with only a modified shift of emphasis, degenerate into the other.

Hitler as orator was not in himself all that remarkable, at least to begin with. Like Wagner he learnt as he went along. All accounts of his performances by those who had been present (recordings and broadcast transcripts are not adequate substitutes) report that the voice itself lacked true resonance and subtle modulation, that its quality lacked richness and that its dynamic range was limited. On the other hand, all attest to its power over its auditors. Clearly, Hitler did not command the deeper subtleties and historical associations of language; there was no hint of *Bar* and *Stollen* from medieval poetry in his harangues. Yet the power he did possess remains unmistakable, and in fact it was achieved through precisely those means that gave Wagner's music its appeal. It touched and sparked off unconscious responses in the massed rallies, reached into the deepest and darkest recesses of the German psyche. In both cases the appeal was to a considerable degree subliminal. In Hitler it specifically encouraged the emotional contagion that is the characteristic of groups. And emotional contagion was also part of the Wagnerian appeal, consciously and intentionally.[6] The entire performance, with speaker or composer and audience drawn ever closer together, had the effect of orchestrating the unconscious.

Hitler's gift was not so much to make the national unconscious articulate as to reach into the Freudian pit and stir the violent and inimical elements in it to break the surface and assume various guises of false patriotism, chauvinism, racial prejudice, social enmity and national assertiveness, all masquerading as noble and sacred ideals. The appeal of ritual and institutionalism was deliberately fostered, as it was in its own context by Wagner. The crudities of Hitler and the subtleties of Wagner may at first seem irreconcilable; but in fact they were no such thing: they were variants of the same fundamental theme.

Wagner saw myth as 'true for all time', its content 'however suppressed is inexhaustible throughout the ages'. True: yet the eternal veracity of myth exposes not only the good and creative in the human psyche but also, as inescapable corollary and constituent part, the most base and destructive.The appeal to myth is not in itself either creative or non-creative: everything depends upon the bias of the myth – its selection and interpretation. Thus the Wagnerian and the Hitlerian resort for the purposes of public address have clearly defined elements in common, even if those elements derive from opposing poles of mythological penetration.

Both make an appeal to the psyche upon ground that may be common in origin but operate from conflicting standpoints. In many respects Hitler represented what Wagner might have become had he not worked through the clearing house of his prose writings and so dispersed his all too human instincts and propensities, his pettiness and malice and ill-will. In so doing he freed his true genius, the genius that turned *Meistersinger* from the malicious and spiteful tract against hostile critics (and against Eduard Hanslick in particular), as he had originally conceived it, into a warm and generous testament to light and life, a burgeoning human comedy of ultimate goodness and benificence. That same demanding genius transformed *Tristan und Isolde* from an Italianate opera in a kind of up-Bellini style, intended to boil the failing pot of his material circumstances, into the greatest paean to sexual and suprasexual love ever perpetrated upon the musico-dramatic stage. The fundamental reason why Hitler's mythological invocations were essentially non-creative and ultimately self-destructive, while Wagner's were essentially creative and ultimately life-enhancing, was that Hitler was animated by deep-seated ill will while Wagner, despite his frequently ruthless and egotistical behaviour, was animated in his creative activities by its opposite, far-ranging goodwill. Or to put it the other way round, Hitler's ill will made all he did and stood for inescapably non-creative, while Wagner's indestructable goodwill ensured that his true motivation was no less inescapably creative.

There was a German schoolmaster, ironically named Wagner, who went off his head and became a mass murderer; and in a lucid moment he said that it is the feeling of impotence that brings forth strong words and that 'the signs of the truly strong are repose and goodwill'. There is no doubt that a sense of impotence was one of the strongest contributory factors in Hitler's incessant resort to 'strong words' and his incurable hostility.

The lines cross at many points. Hitler conceived the public orator as one engaged in a kind of aggressive sexual assault upon his audience, as working towards a triumphant climax by way of reciprocal interaction. And it cannot be denied that Wagner's music, not only overtly as in *Tristan* but all through, exercises a direct sexual excitation on his hearers. That is another reason why, especially to the Protestant, puritan Anglo-Saxon mind, it frequently produces an effect of acute discomfort leading to a specific reaction of hostility, and why total surrender to the impact of his works requires at a certain level a suspension of entrenched adherence to civilized values and to social as well as moral conventions.

It resides primarily in the orchestra. The orchestra in Wagner plays a part similar to that played by Nature in the novels of Joseph Conrad, a vast, proliferating, luxuriating jungle, ever mobile, active, shaping and reshaping cycles of life and death and birth and death, often at its most potent and dominating when the characters are comparatively inactive. The sensuous luxuriance of the Wagnerian orchestra frequently seems to parallel the luxuriant Malayan jungle in Conrad. Nature in Conrad is full of symbols that both echo and instigate the human drama, while always retaining its autonomous identity, is never reduced to a mere cipher of human emotions, never subdued to a form of the 'pathetic fallacy'. The Wagnerian orchestra also exists in its own right as the primary activating principle, is also full of symbols, motifs, elemental energies. For that reason it is sometimes argued that Wagner's music, especially in the later works, can virtually be carried through without the voices, without the 'characters', that is. There is, at one level, a kernel of truth in it. It is technically possible to 'reorchestrate' at least substantial sections leaving out the voice parts; and it has been done, more than once. But it is only possible because of the nature of music itself: it is not true, or possible, without a deliberate ignoring of Wagner's purpose. It would be impossible to conceive of a Conrad novel (or any other for that matter) without the 'characters'. But that too is largely because of the essence of the materials: music can be dramatic without 'characters'; literature cannot, at least not narrative literature. None the less, the parallel between the role of Nature in Conrad and the orchestra in Wagner remains.

There is also the sea; or rather the sea and the river – the water syndrome. In Conrad the sea is the primary element: the bearer of ships and men upon their various occasions, their trade, their trials, their conflicts and frustrations, their voyages of discovery of themselves in the far corners of the globe. But he was not a straightforward writer of 'sea stories', a description to which he took strong exception. The sea for Conrad bears the ship; bears her, buffets her, tests her and all who sail in her until in the end she herself becomes semi-animate and stands in for the *anima,* the feminine principle, the receptive symbol as counterpart of the Earth mother on land. Both the purity and the violence of the sea were leading motifs in Conrad, but only in part as a reflection of the Romantic distrust of industry and mechanization which dissociated Man from Nature. There was a fatal element of sentimentality in that aspect of Romanticism, a kind of William Morris escapism from the consequences of knowledge and its proper scientific application. The objection, with Conrad, went much deeper than that, was bound up with the eternal struggle between man and nature, the inherent conflict.

The birth and death associations of water also loom large in the Wagnerian universe. He wrote to Liszt in 1853 that the poem of *The Ring* 'holds the beginning of the world, and its destruction'. And it both begins and ends in water, with the depths and the floods of the Rhine. But the sea was also important: the sea carried the Flying Dutchman's ship and ultimately consumed it; the sea bore the ship upon which Tristan and Isolde, entrapped, Conrad-like, within the confines of its hull, meet again; and it is the sea that bears the ship carrying Isolde to the dying Tristan, just as it is the river that bears Siegfried on the journey down the Rhine to the fatal encounters at the Hall of the Gibichungs. The water motif in Wagner is as important, as active an agent, as the earth motif.

The genesis of the opening of *Das Rheingold* is significant. In the summer of 1853 Wagner and Liszt spent a week together in Zürich. Afterwards, Wagner went to St Moritz for another of those 'cures' he was always taking, ostensibly for physical maladies but almost as certainly as psychological palliatives. Indeed, he once openly confessed that he wanted to seek a 'cure' for his genius, so that he could henceforth live a normal domestic bourgeois life. (This was another Romantic notion, the idea that genius is some kind of sickness or disturbance of the polarities of nature. It was an idea taken up and worked through by Thomas Mann in different forms and a number of outstanding fictions, including *Buddenbrooks*, *The Magic Mountain* and *Doktor Faustus*, each a brilliant analysis of the post-Romantic situation.)

After St Moritz Wagner went on to Italy. As usual the mountain had for him not proved magical. In Italy he travelled to various towns, taking in Genoa and Turin and finally La Spezia, where he managed to contract dysentery. He was in a low state both physically and mentally; Italy did not enchant him any more than St Moritz. His despondency deepened. His creative vitality, too, seemed to have deserted him.

He returned one day from an outing, tired and dispirited. He tried to rest, to relax both mind and body. An almost exaggerated relaxation began to spread through him. It was as though his entire consciousness was slipping away. He had a strange sensation of sinking into flowing water, a passive sensation of drowning, of being swamped. Then, slowly, insistently, it began to formulate, to centre itself around the chord of E flat. From the depths of his unconscious his musical faculty was taking charge of him. The Prelude to *Das Rheingold*, and so of *The Ring* itself, had taken command of his creative chemistry, had without his conscious volition imposed itself upon him.

This kind of negative capability is by no means uncommon, especially among Romantic, or inspirational, artists. And not only with them: it is, as Keats intimated, a constituent part of all creative activity, in all work where the imagination is unfettered, though it inevitably tends to be more prevalent in those for whom intuition rather than rationalization is the principal motivation. For Beethoven it was what he called a '*raptus*'; D. H. Lawrence, as we have seen, would often cover many pages without knowing what he had written until he read it back. Coleridge's experience with *Kubla Khan* may have been in part induced by drugs; but that in itself is another form of the same thing, a release of the unconscious into the conscious, though frequently in a distorted and damaging form. Wagner himself often seemed to compose in a kind of dream-trance. It tends always to begin in a form of an excessive, on the surface debilitating, sense of relaxation.

Of course, this intuitive process is only the beginning. Once the creative element has been released by the unconscious, the conscious faculty of rationalizing has to bear upon it in order for it to be realized and to impose upon it 'significant form'. Intuitional, inspirational, compulsive (call it what you will) writing or composing is best reserved, at least in its pristine nakedness, for first drafts. But it is for many the necessary starting point.

Hitler referred to himself as a political somnambulist; Wagner, as all those like him, might reasonably be called a compositional somnambulist much of the time. The difference was that Hitler, even with the assistance of the treacherous Josef Goebbels, never worked upon and rationalized into effective terms his 'intuitions', whereas Wagner, the true creative artist, did, not so much because he deliberately wanted it that way, as because that was the way his essentially creative genius worked. Thus Hitler's initial 'inspirations' or 'intuitions' could achieve remarkable successes to begin with, but ultimately fell victim to his own delusions, his unleavened irrationality, while Wagner brought the total weight of his genius to bear upon the task in hand and so succeeded in erecting impressive artworks of enduring stature which left the creative potential continually active. With Hitler the circuit was and remained closed; with Wagner, as with all genuinely creative people, it was always open.

Yet *The Ring*, despite the huge creative effort that went into its making, ultimately remained trapped in its own finiteness. The self-destructive Will of Wotan, ready to acquiesce in his own annihilation and that of the entire race of gods in the interest of a future of new potentiality, ended only in the return to primeval beginnings. The cycle was complete; but because it ended as it had begun, in the waters of the Rhine and the return of the gold to the Rhinemaidens, there was nothing to prevent the whole sorry business of quarrelling, begetting and propounding, of duplicity and manipulation, death and birth and death, constantly recurring. It did not, and within its own terms of reference could not, break through the natural cycle. The beginning and the destruction of the world of which Wagner spoke to Liszt were revealed as in fatal concurrence. If historical time was penetrated, cyclic rather than existential time took its place. The finiteness of Nature rather than the infiniteness of a larger spiritual reality had been established. It was not trapped in historical time; but it remained trapped in the hardly less circumscribing web of cyclic time. As it came out it was not what Wagner intended, if only because he himself was ensnared in the lure of the 'natural'. He foresaw the destruction of Valhalla and the doom of the gods as preparing the way for a new beginning, the emergence of a genuinely new order. But Siegfried was dead and treachery had prevailed. The anomaly could not be explained away, which is why Wagner experienced so much difficulty in encompassing the proper ending for *Götterdämmerung*, why the central enigma persisted even after the work itself was concluded.

He had foreseen this from the outset. By beginning dramatically with *The Death of Siegfried* he had already set the seal on the evolutionary process revealed in his final tetralogy. Within the specifically German context the end of *The Ring* ought logically, as he envisaged, to have led to a genuine new social and national order. But it did no such thing. Bypassing the implications of the pan-Germanism of the Bismarckian empire, which Wagner at first welcomed but soon came to despise, and the cruder nationalistic obsessions of the succeeding Wilhelmine empire, the New Order revealed only the negative and non-creative aspects of the Romantic movement as a whole, Richard Wagner in its van. It might have been otherwise; but for various historical and contemporary reasons it was not, and probably never could have been. It had begun in optimism, the optimism of the Romantic dawn in the wake of the French Revolution. But it declined into war and dissolution; and war is the triumph of pessimism.

It was in essence a matter of evolution. The burden of *The Ring*, its fundamental underlying theme, is the survival of the fittest and the creation of the fittest to survive. Darwin's *Origin of Species* was published in 1859, and through the following decade evolution was all the rage among intellectual Europe. But many of its postulates had already been outlined, not only by Lamarck but also by Erasmus Darwin, Charles Darwin's grandfather. Thus evolution was 'in the air' well before Darwin's epoch-making work appeared. And Wagner, sensitive like all artists to the prevailing currents a good while before they actually broke surface, incorporated, albeit unconsciously, its tenets in the living texture of his works. If Schopenhauer was the conscious 'influence', evolution was the unconscious spur. Thus Siegfried, via Siegmund and Sieglinde and out of Wotan, appears as the active agent of evolution in human form. But Siegfried at this stage was still essentially primitive, a manifestation of the will to survive unseasoned by the civilizing processes which European man had already attained. This was in fact another aspect, a direct concomitant, of the Romantic fancy of 'back to Nature' and the fallacy of the 'noble savage'. In Siegfried it is manifested in the conception of the hero who does not know fear. Yet a man who does not know fear is also one who does not know pity or compassion and cannot penetrate the deeper levels of human understanding. That is why the young Siegfried is often taken for a prototype Nazi. Not until he has undergone a number of trials and confronted suffering in his own person and psyche does Siegfried begin to become 'humanized'. And by then it is too late.

The Ring itself is evolutionary, both in its structure and in its conception. For something over half its span – through *Rheingold*, *Walküre* and the first two and half acts of *Siegfried* (until, that is, he abandoned the huge project in order to write *Tristan* and then *Meistersinger*) – Wagner adhered closely to the principles outlined and insisted upon in *Opera and Drama*. Even here he grew as he went, evolved in assurance of touch and method. And then, after a twelve-year break, when he returned to complete *Siegfried* and write the music for *Götterdämmerung* Wagner himself had undergone further moulding and evolutionary experiences, had been through more sufferings and tribulations, and as a consequence Siegfried too had undergone similar developments of character and personality. But it was still not enough; and perhaps that is why, ultimately, Siegfried had to die, to succumb to the world's treachery and betrayal, and to go through the transformation that always accompanies death in mythology, and therefore in Wagner's works, promoted by Brünnhilde's Immolation, itself an act of transformation through annihilation of the self.

The evolutionary thrust in *The Ring* is thus manifested on a number of different planes. The entire matter of 'evolution' can, however, be dangerous ground to tread upon. Although in nature evolution is biological, and only biological, i.e. primarily physical, in human terms it is essentially spiritual, emotional and intellectual. The evolutionary thrust for man relates to the total personality, the entire consciousness, both individual and collective. And it is in this total sense that it can be applied to *The Ring*, and indeed to all major works of the human mind and spirit. Man as biological phenomenon reached evolutionary fulfilment aeons ago, except for some minor details. It is in his spiritual and intellectual aspects that he continues to evolve, to 'grow', despite apparent setbacks, to enlarge the psyche and the soul-consciousness and the intellectual capacities. Evolution is irreversible; and a necessary part of its internal process lies in uncovering the unconscious and making it articulate. Wagner saw this, for good or ill, as the purpose of all genuinely creative activity.

Siegfried represents certain elements of the unregenerate in the human psyche. But they are elements in all of us, which have not only to be brought out but recognized and even honoured before the evolutionary process can advance a further step; must be lived through as a necessary part of that process.

Jung saw into the heart of the matter. Of a dream he had in December 1913, he wrote:

I was with an unknown, brown-skinned man, a savage, in a lonely, rocky mountain landscape. It was before dawn: the eastern sky was already bright, the stars fading. Then I heard Siegfried's horn sounding over the mountains and I knew we had to kill him. We were armed with rifles and lay in wait for him on a narrow path over the rocks.

Then Siegfried appeared high up on the crest of the mountain, in the first ray of the rising sun. On a chariot made of the bones of dead he drove at a furious speed down the precipitous slope. When he turned a corner, we shot at him, and he plunged down, struck dead.

Filled with disgust and remorse for having destroyed something so great and beautiful, I turned to flee, impelled by the fear that the murder might be discovered. But a tremendous downfall of rain began, and I knew that it would wipe out all traces of the dead. I had escaped the danger of discovery; life could go on, but an unbearable feeling of guilt remained.[7]

Upon awaking, Jung pondered the meaning of the dream, and came to the conclusion that it represented the 'problem that is being played out in the world'. Siegfried 'represents what the Germans want to achieve, heroically impose their will, have their own way . . . I had wanted to do the same. But now that was no longer possible. The dream showed that the attitude embodied by Siegfried, the hero, no longer suited me. Therefore it had to be killed.'

But an overpowering compassion remained, 'as though I myself had been shot: a sign of my secret identity with Siegfried, as well as the grief a man feels when he is forced to sacrifice his ideal and his conscious attitudes. This identity and my heroic idealism had to be abandoned, for there are higher things than the ego's will, and to these one must bow.'[8]

These passages accurately define the provenance of the Siegfried-image in its original form in the modern consciousness. The grief and the killing and the compassion for the slain represent the profound regret at the necessity for suppressing the natural, unregenerate instincts and the transcending of the ego in the interests of 'higher things'; the 'tremendous downfall of rain' the secret desire to overcome feelings of guilt in the face of the suppression. That Wagner himself also discerned it is suggested by the way *The Ring* poem was written backwards, beginning with Siegfried's death and then stepping back into the past to discover his origins and evolutionary growth. And in that discovery the real meaning, not of the fact of Siegfried's death but of the inner necessity for it, slowly emerged and imposed itself on Wagner's conscious mind, through many years of personal and collective trial and difficulty. In the recognition of that inner necessity lay Wagner's cumulative sense of the ultimate necessity for renunciation.

But it did not pass into the more general consciousness. The Germany of 1914 was not prepared to make that kind of abandonment, to recognize the necessity for renunciation; and the Third Reich was still less willing to do so. Indeed, Hitler deliberately reawoke and played upon those very instincts of domination, of heroic imposition of the will, that Jung had seen as needing to be suppressed by the death of Siegfried. It was in every sense a regression; it was also a direct emanation of one aspect of *The Ring*, even though, by a huge paradox, it was also a direct contradiction not only of *The Ring* but of all that Richard Wagner stood and worked for.

At this time also Wagner began reading Arthur Schopenhauer, notably *The World as Will and Idea* in which he discerned, 'to my amazement', that it embodied almost exactly what had been passing through his own mind while writing *The Ring* poems, and that at last he understood the meaning of Wotan. The influence of Schopenhauer is at its most direct in *Tristan und Isolde*; but Schopenhauer's philosophical thought often bears significantly on *The Ring*, even though Wagner had not read the philosopher when he wrote the verse. Again, it was a familiar situation; just as evolution was in the air and could thus bear upon those who had not actually read about it before Darwin, so the philosphy of Arthur Schopenhauer both created and reflected the intellectual and emotional ambience of the period and 'influenced' even those who had not read him.[9]

Although Wagner's primary function as an artist was to make the unconscious articulate, various elements of his personal life and experience also bore upon his compositions, in some cases actually set them into motion. It is well known how his relationship with Mathilde Wesendonk, wife of one of his benefactors, led to the writing of *Tristan und Isolde*, and in fact determined its innermost character. But this association also had its effect upon *The Ring*, and in particular on *Die Walküre*. Before his passion for Mathilde had reached its Tristan-like obsessive intensity, he saw a reflection of it in Siegmund and Sieglinde, twin brother and sister, children of Wotan and intended begetters not only of Siegfried but of the whole future race of Wälsungs. The brother–sister relationship is significant. It permeates much. The incest motif is strong throughout *The Ring*; and it was deliberate. Whether or not Wagner can be legitimately accused of 'glorifying incest', as has sometimes been charged, is irrelevant. The creation of the fittest to survive (and in this case is implied also the creation of a new order of the world, otherwise survival becomes not only itself irrelevant but ultimately impossible: the environment and its inhabitants are mutually interactive) required, as it always requires, some special feature of birth and propagation. The most familiar is the virgin or miraculous birth, found not only in Christianity but worldwide in religious myth and legend.

Incest, though frequently implicit, is more contentious. In virtually every case in mythology, incest not only requires but brings on the head of its perpetrators some form of retribution, often ominous, always violent. It may not always be clear and straightforward; but it is nearly always there. The reasons are not far to seek, but are often difficult wholly to comprehend. It is easy enough to argue that incest is both biologically and psychologically retrogressive; but it is not much harder to demolish that argument. It is at once more direct and more complex.

In *The Ring* both the directness and the complexity are exposed. It appears, to put it in crude terms, that Siegfried, offspring of the incestuous intercourse between the twin brother and sister, Siegmund and Sieglinde, subsequently goes to a considerable amount of trouble to have it off with his aunt. It all looks delightfully uncomplicated. But of course it is no such thing: such relationships and entanglements never are. Fricka, Wotan's lawful wife, goddess of marriage and guardian of its laws, not unexpectedly protests at the incestuous coupling of Siegmund and Sieglinde; and at first one wonders why Wotan did not also sense the danger. But Wotan sees farther. He has deliberately engineered the meeting and he tells Fricka that he did so because only a Wälsung of the pure blood can carry out his Will and redeem the world. He is not, however, on firm ground: Fricka calls upon the established laws and conventions and out-manoeuvres him, so that he has reluctantly to agree to the death of Siegmund in the forthcoming fight with Hunding. And in so doing, he fatally starts down the road to undermining his own power. The creation of the fittest to survive was from the outset hedged with moral debt.

In the confusion and moral chaos which Wotan inherited and had to try to resolve by resorting to all manner of expedients, the one hope appeared to lie in the creation of the fearless hero. But that in itself was not enough. The entire complex had to be accommodated, all the strands pulled together, the tangle not only unravelled but respun in a genuinely new and creative pattern. And in order to accomplish that, purity of stock became of paramount importance.

The implications cannot be evaded. Purity of stock, of race or species, implies and requires a greater or lesser degree of inbreeding. And that in turn implies the potential of incest. It is still not properly recognized how far the Garden of Eden, Adam and Eve, exposed an incestuous relationship which cannot be ignored and certainly cannot be evaded by sideways references and shifty expedients. The great national mythologies are full of both the fact and the fear of incest. In part of the Finnish national epic, the *Kalavela*, set by Sibelius in his early *Kullervo* symphony, the hero Kullervo has an incestuous encounter with his sister, and although it is unknown to either at the time, a capricious accident of fate, the effect is still disastrous. The sister is dishonoured, even though the seduction was 'blind'; and Kullervo himself, struck down with misery and remorse, falls upon his sword and kills himself because he cannot face the unavoidable truth or its implications.[10] The incest motifs in *The Ring* lead to retribution more by implication than directly. There is a temptation to argue that Wagner would have given full rein to the potentialities of incestuous couplings, maybe even have 'glorified' it if he had dared. Yet Richard Wagner was never one to back off from a difficult commitment. If he appeared to justify the incest-taboo by insisting upon the death first of Siegmund, then of Sieglinde (in childbirth, bearing Siegfried), and then of Siegfried himself followed by Brünnhilde, it was not because he shied away from the implications of the relationships, incestuous though they were, but because the larger requirements of his grand design demanded it. There were much greater things at stake, even if the fact of incest was absolutely germane to them.

As a sidelight on the sudden eruption of love between Siegmund and Sieglinde, it is useful to recall that St Thomas Aquinas preached against incest because he believed that the love of brother and sister added to the love of husband and wife would lead to an excessive indulgence in sex. The argument may seem curious; but when one recalls the spontaneous ecstacy and passionate responses of Siegmund and Sieglinde, it is not difficult to see the relevance of that contention.

All the same, the incest motif strikes farther and deeper than any conventional prejudice or traditional concept; certainly deeper than any facile explaining away or psychological evasion. It is deeply entrenched in the entire concept of the survival of the fittest and the creation of the fittest to survive and in that of the idea of the 'master race'. Wotan recognizes this when he argues with Fricka that only a hero with the pure blood of the Wälsungs will suffice. This is not a cynical interpretation, in respect either of Wagner himself or of later aberrations. It is the compulsive logic in the fundamental idea of racial purity and genetic engineering. As in animal breeding, selective mating is designed to ensure the creation and perpetuation of the fittest within a specific context, and ultimately the continued improvement of the breed, as a condition of its survival.

Breeding

But in human terms race purity and masterhood goes still further. It is implicit in one aspect of the whole Romantic movement, in the concept of Romantic nationalism, in the belief in the aristocracy of nationality and nationhood, a concept that, because of the evolutionary differential, continues to distort the relationships between peoples of different parts of the world and to exacerbate national rivalries and enmities.

The most notorious and least correctly understood of Wagner's prose self-flushings is *Judaism in Music*, his most directly anti-Semitic tract. Much of Wagner's anti-Semitism was personal and malicious. In Paris in 1839–41 he had suffered and had achieved no success. Meyerbeer and Halévy, both Jews, ruled the Parisian roost, were rich, successful, prosperous: therefore there was a Jewish plot to keep him, Richard Wagner, from his own due recognition and prosperity. No matter that he had received help and encouragement from Meyerbeer and others: Meyerbeer was successful; therefore Meyerbeer was corrupt. Meyerbeer was also a Jew. *Ipso facto*, all Jews were corrupt. It was not sound logic, and it is possible that Wagner himself knew it was not; but it remains illuminating.

Some aspects of Wagner's attack on the Jews were and remain unspeakably petty and unbelievably spiteful. His cruel jibes at their manner of speech is only one example. Unlike the Jews themselves, whose sense of 'Jewish humour' is second to none and, embracing speech idiosyncracies, is so astute and so valuable that non-Jews have been known to complain that it is exclusive to Jews; unlike, indeed, most racial groups of one kind or another who can see and even trade upon the comical side of themselves, Wagner could not even recognize parody, let alone laugh at it, as he could later laugh at pedantic criticism in the figure of Sixtus Beckmesser. Yet pedantic criticism had done him a good deal more harm than any real or imagined Jewish 'hostility'.

But the anti-Semitic question cannot be left there. And it is inextricably related to racial 'purity', nationalistic fervour and its concomitant, economic self-sufficiency. Bertrand Russell wrote:

Belief in blood and race is naturally associated with anti-Semitism. At the same time, the romantic outlook, partly because it is aristocratic, and partly because it prefers passion to calculation, has a vehement contempt for commerce and finance. It is thus led to proclaim an opposition to capitalism which is quite different from that of the socialist who represents the interests of the proleteriat, since it is an opposition based on dislike of economic preoccupations, and strengthened by the suggestion that the capitalist world is governed by Jews.[11]

In the 1850s, when Wagner was writing *Judaism in Music*, the 'Jewish question' existed in a specific form. It was that period between the liberation of the Jews from the ghettoes and their total integration into the larger national societies. It is possible to argue that from several points of view, assimilation has never been total and that therefore anti-Semitism is and must remain a positive force. But in the mid-nineteenth century the Jews appeared, in both commercial and artistic matters (as in most others), an alien element in the body social and the body politic. And the immediate reaction of any social or biological unit is rejection of the alien. Thus where the Jew is either genuinely thought to be alien or can be seen as a usable excuse for apportioning blame for some specified or unspecified form of disaster, anti-Semitism is the invariable and in the end inevitable consequence. That is not perhaps the whole story, for anti-Semitism has many facets, many causes, many rationalizations; but rejection of the alien remains the central motivating force, the actual or implied invasion of the social, national, biological or psychological cell the primary incitement.

It has become virtually impossible to cast a cool eye upon any form of anti-Semitism, and therefore upon Wagner's tract, because of the appalling consequences that ensued under Hitler and the Third Reich, whose crimes are unparalleled in human history, beside which even the worst excesses of the French Revolution, Stalin's liquidation of the *kulaks*, or the mass exterminations in Kampuchea and Vietnam momentarily pale. Yet a dispassionate analysis of the Nazi case is still required. It is imperative to override the natural horror at the Nazi criminality, to resist the inevitable reaction of undiluted disgust, because that in the end is the surest way to misunderstand the totality of the crime and its implications. And that crime itself might have been at least in part avoided if proper attention had been paid to the innermost meaning of Wagner's argument, its more petty and spiteful aspects seen for what they were, the sharp-toothed snappings of a wounded lion – or a lion who imagined himself wounded.

The essential, the primary truth about the enormity of the 'final solution' was its inevitability. Given the German economic collapse, the resentment it produced, and the preponderence of Jews in the economic arena, the consequent opportunity for a systematically worked-up anti-Semitism allied to the ingredient of unleashed violence in the Nazi pysche, and extermination became the only possible outcome, if only upon the theory put forward by Sigmund Freud that the logical end of all crime is murder. The process, once started, could have no other end. All anti-Semitic movements in history, in whatever country, would have had a similar outcome, given the particular circumstances of the Third Reich and the

102

particular concentration upon a precise objective. The Jews were driven out of one country after another throughout history, but they still had somewhere else to go. After Hitler acquired virtually total control of the European mainland, the overall situation was substantially different. Control could be exercised over external as well as internal policy; and from that evolved, no less inevitably, the idea of total extermination. In addition, the economic collapse of Germany, acquiesced in by the victorious Allies after the First World War, created precisely those conditions in which a scapegoat became not only useful but necessary to the kind of evangelical revival that Hitler and the Nazis launched and upon which they relied for their major public and popular support. The Jews were there; they were alleged to have an economic stranglehold on Germany through their control of international finance, and they were an alien, and therefore hostile, element within German society, undermining national vitality, corrupting the purity of the Aryan race. The arguments, even though they were by no means new, followed an inevitable course, a chain reaction culminating with even more deadly inevitability in a solution that was not only 'final' but in every psychological and genetic sense the only possible one. Much of the horror lies in the inescapable logic. Once set in motion, the process could not be checked and soon became irreversible.

Wagner's part in the historical unfolding of anti-Semitism cannot be ignored. In that he was a primary influence on Hitler and the Nazis, though initially through no choice of his own, and in so far as he gave way to spite and malice of a kind that would appeal to the lowest instincts of the lowest intelligences and encourage the most scurrilous prejudices, he was clearly culpable. On the other hand, his underlying analysis of the situation was accurate, and if it had been heeded, even properly read and understood, it might well have alleviated that situation by defining it with accuracy rather than aggravating it by distortion. That in his own time Wagner's anti-Semitism was not universally resented by Jews, was perhaps not even recognized as such in the most basic terms, is indicated by the way a number of his closest supporters and collaborators, like the conductor Hermann Levi,[12] were Jews, and that a number of Jews acted as pallbearers at his funeral. But that, of course, was long before the most serious consequences of anti-Semitism had been revealed, half a century later. It is another contentious matter; but it is, like the others concerning Richard Wagner, not easily disposed of by simple reference to conventional distate or thinking prejudice.

In one of the most penetrating of the smaller (and least verbose) books on Wagner,[13] Bryan Magee categorically states that Wagner's 'central argument was correct, and decades ahead of its time'. It is difficult, though, to follow Magee's statement that what is true in that argument 'could have been advanced without anti-Semitism' or to see the relevance of Wagner's attacks on traditional Christianity to it. This latter introduces a dangerous

103

misconception, one that has frequently confused and distorted the proper issue. Attacks upon Christianity, or any religion *per se*, have no relevance whatsoever to anti-Semitism or to attacks on the Jews. Anti-Semitism is always racial, not religious. It may embrace an attack upon Judaism as a religious and/or national manifestation; but it is not primarily concerned with religion. Anti-Semitism bears no less heavily upon Jews who have been converted to or embrace another religion, whether it be Christianity, Buddhism, Islam or any other, than it bears upon orthodox Jews. Nor does it matter if the conversion is personal or historical, a matter of immediacy or of a tradition of family through generations. To confuse the two, the racial and the religious, is to subvert the entire basis of the argument from both sides.

There can be no doubt that Wagner's anti-Semitism directly influenced Hitler and the Nazis. Nor can it be denied that the petty and malicious aspects of it, motivated by personal animosity and prejudice, closely paralleled those of Hitler, who also believed himself to have suffered at the hands of Jews (a prostitute in Vienna, initially) and to have been humiliated.But that ignores the more profound and meaningful aspects of the argument. Nor, except indirectly and at more than a single remove, does the socialist and anti-capitalist proposition, seeing Jews as the evil manipulators of commerce and finance, reach any deeper.

To probe far enough into the morass to discover the full meaning, it is necessary to go back to the Greeks, as Wagner himself was always doing. Wagner believed that Greek drama, especially classical Greek tragedy, was the highest form of total, or composite art, precisely because it was genuinely communal, sprang from and was directly related to the public consciousness and the collective as well as the individual unconscious. And he believed that art in his own time, the highest contemporary art — his own art, that is — had to perform a similar social and public function. It thus had to be derived from the same sources. But the Jews were not of the true body communal. They were an alien element, cut off from the source springs, their presence corrupting to the true art and the evolution of the communal consciousness. Therefore their art was shallow, meretricious, 'effective' only. He did not deny that Jews had great talents; but he did insist that these were little more than skin deep. Jews could not create true art, art that touches the sources of the national and communal consciousness and so releases the forces of the unconscious.

Of course, this only applied to Jews in a specific national context. Jews within their own cultural environment, within their own orthodoxies, were a different matter: then they too could no doubt produce true art. But they had no cultural environment of their own; so they preyed parasitically on other peoples', and debased them. In the mid-nineteenth century the Jews were still in the process of becoming integrated into different social, national and cultural environments. Some, like Benjamin Disraeli, brought a widening and enriching influence to bear on their particular societies. All the same, even there it was an alien influence: however much it enriched, its roots were not in the same soil as the general national consciousness, its historical vision outward- rather than inward-looking. It could still arouse resentment, and in any case Disraeli was exceptional, in every sense. Otherwise, the tenet held. It was not until the creation of the state of Israel that Jews had a specific focus for their inner life and aspirations. But by then they were already too widely spread, both historically and geographically, throughout the world, and might have remained so had it not been for the additional pressure placed upon them by Nazism. They had been a species of 'displaced persons' for so long that it had become a norm, and might to a far greater extent have remained so had it not been for Hitler. And in one sense the creation of the state of Israel has exacerbated the situation. When the Jews had no homeland, they could not be told to 'go home': now that they have, a new kind of banishment could theoretically be enforced where the pressure is upon them. Yet it is still, obviously, an improvement — if only because if they have nowhere to go, extermination might once again prove to be the only viable alternative.

Anti-Semitism did not begin with Adolf Hitler and it did not end with the military defeat of Nazi Germany in 1945. It is an inescapable historical *donnée*. The causes are complex and deep-running; but at the core of it is always the sense of alienation and the rejection of the alien by successive closed communities. It only reached its inevitable apogee under the Third Reich.

Wagner in fact probed deeper into the heart of the problem than most who have addressed themselves publicly to it. Few would deny that there is such a problem, both in the historical and the contemporary contexts, since anti-Semitism remains an active force in the general currents of worldwide racism today. It does not apply only to particular epochs of history or to particular countries. If Wagner had not allowed the spiteful and malicious elements in his own nature to supervene, had not wilfully projected it, motivated by the memory of his own Parisian humiliations, onto the Jews, his analysis might have led to necessary understanding rather than, as it did, to encouragement of hatred and incitement to genocide. Even so it was by no means straightforward. The reaction was always ambiguous. Wagner frequently associated with Jews and Jewish musicians, and not always for the sole purpose of furthering his own ends; the Jews themselves have not always taken him at his worst value, as is demonstrated not only by associations during his lifetime but also in the way that a number of later composers, including Gustav Mahler and Arnold Schoenberg, both Jews and the latter persecuted, held him in the highest esteem and owed him overt creative allegiance, and also by the fact that some of his greatest interpreters, even at the height of the Nazi persecution, have been Jews – Bruno Walter, Otto Klemperer, Georg Solti.

There have been militant anti-Wagnerians who have claimed that his anti-

Semitism even percolated his works, that certain uncongenial characters, like Mime, Beckmesser and Klingsor, were either overtly or barely concealed representations of Jews and were intended as part of a general attack on Jewry. But this is precisely what Wagner did not do. Wagner may have been dishonest as a man, but he was not dishonest as an artist. When he spoke of his prose writings as poison he needed to expel from his system, he meant exactly what he said. They were not, of course, all poison; but the poision that was in him came out through them, never in his compositions. In its original conception, *Die Meistersinger* was intended as a malicious attack on hostile critics, and on Eduard Hanslick in particular. In the first draft Sixtus Beckmesser was actually called Hans Lich; and when he was present at a first reading of the text, Hanslick not unnaturally walked out in offence. But that was the petty Wagner speaking. Then his true genius took command and what had begun in spite and rancour turned into a broad human comedy of light and life, Beckmesser, the epitome of bumbling, bone-headed officialdom and pedantry, laughed out of court. All the malice had gone.

Wagner's writings are full of attacks on conventional and hidebound critics, either direct or implied. But on the Jewish question he was more consistently explicit. All the same, his malice remained cocooned in the prose: none of it escaped into the ensuing compositions. Wagner was sometimes generous and warm-hearted despite himself.

Attempts have been made to deny that Richard Wagner was really anti-Semitic at all. But that is no nearer the truth than that he projected his anti-Semitism into his works. The reality is that he adumbrated a principle rather than a practice. He saw the Jews as an alien racial element in the social body, an element corrupting to the true emergence of the innermost spirit and genius of the *Volk*. But he did not advocate persecution, or give any warrant for it. On the other hand, his diatribes, especially the meaner aspects of them, undoubtedly fed the base instincts of lesser humans. In other words, he gave Hitler and the Nazis (inadvertently, it need not be questioned, for he would have been as horrified as anyone by the 'holocaust') the bursting charge that led to the 'final solution'. He thus cannot escape culpability: a man who exorcises the poison from his own system, especially if he does it by public exhibition, has to take care where it goes and what subsequently becomes of it. He cannot relieve himself of all responsibility for it at a later time. Every manifestation of race prejudice, whatever the aspect or direction it takes, is a positive step on the road to Auschwitz.

The history of *The Ring* is curious from several points of view. Not only was it conceived, if not executed, 'backwards'; it also suffered total interruption midway through its progress. After he had composed *Das Rheingold*, *Die Walküre*, and half of *Siegfried*, Wagner broke off for a dozen years and did not add a note to it until after he had written *Tristan und Isolde* and *Die*

Meistersinger. There is no reason to suppose that the great project was put out of his mind through all those years, but work on it certainly was. This has led to an idea that when he did finally return to *Siegfried* and went on to write *Götterdämmerung*, he did so as though there had never been a break, that he took up exactly where he had left off. But this is simply not true. Essentially a developing personality, Wagner had in the intervening years been both tempered and enriched, as both man and artist, by his ever deepening experience of life and art, by further sufferings and existential enlargements. It was impossible for such a man, the true Romantic evolutionist, not to have altered in psychic response and emotional involvement in over a decade. So when he returned to *Siegfried*, in 1868, there was no way that he could have been the same man and the same composer. Not only the musical procedures, the harmonic language and subtlety of melodic interrelationship, but also the depth and direction of the psychological bias had been deepened and enriched by the experiences lived through and worked out in *Meistersinger* as well as the dominatingly chromatic *Tristan*. The enrichments worked from both sides, from the light and the dark simultaneously, and progressively weaned him away from strict adherence to the principles laid down in *Opera and Drama*.

That is not to say that the latter sections of *The Ring* 'revert' to a more established, a more conventional form of opera. Quite the contrary. Most artists given much to theorizing tend to do their best work when they forget, or at least put aside, the 'theories' and allow free rein to their autonomous creative abilities. Wordsworth is a prime example in poetry; Schoenberg, more subtly and significantly, in music. It is not that the theories are necessarily either invalid or expendable; it is simply that they act as a clearing-ground, a kind of preparative signal in advance of the full creative executive. And if the creative act contradicts the theory, it is the theory that must bow down. More realistically, what is true in theory is true in practice: if the practice is unworkable, the theory is at fault. On the other hand, most theories are terminal; that is, they serve a particular purpose at a particular time, but in an evolutionary context must always remain open to revision and modification. Only the incurably third-rate are so tied to their own theories that they cannot, or will not, break or modify them in the light of expanding experience or altering circumstances. The charge of 'revisionism' used in the pejorative sense is meaningless. Without revision all theory is moribund. Thus, if we are tempted to describe *Götterdämmerung* as the grandest of Grand Opera that does not mean it is in any sense a reversion to what Wagner had consciously set out to jettison in *The Flying Dutchman* and had finally exhausted in *Lohengrin*. It meant, on the contrary, nothing less than a totally new dimension of opera/music drama finally and triumphantly achieved after much striving and a huge output of creative energy. Maybe it would not have been quite like that if he had not broken off in the third act of *Siegfried* but had gone straight on through the entire tetralogy as he had originally intended. But he did break off and he did not carry it straight through; *Tristan* and *Meistersinger* did come between, with all that implied in both musical and existential terms, in the fullest and most profound meaning of all that those intervening years meant to him. It is only in the light of that existential meaning that the full impact of the final consummation of *The Ring* can be understood.

The problem of how far the Wagnerian assumption in general and *The Ring* in particular can be taken as a blueprint for national socialism is one that has exercised many minds and troubled many consciences. In its simplest terms, anti-Wagnerians assert that it could and was; Wagnerians deny it hotly (or evade it). The real question, however, is by no means so simple or unambiguous. Part of the difficulty lies within the structure of *The Ring* itself. That Wagner always intended something more than a piece of musical entertainment, even of the most 'serious' kind, is so obvious that it is not worth considering. There was from the outset a meaning to *The Ring*, as indeed to all Wagner's mature works, that went far beyond any established form of musical and theatrical diversion. So much is not to be disputed. But how much was in fact a species of pseudo-political propaganda? That too is a legitimate question, though not a particularly profound one. There is what may be called a 'third element', which contains the essence and provides the clue to the final answer. The two primary elements, the musical and the didactic, as it may be, are comparatively clear, both in themselves and in their relationship to each other. On the one hand there is the music, representing the unconscious, the elemental, the intuitional; on the other there is the verse, the 'argument' representing the conscious, the intellectual, the critical. They are not separate and self-contained entities: there is a continual cross-fertilization, the one all the time 'provoking' the other. But beyond both there is a deeper interaction, which releases a third element that is more than the sum of the other two. We may say that this lies in the symbolism, expertly analysed by Robert Donington;[14] and that is a valid interpretation. But it is still not the one I am seeking; at least not the whole of it. It is obviously related, but it deals primarily, if not uniquely, with the unconscious or intuitional aspect; and what I have in mind, the 'third element', is not biased towards one side or the other: it is neither wholly unconscious and intuitional nor wholly conscious and intellectual, though it partakes of both and in fact is released by that participation.

Perhaps the nearest definition of what I am trying to uncover is a kind of metaphysical intentionality. The term is not precise; but then the element in question is not in itself precise. In so far as every true work of art is the product of both conscious and unconscious processes in the mind and psyche of its creator, there is always some aspect of this 'third element'. But with Wagner, because of the deliberate bias towards the intuitional, because of his declared aim of articulating the unconscious added to the force of the equally postulated dramatic argument, it takes on a particular form and

108

direction. He himself argued that whatever the words in his dramas said, it was music, via the orchestra, that expressed the *feeling*; and he claimed that it was the feeling that mattered above all. So it did, and does. But to play the words, the 'argument', too far down is to throw the total composite artwork out of focus and to diminish both the impact and the meaning of the whole. There is clear evidence that Wagner himself sometimes experienced difficulty in making his meaning perfectly clear; and whenever that did occur he relied on the orchestra to express the feeling and carry through the dramatic enigma. But that does not mean that we are ever justified in either ignoring or negating the importance of the words.

Wagner, as I have said, once told Liszt that the poem of *The Ring* encompassed both the beginning and the destruction of the world. The complex process by which this God-like achievement was to come about went through changes in Wagner's mind before it could finally be accomplished with the completion of *Götterdämmerung*; and even then anomalies remained. But the intention was clear as soon as he saw beyond the originally projected single drama *Siegfried's Death* to the eventual whole of three dramas and a prelude. It was not an easy road he had to travel. The pain of the true, unflinching creator was Richard Wagner's, beginning to end. That is why he sometimes prayed to be released from the burden of his genius; even at one time cherished the illusion that he might take a 'cure' for it and so be enabled to live out the rest of his life in peace and untroubled domestic felicity. But it could not be. It can never be.[15] Genius is pitiless. It requires, demands, renunciation and resignation in one form or another, at its purest and most intense in the tear that Beethoven said hearing the Cavatina from the B flat quartet always cost him. So much lost; but so much more gained. Wagner too had both lessons to learn; and it cost him more than a passing tear.

If in *Das Rheingold*, *Die Wälkure* and the first sections of *Siegfried* Wagner adhered more or less strictly, though with growing flexibility, to the principles he had laid down in *Opera and Drama*, in the latter parts of *Siegfried* and the whole of *Götterdämmerung* he not so much turned his back on those principles as so enlarged and extended them that they now became secondary rather than primary objectives. In the overall evolution of *The Ring* the theories of Wagner's prose theorizings altered significantly. Put in its simplest terms, in the first parts the compositional methods were a demonstration of those principles, in the later parts the extended method was a consequence of them. The differences are subtle but important; and the reason for them was in part Wagner's natural evolution as man and musician, but even more the experiences that led to *Tristan* and *Meistersinger*, the dark and the light side, the night and the day of the existential equation.

But the change, the evolution, was as much metaphysical as purely musical. Still less was it directly political. Marxist interpreters tend to regard this change as a result of the failure of the revolutionary movements in which Wagner had placed so much hope and in which he had been actively involved. No doubt Wagner's disappointment with the revolutionary abortions was profound and did exert a lasting influence on his subsequent life- and world-view. But the real change, on the surface a change from optimism to pessimism, had deeper roots than the failure of political hopes. It was an inescapable part of the movement of nineteenth-century Romanticism itself, a movement from the optimism of the early beginnings to the pessimism of the end of century decline. Certainly Wagner was convinced – and he was not alone in that conviction – that only a new order of society would bring about conditions in which art, and his own works in particular, could have its proper and (as he saw it) appointed place. But he soon gave up any idea of seeing that come about in the immediate future. He resigned himself to compromise, literally in order to live. The reason why he despaired of ever seeing *The Ring* produced was not because of political inadequacy or revolutionary failure; it was that until the creation of the Bayreuth Festival Theatre it made demands far beyond the resources of contemporary opera houses or the techniques of contemporary singers. Even if the revolution had succeeded there is no reason to suppose that the artistic conditions necessary for such an undertaking would have materialized any sooner than in fact they did. And that came about through royal patronage, not through social or political revolution. Revolutionary politics had nothing to do with it, and probably never would have.

The change from optimism to pessimism was, for Wagner, primarily internal. It may have been triggered by external events; those events may have struck deep into him; we need not deny their influence. But the deep and meaningful conditions of change were within his own psychological and emotional life; an emanation of the innermost motives of his creative self. And as always, it had a dual aspect. It was not positively, unequivocally, one thing or the other. It was both dark and light, night as well as day. If pessimism in the end triumphed, of existential necessity, the daylight of optimism did not fade without trace, or without fight.

It is customary, especially among those who cannot see him whole and 'in the round', to speak of *Meistersinger* as a 'sport' among Wagner's works, because it is predominantly cheerful, 'optimistic', warm-hearted, often humorous. And in so far as the characterization of *Meistersinger* is concerned, that is perfectly true. But it is not true in the larger sense; it certainly does not make *Meistersinger* a 'sport'; it does not even make it all that unusual in the overall context of Wagner's ethic and aesthetic. The first sections of *The Ring*, right up to some way into the third act of *Siegfried*, are, if not outright optimistic, at least definitely confident in tone and ambience. It may have been, in Nietzsche's term, a 'tragic optimism', and it may have contained, in Wotan's renunciation of and farewell to Brünnhilde, its cloud of pessimism; all the same, the overall impression is one of hope for the future and a powerful means for creating it. While it is true that Wagner's original contact with the Nibelungen sagas on which *The Ring* is built had begun with *Siegfried's Death*, he did not at first grasp the full implications of what, in creating the hero-character of Siegfried, he was doing. He could see the death of Siegfried as opening the way for a new world order in comparatively direct and straightforward terms. But as he went farther back, as he had to, discovered *The Young Siegfried*, then began to work out the total world- and life-view, the necessity for the change of direction became clear to him. And the nature of that necessity became increasingly clear during the dozen or so years between the abandoning of the third act of *Siegfried* and his subsequent return to it. It is usually argued that Wagner broke off work of *The Ring* because he despaired of ever seeing it staged and hoped to turn his hand to more profitable work. But it did not work out that way, and in the end it could not. *Tristan und Isolde*, originally conceived as an Italianate entertainment, evolved into something very different, under another type of necessity. It was in that necessity, sparked by his passionate attachment to Mathilde Wesendonk, that it was pressurized, so to say, into its ultimate form, than which nothing could be less counted upon for commercial success and consequent profit.

The idea that *Tristan* is 'sick' and *Meistersinger* is 'healthy' is quite untenable. *Tristan* is just as 'healthy' as *Meistersinger*: it simply deals with a different, darker, deeper-seated, perhaps more ominous area of experience. But it is still a valid and essential area, as 'universal' as the other. To regard *Tristan* as 'sick' is to evade existential reality. Nietzsche, whose attitude to Wagner, beginning in idolatry and ending in furious denunciation, was always ambivalent, could dismiss *Meistersinger* as 'German beer music'; but he could not dismiss *Tristan*. Right to the end, Nietzsche's reaction to *Tristan* was a kind of horrified fascination. And that is a common experience to this day. Both those who are deeply moved by *Tristan* and those who are repelled by it are invariably disturbed in a particular and discomforting way. And there is no doubt that, consciously recognized or not, it is a predominantly sexual disturbance.[16] But the audience at *Die Meistersinger* has only enjoyment and good cheer, with a minimum of disturbing or distressing overtones to cope with, the only possible negative a sometimes arduous demand upon endurance. Yet the relationship between the two is much closer and more subtle than is commonly admitted. Both are penetrating depictions of soul-states, the one (*Tristan*) private, the other (*Meistersinger*) public, though again there is constant interplay between the public and the private, a question of bias rather than exclusivity. The motif of love between the sexes is central to both. And although one is secretively chromatic in its structure while the other is openly diatonic, the musical interaction between chromaticism and diatonicism is inescapable. The links and similarities are as complex and as significant as the apparent differences.

They also permeate *The Ring*. The difficulty in any discussion of *The Ring* is that break of a decade-plus between the second half of *Siegfried* and the completion of the total project. It is thus not easy to focus the entire tetralogy as a single continuous whole. Yet it certainly existed thus in Wagner's own mind and imagination. What caused him to shift his course was a matter of inescapable necessity. He always foresaw Siegfried as one whose destiny was to Will What is Necessary. And that, in a slightly earlier stage, is true also of Wotan. It was this, Siegfried as the Freewiller of Necessity,[17] that obliged Wagner to subdue his own will to the deeper necessity above and beyond the nagging demands of the ego. It may have been outwardly true that Wagner turned from *Siegfried* to what he hoped would be more profitable work; but at the more profound level it was because in reaching that specific point, in *Siegfried* in particular but also in *The Ring* as a whole, he found himself confronted by an impasse. And it was a metaphysical rather than a purely musical problem; for that reason alone it was the more inhibiting.[18] The experience of composing and living through *Tristan* and *Meistersinger*, of all the ramifications of his private life, of the disaster of the Paris production of *Tannhäuser*, of his involvement with the Wesendonks, the beginnings of his association with King Ludwig II of Bavaria and with Cosima von Bülow, plus the final collapse of the revolutionary hopes in Germany together with the founding of the German empire under Bismarck, the hopes and disappointments over the production of his works – all these had to a greater or lesser extent driven him deeper into himself, caused him to explore more thoroughly his own subjectivity and in various ways altered the bias of what 'willing what is necessary' really meant. There was also the deepening influence of Schopenhauer, which had come to an imperative head in *Tristan* but which worked its way into the whole of him and helped 'bend' the final metaphysic of *The Ring*.

Up to a certain point in *The Ring* Wagner had seen the way ahead as loosing Siegfried with his sword on the world and letting him hack away the dead wood and outmoded conventions that held back the full human potential; Siegfried, the one without fear created by the Will of Wotan out of the incestuous relationship of Siegmund and Sieglinde; Siegfried, to whom the Gold in itself meant nothing and who through the awakening of Brünnhilde was to procreate the new race free from the old shackles and deceptions. Siegfried had to die, yes, but that was nothing special: all men have to die, even heroes; and the elevation or transformation of Siegfried through and in death would signal the birth of the New Order.

To manoeuvre Siegfried into that position, Wotan was obliged to enter into all manner of alliances, plots, stratagems, diplomatic ploys and pacts so that power should rest where it rightfully belonged or could easily be recovered when necessary. But from the beginning it had not gone as intended. By bringing forth Siegfried from an incestuous coupling of brother and sister Wotan had transgressed the Law. Yet as chief of the gods it was his duty to preserve the Law, upon which the power of the gods rested. So

112

Wotan found himself in a dilemma at the outset, and because of it was compelled to acquiesce in Fricka's demand that, since the transgression could not be reversed, at least the price must be paid in Siegmund's death in the fight with Hunding. But in allowing himself to be defeated on that point, an important one in his overall plan, Wotan had taken the first fatal step towards the ultimate destruction of his own power and the reign of the gods. He then further compounded his defeat by quarrelling with Brünnhilde, his own anima and the expression of his real Will.[19] In an effort to pull the situation back on course, Wotan projected Brünnhilde as Siegfried's eventual bride. True, this was another piece of incestuous manipulation; but by then it was designed that Siegfried would have done away with all the old prejudices and conventions, established a genuinely free society, and disposed of lingering obstacles to true progress like Mime, Alberich and Fafner at a stroke of his trusty sword.

So far so good. Everything had not gone as smoothly as originally envisaged; but then plans seldom do. The bargains had been made and had served their purpose, even where they were disreputable or deliberately dishonest. The end justifies the means, Wotan might have retorted if charged with treachery and deceit. Wotan's power had been greatly diminished, if not actually destroyed. As the Wanderer he can only urge and argue with Siegfried, who is somewhat irritated by the garrulous stranger with one eye and a floppy hat, obviously an old bore trying to impress a healthy young fellow with a sizeable opinion of himself. Siegfried, however, was fulfilling his appointed destiny, clearing the way for the decisive act of inaugurating the New Order.

Then comes the break; and by the time of the return much had changed. Wagner had realized, in part consciously, in part unconsciously, that the New Order, however it might work out, could not be brought about this way; that the world could no more be redeemed by a hero with a sword than by a god with a spear. In other words, the problem had become less political, more profoundly metaphysical. Wagner himself was aware of this development, though it took him a long time to see it with clarity, and even then it could not be finally resolved. And it is the point at which all political systems, especially dictatorships, whether of the Nazi/Fascist or the Socialist/Communist varieties, fail, for no genuinely new, rejuvenated order of society can ever be imposed from without: it has to grow from within or it will be nothing more than the obverse of what is designed to supersede. It was, this new necessity, analogous to what Jesus had established when He entered Jerusalem on Palm Sunday on an ass instead of a warhorse. He had the open choice, and He made it deliberately. But the idea that the Second Coming will be a military coup is by no means discredited in circles claiming to be Christian. 'I bring not peace but a sword' has been misinterpreted through the ages, as much by evangelists as by militarists, because the human intelligence remains incapable of differentiating between Nothung and the sword of the spirit. Wagner himself did not make the distinction at first. He only came near to it when the burden of his experience activating his genius obliged him to accept it. Nothungs may be needed in certain circumstances; but they can never create new worlds and regenerate social structures, whether by war or violent revolution, for both are the decision of pessimism.

The Will of Wotan, even when translated into the Will of Siegfried, was doomed to frustration and disappointment. Schopenhauer had argued that the universal will to live compels men to seek satisfactions that can never be gratified so they are doomed to perpetual suffering; therefore the only way for the intelligent individual lies in resignation and death, the search for Nirvana.

It was not the death of Siegfried that caused Wagner his dilemma. That had been foreseen from the beginning. It was the meaning of that death and the deeper necessity for it that bore heavily upon him and brought about the alteration of *The Ring*'s final evolution. Only by willing his own destruction and that of the entire race of gods can Wotan see any way into the future. That too became a case of willing what is necessary.

It goes back to the passage from Jung I quoted earlier. Siegfried is representative of the Germans' determination to impose their will, to fashion matters to their own desires. But, 'there are higher things than the ego's will, and to these one must bow.' Wagner did see it. More: he saw precisely why Siegfried had to die, though he did not clearly understand it until after the intervention of both the *Tristan* and the *Meistersinger* experiences and all that went with and around them. He then saw deep into the metaphysical truth: Bismarck, Kaiser Wilhelm II, Adolf Hitler, did not, and by the very nature of their calling and activity could not. The problem was never as they and their like, anywhere, saw it, and continue to see it. Every political solution is a falsification and an evasion; and when it is a politico-military solution it is even more false.

Yet it is easy to see how the concept of *The Ring* could be turned against itself and lead to the totalitarian State (with encouragement from Hegel) based on militarism and the predominance of force, i.e. of an imposed solution. *Götterdämmerung* poses one of the great unanswered questions. Though Wagner came to understand it, the answer eluded him, not because it was a straight either/or but because the ultimate question it asked could not even be clearly defined this side of the finite yet still did not break through into the infinite. It was, in short, the central Romantic dilemma. Wotan willed the destruction of himself and the gods and the razing of Valhalla; the Gold is returned to the Rhinemaidens. We are back where we began; we are back with nature, but we are not 'through' nature. And nature is finite. We are still trapped within the circle, the recurrént cycle. We can almost see another Alberich waiting with eyes of greed fixed upon the Gold; another Wotan standing, spear in hand, pondering various imponderables;

114

another Siegfried buckling on his sword. The earthly paradise remains an illusion, a mirage quivering in the waters of the Rhine as they reflect the dying fire that consumes Valhalla. Historical time has been penetrated; but not cyclic time. Wagner himself was aware of the dilemma. He argued that if people could not see that if social injustices and inequalities could not be prevented and cured, there was no reason why the entire cycle should not begin all over again; but he also declared, more penetratingly, that the real questions were 'a matter of metaphysics'.[20] And that is the rub. Political solutions to metaphysical questions are irrelevant. He tried to work out the burden of the argument in political terms; but it would not work. The farther he went into the matter, the deeper he was drawn into pure metaphysics. To some extent it resolved again onto Plato's philosopher kings. But kings are not philosophers. Therefore the dilemma remains. In Romantic terms it took on a specific form; but because of the Romantic postulates the form it took was one of existential crisis of a particularly acute and demanding kind. In Wagner's own terms it was a bold, courageous effort; a tremendous attempt and a memorable achievement. But it failed.

And perhaps it had to fail. Wagner saw with unusual clarity. In working back from *Siegfried's Death* past *Young Siegfried* to the origins of consciousness (in the Prelude to *Das Rheingold*) he alighted upon an important truth expressed in Kierkegaard's dictum that life can only be understood backwards but it must be lived forwards. He adopted the true existentialist standpoint. All the same, he could not break out of the Romantic impasse. He was honest and courageous enough to change course when he understood that necessity demanded of him that he should do so; yet he still remained trapped within the circle, the squirrel in the cage. He was nearly but not quite great enough to break out. The transformation, so dear to the hearts of the Romantic generations, was not complete, and perhaps in the context of his own life- and world-view it could not be complete. For the final dilemma was not Wotan's or Siegfried's only, not even Wagner's own: it was the dilemma of the entire Romantic movement. And it led to a disaster more overwhelming than the Twilight of the Gods, not in one aspect or one context only, but in the depths of the human psyche itself.

CHAPTER SIX

TRISTAN AS WILL
AND IDEA

Arthur Schopenhauer became the voice and conscience of post-Napoleonic Europe. The high hopes released by the French Revolution had collapsed; reaction had triumphed. Napoleon himself, already discredited, was defeated and in captivity. Beethoven, tearing out the dedication of the *Eroica* symphony and seeing that Napoleon was 'after all just like other men', had both articulated and anticipated the disillusion of a generation.[1] The European hangover was severe. It was time for a bracing dose of pessimism and a hard look at the internal causes of the contemporary situation. This Schopenhauer provided, much to the disgust, supported by the cowardice, of the newly entrenched forces of reaction.

Yet the revolutionary fervours were by no means extinguished. Between about 1815, the date of Waterloo, and 1850, when the revolution could finally be seen to have aborted, the dream could still be dreamt. It was not yet burnt out.

In philosophy Hegel, worshipper of the State and authority on and master of massively obscure metaphysics, was the entrenched favourite of the establishment. Hegel's predominantly optimistic pursuit of the Absolute continued the central tradition of European philosophy and earned him both the respect and the favour of his colleagues and his political masters. Hegel attempted to elevate the nineteenth century's belief in progress into a cosmic process. Although it may not be true, finally, to say of Hegel, as Shelley said of Plato, that 'he is obscure only because he is profound', it is certainly true to say of him that he represented the culmination of that powerful philosophic movement of German intellectual idealism of which Kant was the central contemporary figure.

Onto this mound of philosophical optimism Schopenhauer threw a cold douche of pessimism. And in the emotional and intellectual atmosphere of the 1820s (*The World as Will and Idea*, Schopenhauer's *magnum opus*, was published in 1819), with many smarting under the disasters of war and its aftermath and the inevitable malaise brought about by the collapse of early hopes, he found a ready audience. He was not, however, academically respected, even respectable. In the battle between Hegelian 'optimism' and Schopenhauerean 'pessimism', the official victory went to the former; but it was the latter that caught and most accurately expressed the prevailing *zeitgeist*. Rejected by the academics, Schopenhauer was accepted by the world that lay beyond academic reach.[2]

Wagner began reading Schopenhauer in 1854, and the influence struck deep. Yet it was not entirely a matter of influence. As later with Delius and Nietzsche, it was more a matter of convergence of like than of conversion from one to the other. In the catalogue of Wagner's works, Schopenhauer bore upon the evolution of *The Ring* but determined that of *Tristan und Isolde*.[3]

At this time Wagner was in his usual dire straits, both emotional and financial. In 1852 he had met and been befriended by Otto and Mathilde Wesendonk. As usual, he made an immediate and profound impression. Otto Wesendonk was a silk merchant with interests in New York, wealthy and a patron of the arts. He and Mathilde soon became Wagner's benefactors, financing the 1853 Zürich concerts of his music and furthering his cause in many ways. Soon, and again inevitably, Wagner reacted to the charms of Mathilde; and she to his. He found her responsive to his ideas; and before long the relationship ripened, intensified from that of master and pupil into something deeper, something more far-ranging, ultimately all-consuming. He began (as usual) to see it in terms of his own dramas, as a kind of Wotan/Brünnhilde equivalent or Siegmund/Sieglinde conjunction, a spiritual brother–sister mating on the one hand to match the sexual implications of man–woman lovers.

But not at once. The complex physical and psychological situation took time to develop. Early on Wagner became convinced that he must renounce his love, and like Wotan submit to the universal Will. The situation did not, however, remain like that. In the spring of 1855 Wagner went to London, partly in the hope of arranging for *The Ring* to be produced at Covent Garden, partly because he had been offered a much needed fee by the Royal Philharmonic Society which he also hoped to increase by other English activities. He was once again (it was the recurring pattern of at least the first two-thirds of his life) largely disappointed in his expectations. Covent Garden, dedicated to Italian opera, was not interested in so original and uncompromisingly Germanic an undertaking; his concerts only met with any kind of success in part and latterly; and he made no general progress. On the other hand, he was received by Queen Victoria and Prince Albert, made new friends, and met Berlioz again for almost the first time since the bad days in Paris fifteen years earlier. It was a meeting that cheered him, even to the point of making him acknowledge that Berlioz was probably unhappier than he was himself.

On his return to Zürich in the summer, still an exile from Germany, his re-entry proscribed, his finances were in the familiar parlous condition and his health weakened by his London exertions. He worked in a somewhat desultory manner on the score of *Die Walküre*, low in spirits and living more or less from hand to mouth. Then the following year Liszt sent a present of money, which he used to take a rest from work and a cure at Mornex; after which he returned again to Zürich, now in better fettle than he had been for some time, and immediately set to work with renewed vigour and optimism on the score of *Siegfried*. He had hopes of selling *The Ring* to Breitkopf & Härtel; Liszt wanted it for Weimar, and was working to that end by urging the Duke of Weimar to secure an amnesty so that Wagner could gain readmittance into Germany and so take part in the productions. He was further cheered by a visit from Liszt and the Princess von Wittgenstein, which proved rewarding in spite of the Princess's addiction to socializing, and which encompassed a rendition of the first act of *Walküre* in the Baur au Lac Hotel with Wagner declaiming loudly and Liszt transposing the orchestral part onto the piano at sight.

During this period Wagner's apartment was proving not only too costly but too noisy as well. He was constantly distracted while trying to work. He complained to the Wesendonks, who were at the time in Paris pending completion of their handsome new villa by the lake in the Enge suburb of Zürich. Probably at the instigation of Mathilde, they offered him the use of a smaller villa in the grounds of the new one, a pleasant little dwelling called 'Asyl', or 'Refuge', and had it adapted to Wagner's special requirements. It was here, in Asyl, that the deep-running passion between Wagner and Mathilde Wesendonk finally flowered and was no longer secret, and here that the inner seeding for *Tristan und Isolde* came to fruition.

He still despaired of seeing *The Ring* produced, and he still thought of *Tristan* as a Bellini-type opera designed to catch the popular fancy. Like many another, the subject of Tristram and Iseult had been milling around below the surface of his mind for some time. He had made acquaintance with the basics of the story during his years in Dresden when he had immersed himself in medieval German history and legend. It had lain in the back of his consciousness ever since, at times throwing out prospective tendrils while awaiting the right time to take over his creative faculties. This came about under various pressures between 1856 and 1859, though not at all as he originally supposed or intended.

Of course *Tristan und Isolde* could never have emerged as any kind of Italianate opera; and of course it would boil no pot. As so often, Wagner's genius took charge of him and fashioned something he could only vaguely comprehend in the intial stages, if at all. The Will took charge of the Idea and produced a unique masterpiece of the musical theatre. Richard Wagner being Richard Wagner, again it could not have been otherwise.

The precise part played by Mathilde Wesendonk and Wagner's

undiminished and undisguised passion for her in the creation of *Tristan und Isolde* has always been recognized. Nor is the disposal of that influence particularly important. In short, whether he wrote *Tristan* as he did because he had fallen for the lady, or fell for the lady because his unconscious was already pushing him towards the creation of the great love-drama, is hardly a valid question, if only because the strands of meaning and the complexities of the pressures that went into the making of the artwork can never admit of a single or simple answer. Wagner may have thought he abandoned *The Ring* because of the hopelessness of seeing it produced in the foreseeable future; and he may have been driven deep into the subject of *Tristan und Isolde* by his passion for Mathilde Wesendonk; but these are only the outward and manifest signals of a profoundly inward and esoteric process taking place in the depths of his creative being.

In any case, ultimately the crux of the Wesendonk affair lies not in Wagner's passion for Mathilde but in his awareness of the necessity for renunciation. Yet even this is more inward than outward. Outwardly he came to realize that nothing but disaster lay ahead in the *ménage à quatre* in which he had become involved (Otto and Mathilde Wesendonk on the one side, himself and his wife Minna on the other). But the real reason lies much deeper. Wagner was never a man to give up what he wanted because it was dangerous or would upset somebody. As he had proved in the Königsberg days, when he had severely reprimanded Minna for her extra-marital pecadilloes while himself preaching (and no doubt practising) free love and total indulgence of the senses, and as he was to prove again when he made his liaison with Cosima, daughter of one friend, Franz Liszt, and wife of another, Hans von Bülow, Richard Wagner was a strong adherent of the sound socialistic principle 'what's yours is mine and what's mine's my own'. But not this time. He was now in all the throes of making his terms with the spirit of renunciation, as preached by his 'guru', Arthur Schopenhauer. And for once he did not only preach it, he applied it to himself. He had not long completed Wotan's moving Farewell to Brünnhilde, a positive if inevitable, in the circumstances, act of renunciation; and he had come to see that in Siegfried as child of Nature, without inhibitions and with all his natural instincts to be indulged, whether within or outside the Law, he had created, if not a monster, at least a figure only half the hero he had at first envisaged and one who also had to learn the lesson of renunciation. It was in this emotional and psychological climate that *Tristan und Isolde* was written.

Even in 1854, right at the beginning of the Mathilde affair, he had preened himself and tended to bask in the light of his own righteousness, informing Liszt that 'I now take delight in living for my wife'. He went on to announce that since he had never in his life known the joys of true love, 'I will set up a memorial to this most lovely of all dreams'. It was well said. There had never been any pretence that the marriage with Minna was a real love match. It had worked by a kind of mutual interest but with little mutual understanding. They had no children, but a succession of pets who seemed to act as infant substitutes. (Just why Wagner and Minna were childless is not clear; Minna already had a daughter when they were married, and Wagner was far from infertile when he set up with Cosima.) So, and in spite of a number of liaisons along the way, Wagner was justified in saying that he had never experienced the depths of true love. Passions, yes; love, no. On the other hand, he had probably come by a deeper truth and one which seemed to him justified by his 'renunciation' in respect of Mathilde Wesendonk. Just as he had come to see that Wotan had to renounce Brünnhilde and that Siegfried the hero was inadequate, so he seemed now to realize that, at least in worldly and practical terms, the Great Love was only another aspect of the Great Illusion. *Tristan und Isolde* was to be an idealization of what might be in a perfect world; but the ultimate consummation still had to lie in and beyond death.

The intensity of the music of *Tristan* therefore derived not so much from Wagner's passion for Mathilde Wesendonk as from his self-willed renunciation of it. While he was living at Asyl the affair burned hot and openly. The fires blazed, and threatened to engulf two families. Otto Wesendonk himself had also to renounce, had to acquiesce in the situation both because he loved his wife and because he wished to preserve his family for the sake of his children. Minna, whether present in Zürich or away somewhere else, was consumed with jealousy; she meddled with mail, refused to believe Wagner's protestations or accept any explanations. She can hardly be blamed. Wagner himself haughtily maintained that the relationship was innocent and that in renouncing his love for Mathilde he was returning to his wife without a blemish. He could not understand why she would not believe him. The anger and agitation of it all brought on the incipient heart disease from which she eventually died.

Yet Wagner was not being merely cynical and wilfully dishonest. Like his own Wotan, he was probing into what he saw as new areas of experience and a manner of living beyond and outside the inhibitingly social and bourgeois conventions. But of course others did not see it that way. The world at large saw it from Fricka's rather than Wotan's point of view – as a commonplace adultery.

The matter was open between Otto Wesendonk and his wife; but when Minna intercepted a letter from Wagner to Mathilde and confronted her with it, the fur began seriously to fly. It came to a head and it had the effect of bringing the useful arrangements at Asyl to a premature end.

In part, the situation paralleled that in *Tristan und Isolde*: Wagner carrying on a 'forbidden' liaison with his friend's wife. It also related back to the situation of Siegmund, Sieglinde and Hunding. But only in part. The thing was now a quadrangle rather than a triangle; and in any case it operated from within more than from without. It can be argued, and in fact it has been argued, that Wagner's much vaunted (to himself) 'renunciation' of

120

his love for Mathilde was simply a means of escape from an entanglement that was becoming rather tiresome, a liaison with a very ordinary woman whose charms were fading for him. And it is true that Mathilde Wesendonk appears to have been an ordinary middle-class woman of no great quality or accomplishment, rather romantic and easily impressed; the kind of woman in fact of whom someone like Richard Wagner might quickly tire. Their little collaboration in the matter of the 'Wesendonk Lieder' signifies little. The music is infinitely superior to the words; but that was only to be expected. The comparisons on any plane are probably unfair to Mathilde. She almost certainly was a rather ordinary, even commonplace person; but then great men do not invariably love great women: in fact they seldom do. In many respects, they do not need to; even ought not to. They need somebody to elevate and idealize.

Another curiosity intrudes. Schopenhauer had a poor opinion of women; but Richard Wagner, in his quest for perfect love, whether in fact or in the imagination, can hardly be said to have shared it or to have allowed himself to share it. Yet Schopenhauer's misogamy was an inevitable consequence of his philosophy, and that philosophy lay at the heart of *Tristan und Isolde* and to a lesser extent of parts of *The Ring*. Here Wagner, the high Romantic, was nearer to the exalted idea of Perfect Woman, of which he often spoke and wrote, the 'angel' of Divine Origin, than Wagner the devout Schopenhauerean was to the lesson of the master. Certainly hatred of women was not the essence of Schopenhauer's philosophy but a by-product of it. All the same, Richard Wagner was not the first disciple to evade the more uncomfortable aspects of his master's teaching.

But it was the Schopenhaurean concept of the Will that drove Tristan and Isolde inexorably towards the ultimate consummation of their love in Death and Night and away from Life and Day. Wagner confessed that during the troubled time when *Tristan* was forming in his mind and he was floating uneasily on the ebb tide of his first determination to renounce his love for Mathilde Wesendonk, he often cast his 'yearning gaze towards the land of Nirvana. But Nirvana swiftly turns to Tristan again.' Pure Schopenhauer, of course.

Yet there was also in Wagner a parallel strain of Nietzschean life-affirmation, a creative tension between day and night, life and death, light and dark, in the deepest sense of an optimism that enabled him to follow *Tristan* immediately with *Meistersinger* and to write the two virtually side by side.

Schopenhauer's attack on women was, as I say, an inevitable consequence of his philosophy, the cause rather than the result of his own bachelordom, deliberately chosen and staunchly maintained. The universal Will draws the sexes together for the purpose of procreation; nature has ordained that women shall be attractive to men in the interests of propagation of the species. But only for that reason. 'Love' tends to work as the agent of eugenics because when it functions properly it draws the right couples together and thus ensures evolutionary continuity. 'Happiness' is unimportant. But the human animal is full of contrariness, especially the Western-Christian variety, and will insist upon seeking 'love' and 'happiness'. It is an illusion and it causes untold suffering and disappointment; but it still persists. Mankind is incurably dedicated to chasing shadows and rainbows and remains perpetually surprised when they turn out to be delusions. Biologically, men and women are complementary; but in every other respect, intellectually, emotionally, spiritually, women are markedly inferior to men. They are good at motherhood, as procreative agents that is; but socially and morally they are irresponsible and usually trivial. Whenever they have achieved anything worthwhile, they have done so in direct ratio to their taking on of male qualities and characteristics. The idea was by no means new, even if the acidulated tongue of Arthur Schopenhauer gave it a new and sharper twist. Beethoven had once said to Bettina von Brentano: 'Forgive me: emotion is for women. The flame of music must burst forth from the heart of a man.' There have been, and are, admirable women musicians; but it can hardly be denied, whatever excuse is offered, that the ultimate creative force has not so far manifested itself in a searing flame bursting forth from the heart and mind of a woman.

The veneration of women in Europe Schopenhauer put down largely to the influence of a mixture of German sentimentality and Christianity, especially the Roman Catholic veneration of the Virgin Mary. Yet that contention cannot be carried all the way, since St Paul directly abjures men to steer clear of women. He may have been right; but it does little to support the contention that Christianity bears the heaviest responsibility for the veneration of women, at least transmitted Christianity. The Orientals, as Schopenhauer was quick to note, arrange these things better: they do not permit any nonsense about the equality of women or 'love' marriages.

These ideas of Schopenhauer, however philosophically and intellectually tenable they might be, can hardly have appealed to Richard Wagner. Like all the Romantics, Wagner had a more or less angelic view of women, at least in the abstract. Yet his idea that women only completely fulfil themselves in the act of surrender to a man veers significantly towards Schopenhauerean waters. All the same, for Wagner, the arch-Romantic, susceptible to German sentimentalities as well as to German metaphysical realities, Perfect Woman was one of those realities, and in Isolde he created his most passionately projected image of her.

But the danger remains inherent. The elevation of woman can go two ways, and one of those ways leads in the drection of racism and genetic exclusiveness. If the underlying theme of *The Ring* is the survival of the fittest and the creation of the fittest to survive, then the next step is 'racial purity', with women as agents of that creation and therefore as tools in the racial process, as breeding machines for the pure in race as well as the 'pure' in heart. It is inevitable. And indeed that is precisely what happened in Nazi Germany and what must happen in any coincident circumstances, on whatever basis and directed to whatever political or generic ends. Again, only in Death is the final consummation of Love and Desire, which can never be satisfied except through extinction and thus possible transformation; only thus can a couple be freed from the tyranny of the natural and the mechanics of reproduction upon which the universal Will insists, whatever the cost. Nirvana becomes the ultimate reality.

There is also the matter of reincarnation. In the search for Nirvana and the reality of transformation through Love, as with Senta and the Flying Dutchman, as with Elisabeth and Tannhäuser, as above all with Tristan and Isolde, much relates to the Buddhistic elements in the philosophy of Schopenhauer. In *Tristan* there is considerable significance hinging upon the fact that Isolde had encountered Tristan in an earlier time. But symbolically, in the context of the drama as a whole, this might be in another life. There is nothing in the text or in the origins of the legend to suggest such an interpretation, let alone to establish it; yet it is possible to see it as implicit, if only because the idea of reincarnation, of passing through a series of phases in the total life-cycle, gives added, and perhaps final point to the meaning of transformation through death, or death as transition from one plane of existence to another. Different planes of existence, various incarnations, are an inherent belief of Buddhism: it is also inherent in Schopenhauer where his philosophic tenets touch most nearly upon Buddhism.

Wagner's deepening experience of life and art coincided with rather than depended upon external events. He had come to a crux, a true crisis when he gave up the composition of *Siegfried* and turned instead to *Tristan*. That he thought he did so because he needed money and hoped that the new work would earn it is simply another example of the Will at its Schopenhauerean work. So was the Wesendonk involvement, which outwardly turned him from his original intention but at the deeper level was only the 'trigger' that set him to his true work on *Tristan* and then on *Meistersinger* before he could return to *The Ring* and complete the great plan as it had to be completed.

The profound despair and the necessity for renunciation implicit in Wotan's Farewell to Brünhilde, which ends Act III of *Die Walküre*, seemed to lift with the predominantly optimistic music of the first half of *Siegfried*. But it was a false dawn, and when he returned to *Siegfried* more than a decade later the necessary transformation had taken place inside him, an intensifying and virtual mutating as much musical as personal and metaphysical. And it was *Tristan* that exemplified it.

The opening bars of *Tristan* Prelude, or *Vorspiel*, are often taken as the starting point of modern music, in so far as such a demarcation can be admitted in the first place. The way the harmony moves without any point of resolution produces an impression of walking on quicksand, in sharp distinction from the tonal securities of the classical period. True, Wagner had prepared the way in many passages in earlier works; but never had the declaration been made so clearly and so decisively. In fact, of course, it was only a beginning; virtually the whole of *Tristan* is suffused with a shifting chromaticism that moves always away from the finite towards the infinite, from the clear light of day towards the ambiguities of night, from the transience of life towards the eternities beyond death, the flow of 'endless melody' contradicting the contrary pull of the terminal dimension of material nature and desire. The strain is always towards the dark side of the musical spectrum.

The deathward slant is inescapable and intentional. Indeed, Wagner originally intended the Prelude, rather than Isolde's final lament, to bear the name of 'Liebestod'. Death was not only foreseen in the beginning, it was the central motif throughout. The substitution of the Love Potion for the Death Potion by Brangäne was itself an unwitting gesture on the side of death, since an overwhelming intensification of the love between Tristan and Isolde implied an intensification of the death wish and ensured its final inevitability.

Tristan as well as Isolde is already death-set; he as well as she is prepared to drink the Death Potion, as both suppose it to be. After each has drunk the substituted Love Potion, the bias is altered but not the outcome. The substitution is not simply a theatrical device, though it is also that; it acts as the agent of the Will upon the Idea, which is then worked out in the second act love duet in openly Schopenhauerean terms. It is sometimes argued that, as in *The Ring*, the words, the 'argument', are not important: the music is all that matters. This again is only a half-truth, if that. While it is true that the heart of the matter lies within the music, it is not true that ignorance of the words does little to diminish or detract from the whole. Wagner's concept of the total artwork, the overriding synthesis of drama, music and the graphic arts, depends upon the comprehensive combing of all the elements so that a disallowing of any one denies and undermines the whole. In *Tristan*, as in all Wagner's music dramas, the 'argument' represents the intellectual, the civilized or critical element, while the music represents the elemental, the instinctive, the intuitional. If one of Schopenhauer's achievements was to anticipate Freud in revealing the power of the instinctual, and argued that knowledge, or intellect, is the source of pain and suffering, there is still no warrant for asserting that the latter must or can be ignored. Though the fullest implications of the drama lie in the music, and although the words are infrequently heard so that they can be understood in performance,[4] that is no warrant for presenting the music without the words, as is the habit with the 'Liebestod', coupling it with the Prelude to make a concert offering, even if Wagner himself, for practical and material purposes, sanctioned and even encouraged such a procedure.

The Liebestod without the voice misses a number of necessary points, both dramatic and musical. One of these, which is also overlooked in the full version, is its relationship with Dido's Lament, 'When I am laid in earth', from Purcell's *Dido and Aeneas*, a magnificent and noble aria over a chromatic ground bass which almost exactly parallels in musical terms and at a distance of two centuries the 'Liebestod' with its cumulative chromaticism. There is no evidence that Wagner had ever heard, or even heard of, Purcell's *Dido*; nor is it important. What it does demonstrate once again is the essential nature of music as a language of the emotions, no matter what the period or context, and that its means of expression, though they may change outwardly, remain constant and perpetually valid. Nor is this a singular example: Tristan's agonized song upon being awakened by the shepherd boy's pipe in the third act is a direct descendant, at a very much shorter interval, of the half-delirious Florestan's vision of Leonora at the beginning of Act II of Beethoven's *Fidelio*. Wagner as certainly did know every note of *Fidelio* as he probably did not know a single one of *Dido and Aeneas*. But that too is beside the point. It is the totality of music, across the ages and of many different kinds, that determines these coincidences and correspondences.

No doubt the music of Dido's Lament arranged without the voice would convey the sense of loss and agony much as the voiceless Liebestod conveys its own aura of death and its ecstatic embrace. Yet if drama is to be set to music there is no point dismissing the words out of hand and consigning the dramatic particulars to the condition of baggage 'not wanted on voyage'. It certainly will not do with Wagner. No doubt much in Wagner's dramatic and metaphysical thought is now outdated, *démodé*. Yet in so far as the hard core of it was relevant in his own day, and that day has exerted a formative influence on our own, it cannot be thrown carelessly into some disposal bin along with the fashions and ephemera of the time.

The matter is of importance because of the unusually strong admixture of the instinctive and the intellectual, the rational and the irrational, the emotional and the speculative in the German psyche and temperament; and Richard Wagner in a unique way represented precisely those qualities in that specific balance. Because of it, the direction taken at any one time by German politics and social arrangement has tended to be exaggerated, and when the culminating aberration came it was certain to stretch the exaggeration beyond containable limits. Yet that exaggeration, stretched though it temporarily was, remained rooted in the essence of the German psychological and philosophical equation even if it was a major distortion of them. Distorted or not, it grew out of the central German myth.

In fact the optimistic and the pessimistic in German intellectual and emotional life coincided at several points. But the bias invariably came down on the side of pessimism. Schopenhauer's contention that as knowledge increases so does suffering, and 'as consciousness ascends, pain also increases, and reaches its highest degree in man', closely parallels the Hegelian 'tragic consciousness', even though Hegel is regarded as predominantly optimistic in philosophical terms and Schopenhauer was the apostle of pessimism, so that the context and emphasis are both different. And Nietzsche's ethic of life-affirmation only tries, not always convincingly, to reach out beyond and in the end to contradict his belief in 'tragic optimism' and his interpretation of Greek tragic drama as the 'conquest of pessimism through art'.

Romanticism may have begun in optimism, as a brave new dawn. The motto of the early, dawnlit Romantics may have been Wordsworth's 'Surprised by joy!' But it soon had to tune its responses with pessimism if it was not to evade its central issue. After the Napoleonic débâcle it could be said that pessimism became necessary to prevent optimism getting out of hand. The Napoleonic adventure had appeared to begin in high optimism, as Beethoven believed with the original dedication of the *Eroica* symphony. But it was an illusion: since war is always the triumph of pessimism, the end was in the beginning even if it was not seen in the first flush of enthusiasm. In the Napoleonic aftermath, which was also the aftermath of the French Revolution, optimism could only be maintained on a very limited and local scale. Nearer the truth then was Carlyle's

O poor mortals, how ye make this Earth bitter for each other; this fearful and wonderful Life fearful and horrible; and Satan has his place in all hearts! Such agonies and ragings and wailings ye have, and have had, in all times: – to be buried all, in so deep silence; and the salt sea is not swoln with your tears.[5]

– and that is a testament of pessimism.

Schopenhauer recognized that the Will drives men onwards to seek the fulfilment of desires that can never be gratified. But even if the desire is gratified, the result is invariably disappointment. W. B. Yeats quotes a striking phrase from an old prose allegory about 'a hollow image of fulfilled desire'. 'All happy art,' Yeats continues, 'seems to me that hollow image, but when its lineaments express also the poverty or the exasperation that set its maker to work, we call it tragic art'.

Wagner, to his honour, did not opt for the disreputable device of the 'hollow image' but faced resolutely the necessity for a truly tragic art – another example of his honesty as an artist whatever may have been true of Wagner the man. In *Tristan*, above all, he held fast to his principle, to his fundamental honesty, knowing and affirming that the only way out of and away from that 'hollow image' was a consummation and transformation through death – through, that is, the existential movement from the finite into the infinite, the ephemeral into the eternal via renunciation of the gratification of worldly desire and the penetration of the higher reality beyond the ego's will. It was, again, a specifically Romantic attitude; but within the context of Romanticism it was both inevitable and necessary.

What had promised to be the idyll at the villa Asyl proved in the end to be nothing of the sort. The entanglement with Mathilde cost Wagner and

Minna dear. Minna could stand no more, and nor could Mathilde. Minna's health broke; and Mathilde finally came to recognize that she lacked the resolution to go all the way with Wagner, foregoing husband and children. The reality of renunciation now demanded that it be taken seriously; it became not simply metaphysical or philosophical, a speculation in the abstract, but immediate and practical. It caught up with him, and there was no way he could evade the consequences. He had to practise what he preached.

In August 1858 the idyll was over. He left Zürich and travelled to Venice, via Geneva. In Venice he composed more of *Tristan*. The breaking of his hopes and the despair of his lost love went into the music of Act II.

He had learnt a major lesson. He knew now what renunciation really meant; it was no longer a philosophical plaything. No doubt the Great Love for which Wagner had yearned and up until then even thought he could win is always a practical impossibility, a temptation that leads men into the ultimate absurdity and disenchantment: it is an unrealizable dream. But it will not be extinguised in men's hearts for all that. It cannot be realized in this world; but it can be realized through the imagination. It exists eternally in the pages of *Tristan und Isolde*. And it ends there in death, as ultimately it must. Nirvana becomes the final reality. This side of eternity the Great Love had indeed proved to be the Great Illusion.

He left Venice in the spring of 1859 and went to Lucerne, where he finished the score of *Tristan*. He hoped to have it produced in Karlsruhe and thus at last to repair his fortunes. Of course it did not work out that way; it never did. But at last he had another important task accomplished, though it brought him nothing in material terms.

He turned again for help to Otto Wesendonk; and again it was not withheld. Wesendonk purchased the existing parts of *The Ring* and so enabled Wagner to return to his old temptress and deceiver, the city of Paris, where he settled towards the end of 1859 and was reunited with Minna, on somewhat uncertain but temporarily secure terms.

Nothing changes – and if it does it remains the same. In Paris, again without much money or steady employment, he indulged himself generously, took an expensive house and spent more on arranging it to his liking, furnishing it with accoutrements and servants well beyond his means. Towards the cost of producing his works on the most ambitious scale possible, he received a payment from Schott of Mainz, the celebrated German music publishers, for the score of *Das Rheingold*, although the receipts from that source were the right of Otto Wesendonk. He gave concerts of extracts from his dramas, and generally prepared the grand assault on the musical world of Paris by performance linked to negotiation and a kind of diplomacy.

He wanted to have *Tristan* produced in Paris; but there was little promise in that direction. What hope there was rested with *Tannhäuser*, a work he had long outgrown but which he continued to hold in some affection. He engineered, through a pulling of strings and a twisting of arms, a performance of *Tannhäuser* at the Paris Opéra, at Imperial command, in a French translation and with a revised musical score. It was put into rehearsal in September 1860, and presented at the Opéra in March 1861; Pierre Dietsch conducted as Wagner, despite more twisting of arms, had not been able to overturn the rule against foreign composers conducting their own works.

History has blazoned across its pages the fiasco of the 1861 Paris *Tannhäuser*, largely because the cretins of the Jockey Club gave tongue upon not finding their ballet, and therefore their pretty little ballerinas, where they expected and demanded to find it, but also because the anti-German French press seized upon the rumpus further to undermine the success of the proceedings. The fact that many thought, and still do think, post-*Tristan* Wagner's revision of the score introduced a false note is irrelevant, since the majority present were no more competent to judge a musical composition than were their successors at the Théâtre du Champs-Elysées at the riot-troubled première of Stravinsky's *Rite of Spring* in 1913. The protest was social, not musical. Wagner, though disappointed materially, took an acquiescent view of the matter. If it had been his beloved *Tristan* that had been thus traduced, it would have been very different. But it was only his old, if refurbished, *Tannhäuser*. Paris was living up to her Wagnerian deceitfulness, as before promising only to disappoint.

He had still not heard a full performance of his *Lohengrin*, though it was fast becoming the most celebrated of his works and the best admired. Now he heard it in Vienna, where he had gone to try to encourage a production of *Tristan*, which he proceeded to withdraw from Karlsruhe. But it still would not go well: the tenor developed throat trouble; and Wagner as usual was out of money. He made shift, lived day to day, hoped, despaired, railed, recanted. Despite goodwill, the originality of *Tristan* and the difficulties it presented for singers and orchestra threatened the future of the production. And the origins of the *Tristan* intensities bore on him continually. He could not get Mathilde out of his mind. When he met her and Otto in Venice their recovered happiness only served to remind him of his own sense of loss and the hopelessness of his apparently inextinguishable passion. He had poured it all into *Tristan*; but it would not stay there.

Whether at this time or at some other, it seems to have been Mathilde Wesendonk who turned his thoughts back to the subject of the Mastersingers of Nuremberg. He extracted an advance from Schott on the strength of the original sketch. It began to take him over, to dispel the misery of his lost love for Mathilde and to do something to assuage him for the continued failure of the *Tristan* production to materialize. Not for the first or last time in the history of art, the artist created his happiest and most optimistic work while he himself was undergoing one of the unhappiest periods of even his fraught life. As Beethoven produced some of his sunniest music, including the D major symphony, at the time of the bitter and desperate document known as the Heiligenstadt Testament, so Wagner plunged himself into *Meistersinger* when all about him appeared to be in ruin and collapse, his hopes dashed, his future black, his personal and professional situation in turmoil, on every side. Or at least so he saw it. He sorely needed succour from some source. *Meistersinger* provided it from the inside.

But he needed it no less from some source outside himself, some material alleviation of his condition. It came, though not at once, from a totally unexpected and highly prestigious fountainhead.

In the meantime, things continued to go wrong. Work on *Meistersinger* fell behind and Schott stopped the payments. So it was further delayed by the need to raise money or to earn it, both if possible. Machinations to this end took up his time and distracted his mind. He also managed to involve himself with two more women, much to Minna's displeasure and his own consequent discomfort. It was no doubt inevitable, Wagner being Wagner. He needed a sexual or parasexual relationship most times in his life; it was in his nature and part of the motivation of his creative chemistry. The more conventional and non-creative social proprieties meant nothing to him, as they must mean nothing to anyone of spirit and temper. This time he appears to have entangled himself one way or another with both Mathilde Maier and Friederike Meyer, the latter a pert young actress of much charm and initiative. He was also on terms of close friendship with Hans and Cosima von Bülow, though the intimacy with Cosima had not yet ripened into its later absolute passion.

Otherwise it was yet another period of scroutling and makeshift. The world still would not afford him the luxurious living he expected of it and to which he thought himself, as an artist, automatically entitled. In late 1862 he moved back to Vienna with Friederike Meyer, and saw his wife, who had manipulated a belated assent for him to return to Germany, for the last time before her heart complaint finally ended her life at the beginning of 1866. Though never 'faithful' in the conventional sense, Wagner stood by Minna to the end, concerned for her welfare, supporting her with money even when he had virtually none, certainly none to spare, always declaring that whatever else happened he would not divorce her. Athough she blamed him for nearly everything, he never blamed her on any permanent basis – and only did so at all in the short term when the pressures built to intolerable levels. There is no doubt that they were ill-matched. He married the wrong partner (maybe until he was older and wiser and came under Cosima's command there was no 'right' partner for him); but although he strayed frequently he usually kept some idea of marital duty before him.

Meistersinger continued to occupy him; but more practical matters still pressed hard. He was once again reduced to all manner of expedients to keep body and finances within striking distance of each other. And he could not always succeed. Total ruin approached. He gave concerts in Prague, St Petersburg and Moscow, from which he earned money that he immediately and without hesitation spent on the luxuries of his daily living, though he did also send a substantial contribution to Minna. The next year, 1863, he gave more concerts in Budapest, then in Prague, Karlsruhe, Breslau and Lowenberg. With his usual exercise of personal charm he found yet another potential patroness, one Henriette von Bissing, a wealthy widow who at one time agreed to discharge his most pressing financial liabilities (she later changed her mind, ostensibly because she was convinced he would only run up more and bigger debts and because she resented his continuing passion for 'the Wesendonk woman'). Others, too, were beginning to see that helping Wagner only encouraged him to further extravagances and more love affairs. So he was driven once again into the arms of usurers and moneylenders. He hoped for a profitable series of concerts in Russia but they did not materialize, and, as he had been in Paris more than twenty years earlier, he was in real danger of being imprisoned for debt. It did not quite come to that; but it was another near-run thing. His friends saved him just in time, and he fled to Switzerland.

He hoped that the Wesendonks would give him shelter; but even these good and patient friends demurred at the reality of another visitation from this obtrusive cuckoo and his flagrant genius. He was received instead by his old patroness, Eliza Wille, a lady from Hamburg, latterly resident with her husband François in Zürich. François was away at the time, and Wagner took his opportunity. Eliza was the sister of Henriette von Bissing, so maybe he thought he could pull a kind of claim by family default. He was in a bad way, full of remorse and self-pity proportionately mixed, especially in regard to Minna. He refused to see any bright future. He railed that he was not as other men and could not live on a pittance and had no intention of trying to. The world owed him his extravagant way of life, and he would have it.

It was no use. François Wille returned and Wagner had to move on. He went to Stuttgart in the hope of working up an interest in some production of *Tristan* or of raising funds to enable him to finish *Meistersinger*. He was disappointed in both these ambitions. He had a mind to throw in the towel. A short time earlier he had written to his friend the composer Peter Cornelius in despair wailing that '*some* light must show itself'. But no light came to pierce the gloom.

Then, suddenly and miraculously, it came. He was approached by a mysterious stranger who turned out to be the secretary and emissary of the young King Ludwig II of Bavaria, newly ascended to the throne upon the death of his father. Wagner was at first suspicious, fearing some new disaster, some fresh salvo from his creditors or others who intended him no good. He prevaricated. But the emissary persisted. In the end, Wagner agreed to meet him. To his astonishment he realized that the longed-for miracle had occurred. His future was assured, his despair had turned to light after all but dragging him to the depths.

With that encounter Richard Wagner entered upon the most curious and in many respects the most distasteful period of his life, the period when he showed himself at his most self-indulgent and egocentric. His relations with the young king would always be ambivalent, and he showed himself to be one who could be a ruthless and unscrupulous manipulator of fortune when it did smile upon him. But being the man he was he contrived circumstance to his advantage, his art set above all as predominant and triumphant.

Tristan remained for the time being a major preoccupation. He hoped for things to turn his way so that he could complete *Meistersinger*; but the advancement of *Tristan und Isolde* was his permanent concern, his dedicated ambition. It meant too much to him, was too true a record of his innermost experience during the troubled years of the late 1850s and the early 1860s for him to abandon it to its fate in the world's indifferent theatres, at the mercy of careless interpreters. But no more could he bear to see it wasting away unproduced and unperformed.

A final judgement upon *Tristan und Isolde* still abides our question. Charges that it is 'immoral', that it 'glorifies adultery' or whatever, are as jejune and irrelevant as the charge that *Die Walküre*, indeed the entire *Ring* cycle, 'glorifies incest'. With such we need not bother. But the deepest implications of *Tristan*, as with *The Ring*, remain potent and demanding, far beyond commonplace accusations of 'eroticism', 'sensuous indulgence', even some minor form of pornography. The true implications strike deep into the heart of the whole Romantic movement and from there into our own time. And it lay the hand of its most profound penetrations on the culminating drama of *The Ring* also. Richard Wagner had to live through, right to the end, the experience of *Tristan und Isolde* before he could complete his great tetralogy or progress from there to the apparently very different world of *Parsifal*. Yet that world was in fact a direct consequence of what had gone before, of the ethic and aesthetic of *Tristan*, of the conclusion of *The Ring*, forced upon him whether he willed it or not, with all it entailed in the abandonment of former dreams and beliefs and assumptions – that was what brought *Götterdämmerung* into being in its ultimate form, the fundamental direction radically altered, as it had to be, from the original concept, the merely heroic mould in which it had once appeared to be cast. Through *Tristan* the innermost force of renunciation had been forced upon Wagner; and it was a lesson that passed far beyond the personal and the immediately subjective. That lesson needed to be learnt, but it was ignored by the political sophisters and manipulators who followed the breaking of the nineteenth century into the twentieth, whatever they chose to call themselves, the Deutschland of Kaiser Wilhelm II no less than the Third Reich of Adolf Hitler. And in fact the two are more closely related than is frequently comprehended. The latter was in many respects a throwback to the former, and both were emanations of the world created as well as represented by the immense labour and lifework of Richard Wagner. The emanations are direct and fatal; but each was a result of basic misinterpretations and wilful distortions of the movement in the German mind and psyche, accurately adumbrated by Wagner. Yet he did not always fully understand it himself, at least until after the event. He made a mighty effort to see it plain. But it was probably beyond the capability of any one man to encompass the totality of the forces to which he gave conscious articulation. They were the immediate expression of unconscious forces so deep seated that only with the passage of at least a century and in the light of a sequence of disasters can the full implications be grasped.

What, it may be asked, has the superabundant passion, the searing erotic intensity of *Tristan und Isolde* to do with the political and social systems of the Second and Third Reich? Upon the surface, very little. But at the deeper levels of the European consciousness and its evolution it was perhaps the key work. It was through the experience of *Tristan* that Wagner came to terms with the true meaning of renunciation. He saw now that the way ahead lay not in any kind of bland heroic variant of 'optimism', not even, as Nietzsche asserted, in the will to live through the will to power, but through a more profound and penetrating insight which abjured the 'heroic' stand, since that in its material form could not be dissociated from merely crude domination in one form or another. If the heroic ideal could be related back to the Beethoven of the *Eroica* symphony, to the pure objective non-self-seeking ideal, it might have been different. But Napoleon had already betrayed that ideal, exposed the hollowness of the 'heroic' in material terms. Now Europe lay in ruins because of it. Arthur Schopenhauer had placed his finger on the European pulse and blown away the earlier euphoria. The other side of the coin lay in renunciation of the will to live, at least in its more blatant form, as Schopenhauer had preached. Wagner was forced into that position, whether he liked it or not. And in all probability the younger Wagner did not like it and would not have countenanced it. The Young Siegfried of his first association with the sagas of the Nibelung no doubt answered to that description. But it would not do in the Europe of the mid-nineteenth century. If Napoleon had been and remained true, had honoured instead of traduced the spirit of the *Eroica* symphony (which was probably an impossible requirement anyway, since the world of the spirit and the world of political and military domination are so far apart), the subsequent history of European civilization might have taken another course. But it was not, and it could not be. All dawns are false, all hopes are dashed, all desires remain ungratified. Schopenhauer knocked the bottom out of that kind of 'optimism'. It was necessary to begin again, to take fresh stock. That, in the post-Napoleonic context, was the singular contribution of Schopenhauer's philosophy.

In the same way, if Germany rising from the ashes of defeat in 1918 had learnt the primary lesson, had seen the inner cause of the disaster, with its roots in a kind of aggressive Romantic nationalism, and so renounced the will to power and the will to revenge, it might again have been different. But it not only could not have been different, in the emotional and intellectual aftermath of defeat with the twisted legacy of the 'stab in the back' the victors virtually ensured that it could not be. In any case, renunciation was simply not within the scope of the national consciousness. It had to take another and greater disaster and the threat of a more far-reaching genocide, in short the total annihilation of the human race itself, before even the idea of any kind of national renunciation could be contemplated. In the inter-war period of the twentieth century a kind of naïve and crudely aggressive 'optimism' took the place of any possibility of a true following through of the innermost potency of German history. In that context, Romanticism had to be corrupted: it could not be redeemed. And above all it could not be redeemed by that crude form of the 'heroic' which had died but not been interred when, between the breaking off of the third act of *Siegfried* and its resumption a dozen or so years later, Richard Wagner was forced to see the deepest truths.

As it was, every form of perversion and corruption of what Wagner and the Romantics really stood for was possible. The way was open, and it was carried out with a determination awesome to look back on and unnervingly predictable in its consequences. That is why the ultimate Romantic disaster can and must be laid at Richard Wagner's door, though he neither intended nor could have foreseen it in its particular and most gruesome form and would certainly have been horrified had he done so. Yet it was always inherent. It was perhaps even inevitable, if only because men will invariably opt for the easy solution, for the mailed fist rather than the cudgelled brain and the steadfast vision, for the surface emotional reaction rather than the profound spiritual insight; for the 'hollow image'. In the Middle Ages it might have been called submission to the will of God. But these were not the Middle Ages. Yet the Crucifixion is a perpetual fact in the continuing life of the world; betrayal remains the human common denominator, the universal permanent. Richard Wagner was man enough to resist the temptation to take the easy way out, the way he had originally foreseen. He too, in his way, chose the ass in place of the warhorse, the fool rather than the rampant 'hero'. It was not enough, and it was always liable, precisely because it was only partial and therefore not enough in human terms, to be distorted and misapplied. But at least it contained an element of true creative honesty.

And it all began with *Tristan*, with that subjective sense of the necessity for renunciation that was by force of genius raised to the level of universal passionate experience. But if it ended in a kind of transfiguration, it could not end in triumph. Never again. With *Tristan und Isolde* the nineteenth century and its high Romanticism turned finally towards pessimism and night.

CHAPTER SEVEN

LIGHT AND LIFE
IN C MAJOR

If *Tristan* is the music of dusk, *Meistersinger* is the music of dawn. Sunset and sunrise; yet it is not a straightforward juxtaposition of the 'pessimistic' and the 'optimistic'. It goes farther, strikes deeper. The one is the complement or counterpart of the other: without *Tristan*, *Meistersinger* would not have been possible, and vice versa. The one shows the dark side, the other the light side of Wagner's genius. The relationship is close, and more indivisible than is frequently supposed.

Meistersinger is 'dawn music' in more senses than one. It refers back not only to the dawn of Romanticism, which first burgeoned in the latter years of the eighteenth century; it also refers much farther back to the Middle Ages and the fundamental idea of the German nation, both historically and emotionally considered. The German nation as it emerged in the nineteenth century was the product of two basic ideas, both of which appealed strongly to Richard Wagner: a romanticization of the Middle Ages and the drive towards unification out of the squabbling factions of minor princelings and larger kingdoms. Wagner's fascination with the Middle Ages was lifelong. German poetry and literature of the Middle Ages provided the inspiration for nearly all his work apart from *The Ring*. And German unification became one of the foremost of his extra-musical preoccupations. He lived to see and welcome it, though he was soon to be disillusioned by the direction it took. Yet all his life, especially in the earlier part, he tended to delve back into history when things went badly for him and the contemporary world seemed even more shallow and unsatisfactory than usual. Indeed, historicism was one of his foibles: he had a particular tendency to call upon the past to justify his own idea of the present and what he proposed for the future. In this he was again characteristically German, though not only German. It is the habit of all national leaders to indulge in historicism and an appeal to the national past, for it is an essential part of the appeal of the myth-maker and the rabble-rouser (even though the two are not necessarily synonymous). It was true of Adolf Hitler and was a central part of his emotional and psychological power.

Meistersinger is thus no more a subject 'sport' than it is an artistic or ethical one. The commonplace idea that *Meistersinger* lies outside the main current of the Wagnerian ethos as expressed in and through his dramas is, as I say, untenable. The spirit of *Meistersinger* permeates much of Wagner's work, just as its musical evolution is as necessary and as characteristic as that of *Tristan*. The 'optimistic' tone of *Meistersinger* appears in several sections of *The Ring*. It lies behind the first act of *Die Walküre*, comes into the open for at least the first two-thirds of *Siegfried*, and even works its way into *Götterdämmerung*, where the panegyric to Holy German Art which concludes *Meistersinger*, and which Wagner wished to delete but Cosima insisted should be retained, bears a strong resemblance to Gunther's eulogy of Brünnhilde in Act II. But it goes deeper even than that, that specifiable coincidence: the 'pessimism' of *Tristan* and ultimately *The Ring*, even that at the far extremes of *The Flying Dutchman* at one end and *Parsifal* at the other, is only existentially valid bacause of the contrary 'pull' of the 'optimism' of *Meistersinger* and its concomitants in the other works, its essential and necessary corollary. However, it is most directly and meaningfully exposed in the close juxtaposition of *Tristan* and *Meistersinger* as they revolve around the centrepoint of Wagner's genius in a single orbit.

Tristan and *Meistersinger* are in many ways both opposites and complementary. *Tristan* is essentially monolithic, as all true and profound tragedy must be, for it is the innermost ethic of tragedy that it is centrally concentrated; but *Meistersinger* is no less essentially quite different, a vast, sprawling anthill profligate with life and energy. There are no asides in *Tristan*, apart from the touching devotion of Kurwenal and to a lesser extent Brangäne, no small human touches sketched in with sympathetic skill and warmth. But *Meistersinger* is full of them. Wagner's sure dramatic genius grasped the essential distinctions between (to simplify and perhaps over-simplify) tragedy and comedy. Yet both came at the same time in Wagner's life; it is as though his genius elected to express itself in two separate halves of itself which must forever remain in creative coexistence.[1]

In *Tristan* everything is limited, restricted, concentrated, its scope narrowed to the tragedy of the two central figures with only as much additional material as is necessary to *i*motive the drama. But in *Meistersinger* Wagner tells, so to say, the whole truth about the city of Nuremberg and its inhabitants on that summer night and the following day in the sixteenth century. It is the most richly populated, the most superabundant in its human life and vitality, not only among Wagner's own works but among all but a small handful of major operas. Without *Meistersinger* Wagner's *oeuvre* would not have been distorted; his humanity would still have been there, but it would have needed to be inferred rather than been overtly seen and directly stated. *Meistersinger* fills in the total truth about Richard Wagner. Even those passages which have been criticized as pedantic or mere space-filling, like the calling of the roll of the Masters, are essential ingredients in that whole, necessary elements without which the overall picture would be incomplete and greatly impoverished.

The historical bias is important. Not the simple act of reference back to the Middle Ages, but the meaning of it in the context of the emergence of the German nation in the 1860s and 1870s. In its own way and at its own level, *Meistersinger* is a paean not only to Holy German Art but to the innermost spirit, newly found and made politically and socially manifest, of united Germany standing upon the threshold of a new historical epoch.

Bismarck was the prime mover in the recreation of the German nation two hundred years after the Treaty of Westphalia had determined its fragmentation. There followed at least a hundred years of national chaos and isolated provincialism as local princelings attempted to re-establish some kind of order and economy. For Richard Wagner, with his strong historical sense, this was the 'awful century' during which Johann Sebastian Bach represented 'the history of the inner life of the German mind . . . when the German people was utterly extinguished'. It is in this light that the resurgence of German nationalism in the nineteenth century and early twentieth century has to be understood. During the eighteenth century, German soil was ravaged by wars that had virtually nothing to do with the German people. Most of the warring was concerned with the Spanish succession and the quarrel between France and England over possession of territory in India and the New World. William Pitt went so far as to state that the British conquest of Canada would be decided on the plains of Germany. And so indeed it was. Only on one question was the future of Germany involved: in the struggle between the Prussia of Frederick the Great and the Austria of the Empress Maria Theresa, the two most powerful factions and the only ones strong enough eventually to advance the cause of German unification, or to prevent it. In the end, it was Prussia that took the lead and over a hundred years later enabled Bismarck to confirm Kaiser Wilhelm I as Emperor of a united Germany at a grand gathering in the Palais de Versailles at the conclusion of the Franco-Prussian War, in 1871. In the meantime, however, had come the Napoleonic adventure, with further foreign (i.e. French) occupation of German territory and German cities. And largely because of that, the move towards a unified Germany had become an emotional as well as a political and economic necessity well in advance of the first steps taken at the conference of German leaders at Frankfurt-am-Main in 1848. But then, as is usual in such circumstances, there was no agreement; a unified Germany seemed for the time being as far off as a unified Europe. The leaders could not agree.[2]

Yet German unity had to come – and it did come. Wagner saw it, recognized it, welcomed it, strove for it, promulgated it in his works, by inference if not directly.

All this placed Germany beside Italy in the nineteenth century, and also alongside those countries of central and eastern Europe which still had to make that transition. It stood apart from France, England and all other countries that had achieved unity and national identity, whether as major powers or as small ones. It does not quite place Wagner beside Verdi, whose name was made into an acrostic in the service of the Risorgimento, as the hero of national aspiration and unification. All the same, Wagner had the pulse and the deep-seated current of the parallel German spirit of national revival in his blood and at his nerve ends. He served no party, led no faction, either deliberately or by common acclamation. There was no patriotic outburst at the end of any work by Wagner, and his only overtly patriotic pieces were occasional and minor in every respect, in no way an integral part of the true Wagneriana.

Yet at that deeper level *Meistersinger* is a true celebration of German nationhood. By going back to the Middle Ages Wagner was following not only his own natural bent but that of the German nation itself; and in celebrating German art he was both serving his own interests, making a fierce declaration on the side of artistic freedom and independence as he understood it, and in a very real sense promoting the entire ethic and aesthetic of Germanism. And whether he so intended or not, what he promulgated was in profound opposition to that pan-Germanism of Bismarck, emanating from Prussia and militarily based, which was to lead to and become the leitmotif of the European and the Romantic disaster. Yet Bismarck too was traduced and misrepresented. The sacking of Bismarck in 1888 by the reckless, newly ascended Kaiser Wilhelm II was the signal for Germany to take the lead in forwarding that disaster. Indeed, it may be argued that the combination of misrepresentation of Wagner and a turning of the back on Bismarck's political realism were the twin poles of distortion that brought about the European nemesis.

But it does not end there and it cannot be left there. French animosity towards Germany, deeply entrenched after 1870 and virtually incurable, less also to be taken into account. The rift was politically healed in the 1960s; but there is no reason to suppose that it has ever been more than pasted over in emotional terms. There is ample evidence that the French still see the Germans as '*les Bosches*', i.e. as brutish and basically uncivilized, while the Germans still tend to regard the French, while continuing to envy aspects of French culture and refinement, as fundamentally trivial and degenerate. And this comes out even in *Meistersinger* where the dismissal, or 'defence', in the final panegyric is specifically anti-French.

Part of this goes back to Wagner's own love–hate relationship with Paris and the French, and to his well-remembered humiliations of 1839–41 and the *Tannhäuser* fiasco of 1861. But it was also an accurate reflection of the indigenous anti-French feelings in Germany, feelings which the French themselves cordially reciprocated. As late as the Second World War the

German attitude to France, and to Paris in particular, was ambivalent, in part that of conqueror, in part acolyte. Even so, for Wagner it was still not perfectly straightforward. He tended to find the Germans, particularly those of his native Saxony, gross and largely uncultivated. He was drawn towards Paris because of that as much as in the simple hope of profit to his purse and reputation. He thus reveals himself in this respect, as in most others, as a complex and often contradictory character. There is little doubt that if Paris had embraced him as he wished and hoped, had responded to his passionate advances, his Francophobia would have been considerably mollified, if it did not disappear altogether, even against the run of feeling in his nation and its people, to whom he demonstrated his true allegiance.

To call *Meistersinger* 'clean' and 'healthy' and 'optimistic' is true but superficial. It is true as far as it goes; but it does not go anywhere worthwhile. And it goes nowhere at all if it is placed in opposition to Wagner's other dramas. The note and tone of *Meistersinger* is as endemic in the totality of Wagner as that of *Tristan und Isolde*. Although Wagner, especially the central Wagner/Schopenhauer figure, was driven to apparent pessimism, and although the entire Romantic movement slid into pessimism under the impulse of its own conceptual errors and its failure to face up to its own existential problems, the optimistic counterpart was never entirely absent, and could not be if the whole fabric was not to collapse from the centre and disintegrate into chaos. In fact it did virtually that in the twentieth century; but not quite in the way that might have happened in the nineteenth if the optimistic postulates had not held as well. When it did collapse it did so not because it turned from optimism to pessimism but because it lacked a firm centre. It asked questions it could not answer and so opened the way for falsification and corruption.

Beethoven has been called a pessimist trying to convince himself that he was an optimist. But that is a comparatively shallow view. Nearer the truth is that Beethoven was a natural optimist trying to maintain the validity of optimism in the face of every temptation to pessimism, both personal and universal and without shirking any of the issues. To turn back to the *Eroica* symphony after immersion in *Tristan und Isolde* or *Parsifal* is to emerge into a fresh and bracing coolness after oppressive heat, much as to turn to Beethoven's *Pastoral* symphony after, say, the Mahler Sixth is to take plain pleasure in nature after the terrors of a soundscape of formidable discomfort and full of the dinosaurs and pterodactyls and mammoths of the subconscious. A similar process takes place at a different level in Sibelius, where Romantic pessimism confronts hostile nature with the indestructible force of the human will. It is not simply a matter of value judgement. The true ontological meaning of optimism and pessimism goes far beyond and far deeper than a simple matter of looking for, expecting, even consciously willing a hopeful or a hopeless outcome, an encouraging or a distressing future. It depends to a large extent upon 'willing what is necessary', which is not the same as willing what one wants or what one fears. Wagner was right there. It is legitimate to will what one desires, as Shelley put it, to 'hope till hope creates the thing it contemplates'. Yet the central question remains: What is necessary?

The puzzle is not susceptible to any single answer or solution. Since it is primarily a metaphysical proposition, it requires not a quick (or quack) response but a genuinely metaphysical one to match.

Thus *Meistersinger* did not come into being as Wagner's overtly 'optimistic' masterpiece simply because an emissary from King Ludwig had brought him fresh hope in which he could see the resolution of the worst of his material problems and a chance to make the world, or at least some significant part of it, accede to his wishes and grant him its bounty. It had in any case begun while he was still struggling with encircling despair. However, it might still be possible to argue that the completed work reflected his improved fortunes and his personal hopes for the future; but it would not be entirely convincing. *Meistersinger* would have emerged as it did whatever the state of his personal affairs, would always have been a warm-hearted generous human comedy with strong (and intentional) nationalistic sentiments – because that was its innermost nature. It could not have come out otherwise.

All the same, on the purely human and personal plane, the emissary certainly did bring good news. The King, though still only nineteen, was already a confirmed and devout Wagnerian, a worshipper at the shrine, especially of *Lohengrin*. (*Tristan* had still not been produced, nor had *The Ring*, although it was the poem of the latter, with its Preface asking when some enlightened prince would appear to inaugurate the great Festival for its presentation, that had determined Ludwig that he would be that leader of enlightenment.) It was without question an intervention of providence. Wagner was on the point of total ruin; without Ludwig he might have perished, either by his own hand, however unlikely that might appear in retrospect, or under general strain and frustration of a kind to undermine any man's strength and stamina. Or was it – and would he? The question persists: was it perhaps brought about by his own 'willing of what is necessary'? We shall never know for sure. All we do know is that the extraordinary power of Richard Wagner's mind and will could bring most things about that were necessary, even despite Arthur Schopenhauer. The idea that it was nothing but chance and coincidence is too mundane and unimaginative to accord with the life and destiny of a man like Wagner. It simply does not fit.

Even for Wagner his reversal of fortune seems at first to have appeared like something in a dream. But it was not. The secretary–emissary Pfistermeister meant exactly what he said: he came not from the gods of Olympus but from the King of Bavaria, and with an offer no man could refuse – indeed, it seemed like benediction from the gods.

Once he had met Ludwig, in Munich immediately after Pfistermeister's visit, everything changed for him. Back in Vienna he could discharge his debts; ensconced in the villa provided for him by Ludwig he could settle once more to his proper work. All the same, he still felt lonely and isolated. He had no companion of his own mind and temperament. Separated from Minna, he had no woman to love, or to love him. He accordingly begged Hans and Cosima von Bülow to join him with their family. They were not slow to respond and settled in Munich in November 1864. He had previously requested his old flame, Mathilde Maier, to join him; but then changed his mind in terms that looked like another act of deliberate renunciation but was in fact dictated by his growing awareness of his true feelings for Cosima.

It had already begun, back in the 'Asyl' days when he was in the throes of renouncing his love for Mathilde Wesendonk and pouring the emotional turmoil of it into *Tristan und Isolde*. Now he came to recognize that for him Cosima was the only possible companion. It was yet another *Tristan*-like imbroglio: he desired the wife of his friend; but this time nothing would be allowed to stand in his way.

Yet it was not quite a similar situation. Unlike the Wesendonks, Hans and Cosima von Bülow were not happily married. Cosima, the illegitimate daughter of Franz Liszt, forcibly kept apart from her mother, the Countess Marie d'Agoult, resented by Liszt's current mistress, the Princess von Sayn-Wittgenstein, and so estranged from the father she adored, had never found life easy. She did not find it any easier by marriage to von Bülow, a gifted but irascible and neurotic musician with a marked inferiority complex. Cosima, who had grown into an aristocratic figure of considerable intellectual attainment, needed something and someone more substantial to lavish her qualities and her affections on. She found both in Richard Wagner and his genius.

At first Cosima took over the management of Wagner's domestic affairs and professional arrangements. He ensured her continuing presence by having von Bülow appointed pianist and later conductor to the Bavarian Court. In the event, Cosima virtually appointed herself chief champion and second in the Wagnerian cause, the high priestess of the temple. It was exactly what was required: she could not have done better. Wagner always required and needed around him those who would be prepared to devote themselves exclusively and wholeheartedly to his interests; and this Cosima did for the rest of his life and for the rest of her own life afterwards.

And inevitably it blossomed into something else, something that was always inherent and now rapidly established its determining force. Von Bülow was in a difficult position: he worshipped Wagner as an artist, was devoted to his music and his cause; but at the same time he was obliged to watch his idol take his wife, almost literally from under his nose. Wagner himself may have had a qualm or two; but he no doubt assuaged his conscience, if indeed it needed assuaging, by reminding himself that the marriage was a dead one anyway.

His domestic affairs may now have been encouraging and his material prospects more or less assured; but as usual with Wagner there were other factors involved, other knots in the wood. Although he had the support and the absolute loyalty of the king, his presence was resented in many quarters. It was accordingly not long before moves were set afoot to have him removed, to blame him for numerous shortcomings in the public business of the Bavarian state and its officers of government, and in particular for wilful extravagance at the public expense. And being the man he was, outspoken, often domineering, full of a sense of his own mission and his consequent right of patronage from the entire world, he did not always advance or defend his cause to its best advantage. He was disliked and distrusted as a nominal Protestant in a Catholic society; as a former revolutionary; as an obstinate fellow who was interested in nothing but his own art and its promotion; and above all as a bad influence on the young king.

Most of this was unscrupulous political gerrymandering. Attempts to involve him in the machinations of Bavarian state politics and economic affairs proved abortive. He declined the gambit. So, thwarted in their desire to involve him directly, the various factions did their best to unseat him. His art was, and remained, his exclusive interest, its advancement his perpetual concern. Both the clerics and the Jesuits tried to seduce him to their side. He remained adamant. Art or nothing; all or nothing: the Romantic principle held. So the charge of extravagance was stirred against him once more; that he was a voider and waster of the public purse; that taxpayers were being obliged to support his personal indulgences and his grandiose schemes. And of course there was substance in most of it, though not of the kind brought against him by his detractors and denigrators, who resorted to all manner of ploys and strategems to discredit him, ostensibly in the public interest but in reality to advance their own interests and causes. It was the usual and all too familiar sorry tale of political corruption and personal vendettas. The Bavarian state officials ran true to form: corrupt, self-seeking, affecting to serve the public welfare while in fact securing only their own positions and advantages.

Wagner, with Cosima's help, probably made a serious error in attempting to defend himself in public. He thus exacerbated a situation that would have been better served by restraint and a tactful passing over. Yet one can hardly blame him. He was under considerable pressure, and patience and forbearance outside his art were not in his nature. All the same, his action placed the young king in an even more difficult position, in conflict with his ministers, entangled in webs of intrigue and corruption he did not have the experience to understand, let alone deal with. Ludwig was young and still had much to learn. Yet he was by no means the ineffectual weakling some historians have tried to make out. As a ruler, he had the respect of a number of prominent European statesmen of experience and expertise, including Bismarck. In the political interests of Bavaria at a time of considerable confusion and many cross-currents of national and international interest, notably the contention betweeen Prussia and Austria in which Bavaria, partly because of its geographical situation, partly because it represented the Catholic interest against Prussian Protestantism, was in danger of being squeezed like a nut in a nutcracker, Ludwig as he matured proved himself to be both shrewd and tough-minded. He had a penchant for absolute monarchy which, after the French Revolution, had become progressively *démodé*; but he was no mere puppet, nor had he any intention of allowing himself to be manoeuvred into that unenviable position. If he was not expert in kingcraft, and as time went by became more and more erratic as a ruler, he was by no means the milksop of popular legend and interested propaganda.

Nor is the matter of Ludwig's alleged insanity to be accepted at its face value. Ernest Newman once said that Ludwig II was declared insane on evidence so slender that in England it would not have sufficed to have one's neighbour's dog put away. There is no possible doubt that Ludwig was declared insane and driven to an early death from motives of political intrigue and malicious manipulation. There is no evidence, nor ever has been, that he was mad in any meaningful or medically viable sense. Maybe Ludwig could be so declared 'if to be unlike the world be mad'; but on that system of accountancy so was Wagner himself: indeed, so were (and are) most of the world's creative artists, certainly nearly all the Romantics, and most who challenge and question the dead and barren conventions of a dead and barren social order. So certainly was Beethoven – and many have made precisely that charge.

But all this lay in the future, in fact beyond Wagner's own death. For the time being, Wagner found himself at the mercy of the intriguers who managed to persuade the king, against his better judgement and his true will, that Wagner must go and the royal patronage be withdrawn from him. For the common weal, of course. Wagner was a bad influence on Ludwig: therefore Wagner must be removed. Royal favourites are seldom popular favourites, still less political favourites.

So Wagner departed for Geneva and continued to work on *Die Meistersinger*. And soon Cosima joined him. His enemies thought they had won the day and had seen the last of him. He insisted that he would not return to Munich until the offending politicians had been dismissed. And Ludwig appeared to be at their perpetual mercy. They were mistaken: there was never much doubt that they would be disappointed in their hopes. All the same, this temporary banishment acted as a severe setback to Wagner's and Ludwig's plans to realize the great ideal of a permanent Festival Theatre for the sole production of Wagner's works, *The Ring* first and foremost. He had not yet resumed the composition of *Siegfried*, though he worked a little at scoring the second act as hopes had been running high before the blow of banishment fell.

Those hopes had been strongly reinforced by splendid productions of *The Flying Dutchman* and *Tannhäuser* in Munich, and even more by, at last, that of his beloved *Tristan*. Even then things had not gone smoothly. Owing to the illness of the famous tenor, Ludwig Schnorr, who was to sing Tristan, the opening had to be postponed until June, by which time many who had taken time off especially to attend the performance had been obliged to return home. For years *Tristan und Isolde* seemed jinxed. However, when the production eventually took place, it went off well and Wagner was delighted, vindicated in his faith in his masterpiece. The king demanded more performances. Euphoria reigned. Then disaster struck: Schnorr took a chill and died of rheumatic fever less than a month later. The *Tristan* jinx still would not go.

Yet *Tristan und Isolde* had been produced. It lifted a heavy weight from Wagner's spirits. There had been times when he despaired of ever seeing that work, which meant so much to him and was so close to his heart, effectively staged. And in its wake plans were advanced for the building of the Festival Theatre – in a spectacular setting, as Ludwig was of the Wittelsbach line and lineage and had inherited, even expanded, their taste for architectural extravaganzas. There were also to be schools of music and singing, plus a newspaper devoted to Wagneriana; in short, a total Wagner establishment.

But it was not to be; not yet, at any rate. Disfavour won the day and the plans and projects collapsed behind the retreating figure of the discredited master. As it turned out, it was to be only a temporary collapse. But at the time none could know that for certain.

There was also the alliance with Cosima, a situation sure to excite suspicion, calumny and opposition even at the best of times and in the most propitious circumstances, which these were not. The true nature of the tangle has never been entirely clear. For many years it was assumed that von Bülow knew little or nothing about the relationship between Wagner and Cosima, that he was the unsuspecting cuckold denied access to the truth and therefore made to look even more ridiculous. But later research and analysis, led by Newman, established that von Bülow knew very well what was going on, at least for most of the time, and that he in fact acquiesced, partly because he had to, partly because he recognized that his own marriage was a failure, partly because he was so passionately devoted to the Wagner cause that he was willing to sacrifice even his own domestic life to it. If the latter sounds altogether too altruistic to be credible, that is perhaps another facet of the extraordinary spell Wagner tended to cast upon all those who became intimately associated with him.

The Wagner–Cosima affair also angered King Ludwig, who saw in it the spectre of public scandal threatening his already precarious position.

143

Wagner promised to conduct himself correctly, with at least an outward show of propriety. But Wagner's idea of propriety and other people's were not and never would be the same. His entire life and work were dedicated to creating a new moral and aesthetic climate in which art (his art) would lie at the heart of a rejuvenated social order. It was one of the leitmotifs of his career.

It was already clear that Wagner and Cosima were destined for a permanent liaison. It was inbuilt from the beginning. Whoever it displeased – and at one time or another it displeased many people, including Franz Liszt, King Ludwig, and most of the Bavarian Court and society – it meant very little to Wagner. If it upset people, if it required sacrifice and rununciation on the part of those closely involved, *tant pis*. He was not cynical and heartless: he was simply convinced he was right.

All the same, there was some attempt at concealment. Although the pair settled in the house known as Triebschen on the shores of Lake Lucerne, Cosima made duty visits of some length to von Bülow in Munich. That unfortunate man was now in a more than miserable situation. As Hofkapellmeister he had to direct performances of Wagner's music; his devotion to it was not hidden, nor did he seek to hide it. But von Bülow had his pride, and that pride was further wounded by undisguised rumours that he owed his position to his acquiescence in his wife's relationship with his idol. In order to dull these rumours, Cosima for a while kept away from Triebschen. But Wagner was a frequent visitor to the Bülows' house in Munich. The situation was explosive; it could not continue. Minna Wagner had died in 1866, but the unsatisfactory triangle continued for something over a year. Then, towards the end of 1868, Cosima left von Bülow for good and became Wagner's inseparable companion for the rest of his days.

In the meantime *Die Meistersinger* had been finished. It was given, under von Bülow's direction and with Hans Richter as chorusmaster, on 21 June 1868, with great acclaim and resounding success. Wagner received extraordinary and public royal favour. None the less, sections of the press were decidedly hostile. Wagner had offended many influential factions, musical as well as social; and they were unforgiving. It soured the success, and Wagner left for Triebschen swearing that never again would he set foot in Munich.

It was a turning point. The king was furious because Cosima had sworn to him the 'innocence' of her relationship with Wagner. He, Ludwig, blamed her but not his beloved Wagner. Von Bülow was torn again between loyalty to Wagner the artist and enmity towards Wagner the man, who had betrayed him in the world's eyes. In the end, von Bülow filed for divorce, sent the children to Cosima at Triebschen, left Munich for Italy, and had no further personal association with Wagner, ever.

There had been anomalies and curiosities in the situation all along. To begin with, only Cosima's first two daughters, Daniela and Blandine, were von Bülow's; the second two, though christened von Bülow for the sake of appearances and social convenience, were Wagner's. It was no great cause for astonishment: Cosima herself was one of three illegitimate children born to Franz Liszt. So in one sense Wagner may simply be said to have been continuing a family tradition. And in any case, the marriage of Cosima and von Bülow had irreconcilably broken down long before the severance became official.

Then there is the complex question of the real relationship between Wagner and Ludwig II. That Ludwig was homosexual seems beyond doubt or contradiction; but that there was a homosexual relationship between him and Wagner is not only unproven but can hardly be launched as a serious argument, not because Wagner was obviously heterosexual (he might also have been bisexual) but because nothing in the record or the evidence suggests it, despite every effort, both contemporary and historical, at one time or another to discredit both. The flowery language of their correspondence means nothing: it was simply the idiom of the place and time, of the Romantic era plus the nature of the German language as then deployed and which when translated into English (or French) tends to have very different overtones from the original. On the other hand, Ludwig's anger and resentment at Wagner's 'betrayal' in the liaison with Cosima, though it was principally directed against Cosima, may well have been at least in part due to his homosexual feelings and nature. Indeed, the fulmination against Cosima rather than Wagner confirms rather than contradicts that view. Probably Ludwig did not consciously recognize it himself; but that too is tangential evidence. It is recorded fact that Ludwig's disenchantment with Wagner as an 'honourable man' came about not because of financial misdealings or shiftiness over the assignment and completion of works but because of the Cosima affair. And that may further indicate that the disillusionment had a homosexual origin; but it still does not signify a direct homosexual tie between Wagner and his royal patron.

None the less, at this time, when he was enjoying royal support, and afterwards, some of the less attractive aspects of Wagner's character were definitely to the fore. Always extravagant and self-indulgent, he now carried luxurious living and a haughty attitude to new excesses. As Alexander the Great after the defeat of Darius, King of Persia, in his middle or Oriental period set himself up as a potentate, surrounded himself with sycophants and toadies, turned his back on old friends and became generally aloof and unapproachable in direct contrast to his earlier self, so Wagner now became so centred in his own egotism and extravagances that he too became remote and the cause of distress to his old friends and colleagues. During this, his Alexandrine period, success and good fortune appeared to go to his head. Like Alexander, he had conquered large parts of the world, and more than ever he demanded not only its allegiance, but virtually that it fawn upon him. And in this he was certainly encouraged by Cosima. Alexander grew out of that period of self-indulgent vanity, and before the end of his short life resumed his former honourable and direct ways as a more or less straightforward warrior king who could trust and be trusted. Richard Wagner, an altogether more complex modern man, never had quite that estate to return to. The indulgence and extravagance were inbuilt from the beginning. But the better things went for him the worse he tended to behave, for a time. Then, as he grew older and entered the last years of his life, he seemed to recover his equanimity in the face of a world that still appeared hostile but which from now on had to pay him homage, whether it wanted to or not.

For the time being, life at Triebschen maintained something of the character of an idyll. He and Cosima led their lives, entertained their friends, just like a pair of newly weds, which after Cosima's and von Bülow's divorce had come through and been made absolute in the summer of 1870, they were. But that was only a nominalization, the setting of a seal of custom. The actual situation was not changed. Wagner's and Cosima's son Siegfried had been born in June 1869. Visitors to Triebschen described the life there in various terms, but all remark and agree upon Wagner's comparatively relaxed state of mind, on his obvious love for Cosima, and on the way she shielded him from the still rampaging hositility of a number of musical and social circles. And it all gave him freedom to work. With *Meistersinger* behind him, he had returned to the abandoned third act of *Siegfried*, and when he had completed that went on to the composition of *Götterdämmerung*, which he finished in February 1872. He thus rang the curtain down on the great tetralogy of *The Ring* more than twenty years after he had raised it in his imagination. And what twenty years they had been. It was a stupendous achievement: hardly another man could have accomplished it.

During these years at Triebschen and alongside work of the final sections of *The Ring*, Wagner was also recharging his batteries for a fresh advance into the field that lay always close to his heart – the creation of the Festival Theatre that would accommodate his art in the only way he believed possible if it was to justify his lifelong ideal and establish his creative stature for all time. Now that *The Ring* was finished at last, the undertaking became more than ever necessary. Of all his works so far *The Ring* most imperatively required the resources and conditions only possible in such a specialized theatre and with its attendant organization. At the same time, and in pursuance of this objective, he continued to write papers and pamphlets on art, opera, national politics, as usual anything that came into his head and struggled to get out again. Among these, from the years between 1864, when King Ludwig rescued him, and 1871, when he set forth to create Bayreuth, were *State and Religion* (1864), *What Is German?* (1865), *German Art and German Policy* (1867), *The Destiny of Opera* (1871), as well as the somewhat fanciful study of *Beethoven* (1870) and *On Conducting* (1869), which along with *Actors and Singers* (1872) might well be taken to heart today by all who practise these professions but pay scant attention to their true meaning or to that of the works to which they address themselves.

It is sometimes argued that on the evidence of these further writings Wagner went back on, or at least significantly modified, many of the ideas and ideals he had promulgated earlier, in *Opera and Drama* and the other prose works of the 1849–51 period. This is both true and untrue. Certainly Wagner did appear to modify both his theory and his practice in a number of important respects, in artistic as well as more general matters. He no longer saw himself as a political revolutionary, with his own art taking the lead in the formation of a New Order. But there is nothing special in that. Youth always tends to expect that its ideals, however starry, will be translated into reality with the next morning's post; but as one grows older such expectations become recognized as destructive illusions. The ideals themselves remain, though modified as they must be in the light of experience, but they necessarily become longer term objectives. Wagner had by this time outgrown his more naïve dreams of the immediate transformation and redemption of the world through art and revolution. But he still retained the essence of his ideals, saw his art as the expression of a reborn Germany and with it of a new political order. In much the same way, his art itself had been slowly and subtly modified by experience. It was no less necessary that it should do so. The man who wrote *Das Rheingold* and *Die Walküre* was the same man who wrote *Tristan* and *Meistersinger*, then *Götterdämmerung* and finally *Parsifal*. But the artist grows and matures as the man grows and matures; the two are indivisible, particularly with one like Richard Wagner. It is a matter of total evolution again.

In no sense was *Meistersinger* a reaction from *Tristan*, any more than night is a reaction from day. Indeed, this juxtaposition of night and day in the work of creative artists is by no means unusual. It might be an exaggeration to see the *Iliad* and the *Odyssey* in such terms; but in music Manuel de Falla's ballets *El amor burjo* and *The Three-Cornered Hat* can be seen as the Spanish equivalent of *Tristan* and *Meistersinger*, though on a smaller scale; and James Joyce's *Ulysses* and *Finnegan's Wake* are quite clearly, and deliberately, day music and night music, the latter in particular probably as far as language can go in making the unconscious, the world of night and dream anyway, articulate.

There are several aspects of *Meistersinger* to which attention needs to be drawn. Firstly, although it appears, on the surface at least, to be some kind of 'reversion' to opera and even to operatic convention with its set pieces, choruses and arias, it is in fact no such thing. *Meistersinger* demonstrates that Wagner, the totally honest and ruthlessly uncompromising artist, had learnt the primary lesson, that the artist subdues his hand to the immediate task before him and not to any theory or *a priori* rule of law, whether his own or someone else's. If *Meistersinger* does not obey the strict Wagnerian laws and

147

tablets of music drama, it is the 'laws' which must bend or, if necessary, bow out. The warm-hearted humanity and humour of *Meistersinger* could no more have been expressed in terms of the *Tristan* chromaticism or the *Götterdämmerung* synthesis than those two masterpieces and *Parsifal* to follow could have been deployed and carried through via *Meistersinger* ways and techniques. The form of a work of art, any work of substance and significance, is determined by its content: all else, all superimposed theory and preconception, is vanity and irrelevance. That does not invalidate the function, indeed, the necessity of theory; it simply establishes the priorities.

Secondly, though it is apparently a work of cheerful 'optimism', *Meistersinger* is still the creation of a dedicated Schopenhauerean. Hans Sachs is constantly aware of the Will at its unruly work. The great 'Wahn' monologue at the beginning of Act III is two-edged. It encompasses both renunciation and resignation. The two, though related, are not the same thing, in Wagnerian terms anyway. And their operation is on both the personal and the universal plane. It is not only, perhaps not principally, in the famous *Tristan* reference in Act II that Sachs' Schopenhauerism is revealed. It lies deeper and permeates the entire character. That is another reason why *Meistersinger* is in no sense a 'sport' among Wagner's works. The optimism of *Meistersinger* is tempered throughout by a counterbalancing pessimism[3] without which it would be no more than a healthy and hearty piece of time-passing entertainment. And it is in the figure of Hans Sachs that the 'pessimism' largely reposes, not because Sachs takes a particularly gloomy view of the general proceedings, but because he knows human folly and understands that even the natural exuberance of youth and young love have to be, not so much tempered, certainly not deflated, as set in a viable context if subsequent disaster is to be avoided.

Sachs, who loves Eva himself but knows that from every point of view, not only that of disparate ages, it is forlorn, resigns himself to the inevitable, and in encouraging the love of Walther and Eva serves the evolutionary process by 'willing what is necessary' in this specific context. He in his turn, like Wotan, like Siegfried, like Tristan and Isolde, knows the tragedy of consciousness and deliberately wills what has to come about. And in directing matters at least to a nominally satisfactory conclusion, he wills what is necessary on the public as well as the personal plane. In dealing with and finally disposing of Beckmesser, Sachs in fact prevents the destruction of what is necessary, prevents, that is, the conventional and the hidebound from aborting the new and creative and original. But the creative and original itself cannot be allowed to run amok, to take over with no thought for the consequences, to act only by instinct and uncontrolled intuition. That is why he prevents the elopement of Walther and Eva: Sachs knows, as they have not yet learnt, that problems and difficulties have to be confronted and surmounted; that they will not go away by themselves if merely avoided or evaded. Midsummer madness is not the answer.

Musically, *Die Meistersinger* has a number of salient features which are by no means unusual in Wagner but which take on a more or less specific importance here. One is the matter of orchestral and vocal polyphony, always latent in his dramas, sometimes explicit and sometimes not, but in *Meistersinger* turned into a leading principle. And in some ways it is odd: polyphony is usually indicative of a strong element of self-abnegation on the part of the composer; and self-abnegation is about the last characteristic one would associate with Richard Wagner. It is once again an example of his supreme honesty and integrity as an artist that he could, and should, so subdue the self in a work as near to his heart and as accurate a reflection of his innermost experience as this.

The musical structure offers further evidence of his courage as a composer, of his willingness to take enormous risks in order to achieve his aims. In *Meistersinger* he staked everything on his ability to write a great popular melody towards which the entire dramatic sequence moves. As in *Tannhäuser*, the central event of *Meistersinger* is a contrast of song. Originally, Wagner had intended it as a kind of satire on the Wartburg contest, much as Beckmesser was at first conceived as a direct attack on Eduard Hanslick. But that soon went, along with the assault on hostile critics when Wagner's true genius took over and expurgated the waste matter (in the same way that it directed his first intention in respect of *Tristan und Isolde* away from a Bellini-type Italianate opera to its proper course). Even so, the contest of song, though on a different level, remains the centrepiece of *Meistersinger*. And Wagner had to live up to his own challenge, or the entire fabric would collapse around his ears.

And he did rise to it. There are and always have been those who think the 'Prize Song' a commonplace melody, by no means sufficiently distinguished to carry the burden of a full three-act, five-hour opera. But that is not the point. Wagner might well have written a better tune, a more clearly recognizable aesthetic masterpiece of song, a more subtly structured and contoured melody, without achieving his end as cunningly as in fact he did. For the point about the 'Prize Song' is not that it is, incontestably, a great melody but that in its context it sounds as if it were. It is the kind of tune the people can take to, and have taken to. There is no doubt that both Sachs's monologues are in musical terms superior; but the 'Prize Song' is the one that has caught the popular ear, as it was intended to. And that is the real point, for to Wagner it is the people, the *Volk*, 'to whose judgement art in the end must bow'. If the melody had been too complex, too erudite, however pleasing to the pundits and the academics, too far that is from public appreciation, it would have failed. It might even have pleased Beckmesser. But Wagner knew better; he knew that truly great art, as opposed to merely learned art, will always reach its target, even if it takes time, but that a truly popular melody must strike home at once. Again, his instincts were surer than the homilies of his learned critics.

149

Thus *Meistersinger* is on virtually every plane nothing like a 'sport' among Wagner's compositions. The longer one looks into it the more naturally at home does it appear in the Wagner canon. There is hardly a point at which it does not coincide with some otherwise familiar aspect of his compositional practice. If the element of comedy seems outside his normal range it has to be remembered that most who knew him spoke of his great natural ebullience and sense of fun, and that in any case only one who is an overwhelming bore or a disastrous pedant is entirely without some gift of comedy; also, as a man grows older his comic faculty frequently comes closer to the surface, especially if most of his former work had been concerned with the other side of the existential coin. *Meistersinger* fills out the total picture, but it does not alter its essential nature and character.

In one respect *Meistersinger* opened a pit into which Wagner might easily have fallen. At the time of its composition, the matter of German unity was much in the air; and Wagner, as always, desired its fulfilment and willed its achievement. Under Bismarck, Prussia was rapidly assuming the lead; the influence of Austria was declining. Bavaria remained in danger of being caught between the two. Wagner was not particular how national unity came about, so long as it did. It was the innermost spirit of a reborn Germany that interested him, not the precise details of social and political arrangement. *Meistersinger* was, on one plane at least, dedicated to that inner spirit and a deliberate celebration of it. In *Art and Revolution* he had written, 'the Art-work of the Future must embrace the spirit of a free mankind, delivered from every shackle of hampering nationality; its racial imprint must be no more than an embellishment, the individual charm of manifold diversity, and not a hampering barrier.' That had been seen and written as early as 1849, all but twenty years before the completion of *Meistersinger* and when the idea of a rebirth for Germany through revolution into a rejuvenated New Order was still in the air as a practical possibility, even seemed likely. By 1868, when *Meistersinger* was first produced, the idea of revolution had subsided but the pressures towards German unification were gathering increased momentum. Wagner was deeply sensitive to them; and his own feelings went into *Meistersinger*.

Yet it remained necessary, in obedience to his belief and his artistic integrity, to keep them under firm control. They had to be implicit, rather than explicit; *Meistersinger* must not become a nationalistic tract, or he would be back in the days when it was little more than a sarcasm at the expense of Hanslick and the jealous critics. If that happened it would not escape the 'shackle of hampering nationality'. That no doubt is why he wanted to delete the final panegyric, for although this is offered in praise of German art, it amounts to the same thing in the end. It allowed *Meistersinger* to end on a false note. But Cosima ruled, and in this case overruled. And ironically, it was precisely that last hymn of nationalism that appealed most to successive political parties of the nationalistic description, the Nazis most of all. For the sake of a stentorian conclusion in praise of the spirit of national identity through its art, a whole nation could be corrupted from within. In an intelligent and perceptive world this originally proud but inoffensive conclusion to a masterpiece of warmth and generosity embracing 'the spirit of a free mankind' would have been taken for what it was. But it is not a perceptive, let alone an intelligent world, and instead of embracing a free mankind, even *Meistersinger* could be used to distort and destroy. The irony is savage.

Wagner sensed the danger. But Cosima, who was in so many ways his loyal supporter and comrade, had also a will of steel, and probably because Wagner at this time and in the particular social and political circumstances felt a strong desire to sing the praises of the emerging German nation and its art, he succumbed to her persuasions. And the even deeper irony is that Wagner would have been the most vigorous and embattled opponent of all that Nazi/Fascist totalitarianism which dishonourably drew upon his work for sustenance, of all the impertinent political interference with art and artists, that denial of the spirit of a free mankind he desired, of what he referred to as 'our modern State-and-Art barbarism'; and that goes equally for the Socialist/Communist variety. Though a firm believer in a kind of socialism, he would have bared his teeth and set his resolve against what passes for that belief today, no less than for the 'national' brand.

The danger is always inherent in nationalism. The nation-state, extolled and promoted for its own sake and in its own sovereign right, is in inevitable conflict with other nations, with other nationalisms. Hostility between sovereign states is inescapable; but it is only part of a more comprehensive process. It begins with the individual. The search for individual identity through Protestant individualism implies hostility to other individualistic identities;[4] and the process continues up to and beyond the sovereign nation-state, through the family, the tribe, the region, the nation and into, in science fiction terms, the warring galaxies.

It is the same with revolution. Edmund Burke was remarkably prophetic when he foresaw that the upshot of the French Revolution must be the rise of a great military figure, thus anticipating the career of Napoleon Bonaparte. Yet all revolutions either rely upon or lead to militarism and are therefore pessimistic and self-doomed: in other words, all revolutions are reactionary. Whether originally intended or not, militarism is the concomitant of revolution no less than of nationalism.[5]

Yet a vague, nebulous, rootless internationalism or cosmopolitanism is no better, for where a society or community feels, and transmits that feeling to its individual members, that it has no permanent establishment, no place or habitation 'beloved over all', a kind of restless disaffection takes over which may lead to other forms of disintegration and social devastation as destructive as that of war or revolution.

The problem therefore is to transfer valid national and communal feelings from the military and the rigidly institutional to the metaphysical and the ontological. Wagner sensed it even if, in his time and place, he was not able to comprehend it fully. Indeed, it was probably impossible to take the full measure of the problem until scientific development had produced nuclear fission and thus given the militarists weapons they could only use at the risk of self – as well as universal annihilation. It took a persuader of that import to define the fundamental issue with inescapable clarity. Clausewitz's definition of war as the continuation of policy by other means postulates the failure of policy, unless policy is consciously directed towards a military solution in the first place.

For the danger of the immolation of the human race itself to have passed, a transformation of consciousness will be required. And art is one of the means by which that may be promoted and, however slowly, perhaps brought about. Yet it cannot be promoted, let alone brought about, by vague and insubstantial utopianisms, by expectation of the verdant millennium to be inaugurated by the simple expedient of the forcible overthrow of things as they are. Least of all will it come about by ignorant evasion of the tragic implications in too great a renunciation of primitive, elemental passions and animosities inherited from the natural world and therefore innate in the animal side of man. That is another place where the Romantics went wrong; by the cry of 'back to nature' they sought to return man not, as they thought, to a lost paradise of innocence but to the Freudian jungle of violent instincts and hostilities repressed in the unconscious. They did not see or understand it that way; but the disaster which followed was in many respects a direct result of it.

Wagner was no iconoclast. He understood that a nation or a society without roots is without the possibility of true evolution. There was a strong conservative element in Wagner's thinking. He wrote of the Art of the Future: 'This art will be *conservative* afresh'. And it is laid out in *Meistersinger*. Hans Sachs, although an ardent supporter of the young idea as represented by Walther von Stolzing, insists that the rules of the Masters must be upheld and honoured before the new free style can be admitted and accepted. The 'new' is valid, is necessary and enshrines the vision by which alone Art can serve the *Volk* and regenerate society; but only by a form of reconciliation with the 'old'. The two are complementary, and both must be honoured.

And in this too Wagner stood near to Hitler and the Nazis, which again shows the two-sidedness of any moral, ethical or metaphysical hypothesis. To some extent it is always a case of thesis, antithesis, synthesis. When it goes wrong, as in Hitlerism, it is because the synthesis is displaced and wrongly deduced.

The Nazis appealed to the conservative elements in post-1918 German society, to those who saw, and feared, the encroachment of economic chaos and moral disintegration on the one hand, and the advance of rampant

Bolshevism on the other. Nazism was essentially a bourgeois phenomenon. When Goebbels said: 'We have laid the ghost of 1789' (the storming of the Bastille), he was appealing directly to that strong conservative core of the German bourgeoisie, especially the petit bourgeoisie who had suffered most from the economic collapse and hyperinflation of the late Weimar days. That was one side of the picture. But as Edmund Burke again insisted: 'A state without the means of some change is without the means of its conservation.'[6] In *Meistersinger* Wagner paid homage not only to German art but to German bourgeois life and stability, as well as to the free spirit in art reflected in society he saw for the future. He was preserver as well as prophet; so much so that Gustav Mahler was moved to remark: 'If the whole of German art were to disappear, it could be recognized and reconstructed from this one work.'[7]

In *Meistersinger*, as in each of Wagner's music dramas, it is necessary to listen to the orchestra to find out what is really going on. Although this is true of all Wagner, and is one of his leading principles of work, it is of particular significance in *Meistersinger* because of its populous nature and deployment. The deeper feelings and subconscious impulses and motives of the manifold characters can only be understood by reference to the orchestral textures and to the motifs and combinations which underlie the vocal carryings on. In several respects the Wagnerian orchestra performs a function analogous to that of the chorus in the Greek theatre, but as a continuous commentator.

In Wagner, this process of interaction between the instinctual, represented by the orchestra, and the intellectual or critical, represented by the voices, is more than nominally significant. It is the innermost essence of the Wagnerian drama. The juxtaposition of the two generates the real dramatic tension. In many ways it occupies the place of the tension between keys in classical sonata form. Of course, Wagner too makes use of the tension and expressive power of key relationships, although his development and use of progressive tonality gives it a somewhat different effect. But in Wagner's dramas it is the tension between the unconscious and the conscious, between the feeling and the thought, between, that is, the orchestra and the voices, that constitutes the kernel of the dramatic action.

But it goes even farther than that. There is a widely held theory that there are two sides of the human brain connected by a complex nervous 'link'. The left side is the scientific, the side that determines the outer character, the self; the right side is the instinctual or receptive side. The right side determines the creative capacity and response, the left side the controlling force. The connecting 'link' enables a proper interaction between the two to be possible. Thus the right side is the motive power of the creative faculty, while the left directs and channels the energy so that it can assume forms and aspects which, in the right context, serve to release rather than inhibit the intrinsic energies. If this is so, if the theory is accepted, as it widely is today, then it has particular relevance to Wagner and his work. It has direct relevance to all creative activity; but in view of Wagner's specific method and intention, it throws unusual light onto his dramas. The right side, in these terms, is the orchestra, the left side the voices; and when the connecting link is functioning correctly, the interaction between the two is complete and the full force of creativity released.[8]

Both *Tristan* and *Meistersinger* reveal the process at work in different but closely related forms. In *Tristan* it is tight and concentrated, relating specifically to the central tragedy; in *Meistersinger* it covers a wide musical, psychological and emotional spectrum in accordance with the various and varied nature of that populous drama. But in essence it is two sides of the same process, just as *Tristan* and *Meistersinger* themselves are the two inseparable and complementary sides of Wagner's genius.

In no sense was *Meistersinger* a reaction from and against *Tristan und Isolde*. The opposite is more nearly the truth. Only by a combination of *Tristan* and *Meistersinger* can Wagner's genius at the critical middle point in its evolution be properly understood. He had no need to 'react' against *Tristan* and its dark tragedy and doomed chromaticism with the warmly diatonic human comedy of *Meistersinger*. Neither musically nor emotionally can the juxtaposition be seen as in any sense contradictory, let alone inimical. Without the twin experience of *Tristan* and *Meistersinger* the final emergence of the Wagnerian music drama in *Götterdämmerung* and *Parsifal* could not have come out as it did. Wagner, essentially a developing personality, learnt much as he lived and worked; matured as he grew. He was a true evolutionist. And *Meistersinger* is as much and as irreversible a part of that learning and that evolutionary maturing as *Tristan* had been. And he learnt and evolved not only as an artist and a musician, but no less as a man in both his private and his public selves, as private individual and as loyal exponent of the newly emergent Germany at last reaching the point of unification. But, except perhaps in the final flawed panegyric, he did not overshoot the mark. *Meistersinger* otherwise has in it no kernel of malice. It has fun and it has ridicule; it has love and it has laughter; it even has shadows of doubt and sadness; but nowhere does it exude that spirit of animosity, personal, national or racial, which has saddened men of goodwill, few though they may be, and which made Wordsworth lament 'what man has made of man'.

If the world were to be like *Meistersinger*, it would still not be a perfect world. But at least it would be a world well worth living in, which is rather more than can be said for the one we have fashioned for ourselves ever since.

CHAPTER EIGHT

THE TWILIGHT OF AN AGE

Because sequence and chronology do not coincide it is easy to forget that Wagner's penultimate drama was not *Meistersinger* but *Götterdämmerung*. In fact the last part of *Siegfried* also post-dated *Meistersinger*. That is not in itself significant, except that in returning to *Siegfried* and then passing straight on to *Götterdämmerung* Wagner was not so much returning to an old project – although that of course in one sense was true – as shedding a skin and finding a new existential self underneath it. The shedding process had begun with *Tristan* and continued with *Meistersinger*, the two, as we have seen, twin and complementary aspects of the same creative emanation, and it was to be fully revealed in his last drama of all, *Parsifal*. Thus *Götterdämmerung* is not only the apotheosis of the entire *Ring* cycle; it is also the 'bridge' work between the revelatory *Tristan* and *Meistersinger* and the culminating *Parsifal*.

Relating *Götterdämmerung* back to *Das Rheingold* is to see how far the inner evolutionary process has gone. And the musical evolution kept accurate pace with the metaphysical one, as it had to if the huge edifice was not to crumble into ruin and anticlimax, to reveal a fatal hollow at the centre. It was not within the scope and possibiity of an essentially developing personality like Richard Wagner to progress through a whole immense four-part project over twenty-five years without it revealing significantly advanced steps in its own and his process of growth and development. As it turned out, and because of the twelve-year break in the middle, the evolution of *The Ring* went farther and took directions other than those Wagner himself or anyone else could have foreseen. Even without the 'break', even if it had been written straight through as Wagner originally intended, and then produced as a composite whole upon completion, *The Ring* would have been essentially evolutionary, if only because its fundamental postulates were concerned with evolution. But because the scope became wider, the range longer than even he had at first suspected, it came out in a way that was both unforeseen and unpredictable. Not only the character of the central figure, Siegfried, underwent radical change and transformation; far more importantly, Wagner's attitude towards him was transformed, and along with it the entire cast of the metaphysical premise upon which it was built. It became changed, changed utterly, between his conception of the fearless hero as love-child of incest between brother and sister, Siegmund and Sieglinde, and his death at the hands of the treacherous Hagen. The whole of *The Ring* concept had originated with the death of Siegfried; but in the progression towards it everything was altered. The hero born to redeem the world had changed into the lost leader whose inadequacy Wagner was forced, whether he wanted to or not, to admit and confront.

Götterdämmerung in fact represents the high point in Wagner's mature style in music drama. *Tristan* may be more *echt*-Wagner in one sense, a more concentrated example of his manner of work; *Meistersinger* so in another, more varied but equally representative way. But *Götterdämmerung* is a compendium, a summing up of all that had gone before, a pathfinder for the musical and metaphysical concluding drama to come, and in a certain sense for the next fifty years of European music and literature. And if on the surface *Parsifal* appears more passive, more renunciatory still, more steeped in a kind of religious aura, the fuse more slow-burning, it is all predictable from *Götterdämmerung*, is all implicit in that final consummation of the great central tetralogy that occupied many of his waking and more of his sleeping thoughts through virtually the whole of his middle manhood and had originated still earlier. Just as the musical subtlety surpasses anything in the previous dramas, so the metaphysical subtlety advances beyond the hypotheses of those earlier works, even though it emanated from them as an inevitable outcome of their tenets.

What is by no means always properly understood, and what cannot be understood if *The Ring* is seen only in political, economic and deterministic terms, is the full import of the change *Götterdämmerung* represents from the original postulates of *Das Rheingold* and *Die Walküre*. And it amounts to precisely this: that in his primary creation Siegfried is the hero sent to redeem the world and found the New Order and the new race, his death the signal for a race of heroes in his own image to arise; but after the 'break' and to the final bars of *Götterdämmerung* and Brünnhilde's Immolation upon his funeral pyre the import is that that conception is flawed and the death of Siegfried is not, Christ-like, the death of the hero that will release new life and fresh hope for the world through his example, but recognition that the light and the way do not after all lie in that direction at all, that in fact the Siegfried hero-image is but another illusion. In short, the lament over Siegfried's death is not, as had once been predicted, the cause for dedication to the new life he had opened, but sorrow at the failure of a mission. Siegfried, in other words, represents not, as Wagner had at first envisaged and as too many, especially in Germany, have imagined since and still in some quarters do, the beginning of a new line but the end of an old one. The irony is again acute: Siegfried is in the end the opposite of what he was originally created to be. Jung's interpretation thus takes on even more positive meaning as the drama unfolds. The difference is that Wagner himself had become aware of it; and this is implicit in the music and the drama of *Götterdämmerung*. The best that can be said is that Siegfried represents some of the nobler aspects of heroism. But he also represents some of the worst, and in the end fatal aspects of it. He is arrogant, cruel, one who is determined to have his way at whatever cost to other people. He still has much of the savage and the barbarian in him. And from these facets of his personality he can be released only by death, as can the world itself, provided it avoids the temptation and the trap of gesturing on the side of 'heroic' emulation.

The dramatic structure of *Götterdämmerung* contains all the necessary clues. At the end of the previous drama Siegfried had awakened Brünnhilde on her mountaintop and together they had released a long, lyrical outpouring as they looked into a new dawn and a new future they would create for mankind. But in fact Siegfried, despite a certain element of his own as well as Brünnhilde's awakening, had learnt very little. At the beginning of *Götterdämmerung* he sets off down the Rhine in search of new adventure like any adolescent on the rampage, and as likely to get up to mischief as to do anyone any good. And so it turns out. He learns some necessary lessons; but it is too late and his own psyche prevents him from recognizing, let alone grasping, any of the fundamental implications. He remains bent upon self-indulgence.[1] The magic potions dispensed by Hagen, like that given by Brangäne to Isolde in *Tristan*, are dramatic devices for opening the unconscious, for revealing the recipients' true instead of their conscious and assumed thoughts and motivations. They are called 'magic' because they expose things that cannot otherwise be understood or accounted for. In this case, Siegfried susbstitutes the gentle Gutrune for the formidable Brünnhilde, possibly because at heart he himself is becoming aware of the hollowness of the 'heroic' role and image in which he has been cast and in which he has cast himself. Then he goes back and recalls from the inside his past and his understanding of the natural world, the bird's song and the forest murmurs. Under the spell he is made to seem as though he betrays a trust, again perhaps in his subconscious sense that all this warring and adventuring are as empty as the old ways he is supposed to be supplanting and are in fact only another aspect of them.

Götterdämmerung is full of keys and clues, some concealed, some clearly delineated. By the end of Act II much has been revealed. Both musically and dramatically this act is perhaps Wagner's finest single achievement. Then the opening of Act III is virtually a classical fresco, a *pastorale* after the manner of Diana the Huntress and the Water Nymphs. Siegfried has been out with a hunting party. He has become separated from the others and is looking, without success, for game on his own account. He arrives by the banks of the Rhine where the Rhinemaidens are swimming in what might be taken for a kind of formal waterdance. They chide Siegfried and warn him: chide him for being subservient to a woman's threats and angers, warn him of the Curse of the Ring that means death to anyone who holds it unless it is returned to them. And now the flaws in Siegfried's mind and character re-emerge. He has still not learnt fear, so he is incapable of deep understanding and sympathy. He laughs off the warning, saying that the sword which shattered Wotan's spear can deal with any threats or dangers. The chiding he ridicules, and returns. But the note struck by the Rhinemaidens is ominous. Even if Siegfried does not recognize it, does not understand that this is no idle threat or passing pleasantry, everyone else does. Siegfried still thinks he can gain his ends and subdue the world to his will by strong-arm tactics. He has reached the point where he is incapable of learning much more and has too little time to learn anyway.

Siegfried's Funeral March thus represents the end of the old order rather than the beginning of the new. Wotan and the gods have retired to Valhalla, their reign ended. Siegfried was of the line and lineage. He had been created to inaugurate the new order; but his death, even though it had been brought about by treachery, only signalized the failure of that order to materialize. And the reason it did not materialize was inherent in the conception itself. It was all part of the reactionary nature of revolution. Ironically, the reason for Wagner's change of heart and mind was precisely the opposite of what it is usually held to be. Far from being the result of disappointment at the revoutionary failures of the late 1840s and early 1950s, as Marxists and others of their kidney proclaim, it was Wagner's recognition of the futility of such manifestations that led him to seek new and reorientated metaphysical boundaries and eventual horizons. The treachery, in short, was inherent in the revolutionary process, just as militarism and a false 'heroism' was, is, and always will be.

It is for this reason that the musical subtleties of *Götterdämmerung* coincide exactly with the new metaphysical subtleties. Whereas in his earlier works, including the previous parts of *The Ring* itself, Wagner had used the techniques of the leitmotif in a comparatively direct and straightforward manner, in *Götterdämmerung* they are so far advanced that the usage takes on a multitudinous attribute in that each situation or aspect of a particular character now requires a searching combination of motivic 'germs' to satisfy it: there is no one motif for any one situation or character. And it is so precisely because the metaphysical foundations and motifs are no longer comparatively direct and straightforward but increasingly subtle, refined into a new and more potent complexity.

If, as Mahler intimated, the whole of German art could be deduced from *Meistersinger* should all else be lost, so Richard Wagner's particular contribution to it could be deduced from *Götterdämmerung* upon the same potential consideration, both musically and metaphysically.

Meanwhile Wagner's dream of a permanent Festival Theatre was taking practical shape in his mind. *Götterdämmerung* was finished in early 1872; but he would not allow production in Munich, as Ludwig and the Bavarian Court desired, because he would no longer countenance piecemeal production of *The Ring*. He had been obliged to acquiesce in the independent presentation of the first two sections, *Das Rheingold* and *Die Walküre*, for financial and practical reasons, even though he always intended the three dramas and a prelude to be given on consecutive nights. But he now felt in a stronger position. With successful productions of *Tristan* and *Meistersinger* behind him and his material situation secured by royal patronage, he felt able to insist on his intentions being honoured and to brush off the opposition and calumny of the musical and social circles that were still trying to undermine him and his reputation. He returned to Germany in 1871 to look for a site for his theatre, which he eventually found outside the small Bavarian town of Bayreuth. In that same year German arms triumphed in the Franco-Prussian war and Wagner wrote a *Kaisermarsch* in celebration.[2] He also scribbled some rather atrocious doggerel, which he addressed to Bismarck. All this may sound like typical Wagnerian-Germanic tub-thumping; but what is probably nearer the truth is that it was another facet of his ambivalent but basically hostile feelings towards France and the French, a minor chip off the impulse that had led to the false ending of *Meistersinger*.

A more memorable offshoot of Wagner's genius, and one genuinely reflecting his mood of the Triebschen years, was the *Siegfried Idyll* for thirteen solo instruments[3] which he wrote for Cosima's birthday on Christmas Day 1870, and was performed on the staircase on that day by a group of musicians who had rehearsed it in secret, including Hans Richter on the trumpet. The *Idyll* shares melodic material with the latter part of the third act of *Siegfried*, material that derived originally from a string quartet Wagner had planned to write for Cosima after he had first set his sights upon her at Starnberg in 1864. The interpolation of this, apparently alien, material into *Siegfried* was obviously a private allusion between Wagner and Cosima, and the basing of the *Idyll* upon it both emphasizes its relevance to their private lives and helps to give a clue to the allusion. The *Idyll* is often held up as Wagner's single purely instrumental work of any consequence and an indication of how he would have proceeded had he lived longer and carried out his post-*Parsifal* idea of writing one-movement symphonies. It is not a convincing argument. The *Idyll* is only nominally Wagner's sole instrumental work, and it gives little idea how he would have proceeded in full orchestra symphonies. Even if we ignore the early *Faust Overture* (and it should not be ignored) and do not admit the validity of many dramatic preludes to various acts in the stage works, several of which are full-scale orchestral compositions in their own right, his entire procedure in the music dramas is based upon principles that can legitimately be called 'symphonic' in the correct sense. Some, like *Das Rheingold* and *Die Walküre*, are based upon structural principles and constructional laws derived from Beethoven, while the later dramas are extensions and evolutionary elaborations of those laws and principles.

During the latter Triebschen years a new, vital, intellectual force entered Wagner's life in the form and person of a twenty-four year old professor of philology at the University of Basle. His name was Friedrich Nietzsche. Nietzsche became a frequent visitor to Triebschen, and he and Wagner soon began striking sparks out of each other. Both were disciples of Arthur Schopenhauer; both revered the Greeks and their tragic art. For the next decade or so the two were in constant contact, the relationship deepened by Nietzsche's addiction to music and his ambitions as a composer. Wagner largely ridiculed, frequently without kindness, Nietzsche's musical productions, no doubt justifiably in retrospect. Nietzsche was not a very good composer. All the same, that ridicule may well have had a tangential bearing on the philosopher's later furious denunciation of the composer-dramatist. Nietzsche's *The Birth of Tragedy* contained a 'Foreword to Richard Wagner', which extolled Wagner as the true reviver of the spirit of the Greeks, albeit with some personal reservations which he suppressed out of loyalty to the Master.[4]

The Wagner/Nietzsche association was important to both, and so to the evolution of European art and philosophy during the latter part of the nineteenth century. Nietzsche's later denunciation of Wagner, after his previous adulation, was complex and revelatory, though it was not always quite what it seemed at the time and has tended to seem ever since. It was not even what Nietzsche himself supposed it to be. The usual explanation is that Nietzsche came to believe that the art of the Greeks expressed life affirmation while Wagner's ultimately expressed life negation and degeneracy. But the nearer and deeper truth is that in the contemporary context Nietzsche had to allow that Wagner was more right than he wanted to admit; and the dichotomy helped drive him to mental breakdown. The turn against Wagner was to some extent Nietzsche's own self-compensation for the validity of ideas he was struggling with himself not to accept; a sign of recognition of unwelcome truths. Certainly Wagner and Nietzsche drew apart, both personally and existentially; and the personal disaffinities, though never complete, undoubtedly influenced Nietzsche's about-turn in the face of Wagner's music. On the other hand, when Nietzsche came to realize that the motif of renunciation, brought to its consummation in *Parsifal*, was inherent at least from *The Flying Dutchman* on, he was doing no more than acknowledging what was always there and what he, as a professional philosopher, should have been aware of all along.

Philosophically valid though in many respects it was, there is something specious about Nietzsche's furiously assumed anti-Wagnerism. That the apostasy caused the philosopher as much pain as his previous adulation had given him ecstatic pleasure is no argument for the contrary case. There was an element of the neurotic in Nietzsche, leading to the sad circumstance of his insanity, which made a number of his judgements, however brilliant, suspect and unreliable. The Wagner/Nietzsche relationship remains important;[5] but in so far as Richard Wagner is concerned it is a major issue only in respect of Nietzsche's own standing in the history of European thought and philosophy.

Wagner and Cosima were on terms of intimacy with him throughout most of the 1870s, though by the end of the decade Nietzsche's disenchantment had set in, beginning with the publication of *Human, All Too Human* in 1878. This tract deeply offended Wagner, who retaliated with one of his own entitled *Public and Popularity*. The rift was still not complete; but the flaw had opened and was soon to prove fatal. Nietzsche's own position was ambivalent. He began by lauding militarism and Prussianism. He served as an ambulance attendant in the Franco-Prussian war; but he could not stand the sight of blood and had to return home, a nervous wreck. Yet he continued to uphold the 'military virtues' and cheered the Prussian cavalry into action. True, he came later to despise the more blatant aspects of Prussian militarism; all the same, he was one of those who, weak in physique himself, tended to compensate by singing the praises of 'manly exploits'. In Nietzsche's pagan hedonism there was a discomforting element of 'strength through joy' that was to have disastrous results in the next century. For Wagner, unlike Brahms, militarism was never an issue at all. If he cheered the victory of German arms at Sedan and afterwards, it was, as I say, largely because of his hostility, shared by most Germans, towards the French.[6] For the larger aspects of Bismarckism and the pan-German empire he had little time or real patience.

But that did not prevent him from trying to solicit Bismarck's help and support towards the founding and building of the Festspielhaus. Bismarck was not particularly interested; but by then Wagner was already launched into his project. The civic authorities of Bayreuth had proved sympathetic to the general idea; Wagner himself was expending time and energy rallying support among the influential and generally turning over stones with his usual demonic vitality. He spared himself nothing. Many thought to begin with that the whole scheme was just another of his extravagent dreams. But Wagner would brook no obstacle, pushed his idea and its realization forward with ruthless determination, set himself without stint to bring it about. It was another instance of willing what is necessary. It was the Will that carried it through, despite all checks and hindrances.

One of the latter at one time appeared to be King Ludwig. Enraged at Wagner's intention to settle himself in Bayreuth and not return to Munich,

Ludwig threatened to cut off his subsidy. He relented, but it was a bad moment. Without Ludwig's support, not only the Festspielhaus project but the entire foundation of Wagner's life and work would have collapsed. No doubt Wagner did, by conventional standards, renege on assurances,[7] go back on promises given, explicitly if not directly, to Ludwig about the production of his works and even about the building of the theatre itself in Munich. But as usual it was in the interests of the larger cause, which for Wagner remained at all times the paramount consideration. If Wagner saw himself at various times as the Dutchman, as Lohengrin, as Siegfried, there was also an element of Alberich in him, in that he would give up anything, even love, to obtain his way and conquer his chosen fields. He would in that interest turn his back on friends, patrons and supporters without hesitation and apparently without a qualm. It was characteristic of him and of all he did and stood for. He had the total ruthlessness of the utterly dedicated, for the end that justifies all means. It is a dangerous assumption, and it has led to much evil. But it is inescapable in all those of passionate conviction.

Bayreuth appealed to Wagner for several reasons. It was small, it was provincial, it was off the tourist track, it had no established artistic tradition or reputations. It is clear that Wagner saw it, unlike the major centres, as a more or less blank page on which he could imprint his permanent seal. It was also within the boundaries of the kingdom of Bavaria, and therefore under Ludwig's protection. Things did not go smoothly at first: the chosen site could not be obtained because of the recalcitrance of one of the landowners, who would not sell his portion; but a second site on a nearby hill was successfully negotiated and Wagner secured an adjacent plot on which he proposed to build a private villa for occupation by himself, Cosima and the children.

He was, also as usual, over-optimistic. The original architectural plans were hopelessly ambitious and extravagant. Then, contrary to Wagner's hopes and expectation (but to no one else's) the necessary funds, though first computed on a surprisingly modest scale, were reluctant to materialize. Indeed, many continued to believe that it was all just another Wagnerian pipe-dream that would never come to fruition, especially since he had planned the first great festival for 1873, a year so early that even he must have realized its impracticality.

But the project did proceed, although the date had to be put forward to 1876. Various societies and organizations were formed for further fund-raising, and much propaganda undertaken on a permanent basis. Wagner himself was obliged to travel, giving concerts and looking for suitable singers, tasks that he undertook with great reluctance as they interrupted his work on the completion of *Götterdämmerung*. Yet in the end it was accomplished. Kaiser Wilhelm I attended the first festival presentation of *The Ring* in the summer of 1876, remarking, not without some element of both envy and admiration, to Wagner: 'I never thought you would pull it off!' The Emperor was by no means the only one to express surprise. All the same, if it had not been for the loyal and often traduced Ludwig II, it never could have been pulled off, or even launched at all.

History has not dealt kindly with Ludwig II, presenting him too often as a vain, largely ineffectual young man, mentally and emotionally unstable, homosexual, irresponsible, altogether unfit for the task that lay to his hand. Yet many, in addition to Bismarck, were struck by his grasp of government, by his shrewdness and diplomatic skill, by his firmness of character. He found himself in a difficult position, and it was not made easier by his ardent championship of Wagner and his works, which gave his enemies ample opportunity to denigrate him further and laid him open to charges of conduct unbecoming in a monarch. But history does not do him justice. But for Ludwig II there would have been no Bayreuth. More than that, but for Ludwig there might have been no mature Wagner, *The Ring* unfinished, *Meistersinger* a torso at most, not a note of *Parsifal* set down. That Ludwig was not the most stable and reliable of characters is clear; but further evidence suggests that he was in the end humbled by people less gifted and less imaginative than himself, and that he possessed a kind of personal integrity rarely found in conventional people and virtually never in political manoeuvrists. It is not in the end Ludwig, or even Wagner – those two understood each other even though they sometimes fell foul over passing entanglements – but the courtiers and politicians who come badly out of the business. Ludwig, vulnerable, sensitive, imaginative, inexperienced, haunted by unfulfilled creative aspirations, struggling against his homosexuality, was exploited and then cast out by the schemers and sycophants of government.

From now until the end of his life Bayreuth became Wagner's passionate involvement. He had left Triebschen, not without regret, in 1872, and was eventually installed with Cosima and the family in the Bayreuth villa, Wahnfried. It was from Wahnfried that he organized, composed, held court, spoke and wrote, with occasional breaks for holidays and surcease, mostly in Italy. Though there were loyal colleagues and supporters always at Bayreuth, it was his own ceaseless efforts that kept the machine running, ensured success and maintained the quality of the productions. Inevitably, it took time to get into its stride, and some of the earlier productions were substandard. But that was not decisive: what mattered was that the comprehensive idea of a permanent Festival Theatre had been realized. The future would see to the rounding off of corners and the polishing of surfaces. Critical hostility, of which there was plenty, with Eduard Hanslick in the van,[8] could not abort or even in the long run influence the maturation of the Bayreuth project, just as two world wars, social and continental upheaval, disaster, impoverishment and all the rest, including the Nazi aberration, have not been able to destroy or undermine it and its relevance since it was established over a hundred years ago. Though political, administrative and above all financial difficulties continued to press and to absorb Wagner's time and energy while he lived, and continued after his death, Bayreuth proved indestructible, as he himself in his darkest days had proved to be.

With the Bayreuth Festival founded and launched, Wagner could return to composition. The musical as well as the metaphysical questions left open in *Götterdämmerung* demanded such a return; in any case, apart from the need to produce new work to stimulate Bayreuth, his creative power was by no means exhausted and he was, like any other artist, still under irresistible inner compulsion into the act of creation.

Back in the 1840s, when he was immersing himself in German medieval literature, Wagner had come upon the legend of Parzival, alongside those of Tannhäuser and Lohengrin. It had planted a seed, one among many, and it was the last of those seeds to break through the surface and burgeon forth into a major work. When Wagner said that the sin of Tannhäuser passed through Tristan to Amfortas he was recognizing also the way certain motifs and situational themes ran through his dramas in one form or another. Just as a contest of song is common to both *Tannhäuser* and *Die Meistersinger*, so the temptations of the flesh, the abandonment to sensuality is common to *Tannhäuser* and *Parsifal* – yielded to in one case, resisted in the other, but a leading motif in both. It had its central place in *Tristan*, too, but there it had been both sublimated and indulged at one and the same time and so given another and more complex direction. *Parsifal* also inherits from *Lohengrin*, and greatly extends, a central quality of spirituality, via the motif of the Holy Grail. Because Wagner was a comparatively young man when he wrote *Lohengrin*, and an ageing one near the end of his road when he came to *Parsifal*, the spiritual density is different. But it remains an essential part of the creative process in each case.[9] In addition there is the motif of Redemption, which runs all through Wagner's work and which finally turned Nietzsche's allegiance sour when he realized that it did not belong to *Parsifal* only.

Many misconceptions of *Parsifal* are possible, and most of them are made. Nietzsche's almost paranoid hatred of Christianity led him to condemn *Parsifal* as a weakminded submission to ritual and to accuse Wagner of collapsing in tears at the foot of the Cross in a spirit of defeat and life negation.[10] This is one of the most prevalent of errors about *Parsifal*. The fact is that *Parsifal* is a religious work in the larger sense, but it is not specifically Christian any more than it is specifically Buddhist, although it contains elements of both. The error arises from the way in which Wagner uses the trappings of Christian myth and legend as a ritualistic framework for a dramatic presentation which in essence has very little to do with Christian dogma, still less with Christian orthodoxy. It cannot be denied that part of it comes near to religioso; the sense that Wagner the born dramatist was deliberately using and exploiting ritualistic props for a dramatic structure. But he was not insincere; once again he was probing into the future, delineating an extension of his own dramatic and metaphysical principles, combining the ingredients of stagecraft for his own unique purposes. Faced with the dilemma left by the conclusion of *The Ring*, he was obliged to renew the metaphysical enquiry from a different angle; and because he was essentially a musician his new approach led to further evolutions and enrichments of his musical language. *Parsifal*, whatever else may be said about it, contains some of the subtlest and most far-reaching musical thinking in all Wagner. Like *Tristan* the dramatic structure is, apart from the somewhat hectic second act, predominantly static; and like *Götterdämmerung* it breeds an inexhaustible flow of musical invention resulting in exceptionally rich and subtle thematic, harmonic and structural relationships. The evolutionary process in Wagner continued to function; and because he had now all his life experience behind him, it threw up a musico-dramatic texture of endless potential.

The metaphysical dilemma could not be avoided. It amounted to simply this: If the world cannot be redeemed by a god with a spear or a hero with a sword, then who can redeem it? If Wotan's renunciation of power and Siegfried's inability to use it creatively had aborted, and for much the same reasons, then what was left? A fool with a spear he cannot use?[11] A 'holy innocent' who is so gullible that he actually out-manoeuvres the wordly ones? Is it therefore G. K. Chesterton's greenhorn who is taken in while the all-too-knowing ones are cast out? Certainly the heroic hypothesis had to be abandoned. It had failed; it had left a world still without redemption. But whatever might be the way of the fool or 'holy innocent' it can only be in a general sense 'religious'; it cannot have a dogmatic centre. The world will not be redeemed by dogma any more than by swords and spears.

At one time Wagner planned a dramatic work on the subject of Jesus of Nazareth; but *Parsifal* was not it, nor was intended to be. Parsifal is anything but a Jesus-figure. Jesus was no fool or holy innocent. Everything about Him suggests the exact opposite. And although He too may be seen as 'anti-hero', and in the more obvious sense He was, the true character and person of Jesus has been overlaid by sentimentality. This was particularly true in the nineteenth century, especially in Germany and England. The Latin Roman Catholic view gave Him greater strength, saw the essential 'suffering Christ' in more realistic as well as more profoundly spiritual terms, saw that figure as active rather than passive; but it still produced a concomitant effect of undermining the Christian assumption as a whole by sentimentalizing the figure of the Virgin Mary. In fact the sentimentalizing of Christ lies deep in the world history of Christianity as organized religion. It is particularly prevalent in Pietism, another German phenomenon, with its cloying and at times homosexually biased emotionalism, something which even affects many of Bach's church cantatas, beautiful and profound though they are.

One of the curious results of the Catholic veneration of the Virgin is to bend the Christian religion away from homosexual implications. Wagner himself did not wholly avoid either the sentimental or the homosexual undertones in *Parsifal*. In its sentimentalities it contains flaws and metaphysical impurities absent from *Tristan* and *Meistersinger*, from *The Ring* and even in a different form from *The Flying Dutchman*; and in its homosexual implications it takes in a wider range also than those productions. In this respect *Parsifal* is nearer to *Tannhäuser* than to *Tristan*. Though *Parsifal* avoids the crudeness and bombast that disfigures *Tannhäuser*, it too slips on the treacherous slopes of the Kundry/ Venusberg lure of sensuality and a somewhat self-conscious resistance to it. In *Tristan* the element of passionate sensuality is integrated into the drama and adds significantly to its true tragic dimension. But in *Parsifal*, as in *Tannhäuser*, it constitutes a trap which even the totally mature Wagner did not altogether avoid. And it was in many ways inevitable, for one reason why he could not avoid it was that the dichotomy was inherent, like so much else relating to his life and art, in the Romantic assumption itself.

The specifically Christian elements in *Parsifal* are misleading. It refers to Christianity in its use of Christian symbol and legend as dramatic framework; but in several important respects it directly contravenes Christian doctrine. In particular it avoids the focal point of the Crucifixion. In this respect it rebuffs Nietzsche's charge of life-negation. By turning away from death on the Cross, it affirms life against death. This lies at the heart of the conception of Parsifal as Fool. Jesus's death by crucifixion was a direct result of His intransigence. He would not compromise. He rejected the armed force solution, though He was offered it; He refused the dialectic letout, though He could easily have accommodated it without relinquishing His central message. But He would not. So He was put to death. The fate of Socrates was not dissimilar. But Parsifal saw it differently. Parsifal did not so much compromise as side-step. Thus the *Parsifal* drama as unfolded by Richard Wagner was 'religious' in the larger and deeper sense of attempting to penetrate to some ultimate spiritual reality. For the committed Christian of course that means the specifically Christian way. But it is not so for non-Christians, though they may according to their own lights and beliefs be no less genuinely religious. *Parsifal* is in no sense sectarian. Sectarianism is essentially irreligious. Sectarianism leads to dogmatism, which in turn leads to atheism. Dogmatic sectarianism makes belief in God impossible. A BBC radio broadcaster, Pauline Webb, once said that when confronted with an atheist she wanted to retort: 'I don't believe in the God you don't believe in either.' The shaft was well aimed: atheism is the inevitable consequence of the usual degraded idea of God and religion. Orthodox, organized religion is in any case a contradiction, for as Kierkegaard asserted, 'officialdom is incommensurable with Christianity'. And not only with Christianity:

officialdom is incommensurable with any religion. Dostoevsky's Grand Inquisitor charges Christ with laying the intolerable burden of freedom on men and thereby showing no pity towards them. And that is the crux of the matter: a spiritual movement from determinism into freedom with all that implies in terms of natural human limitation. The truly religious nature, whether Christian or other, subsists in the liberation from dogmatism and its concomitant authoritarian officialdom, and the recognition of symbol and ritual as the mirror-image of the surface only of the deeper spiritual reality.

Parsifal represents Wagner's last attempt to break out of the Romantic dilemma. Paradoxically, it is also the apotheosis of the Romantic–religious attitude. Like *The Ring*, it failed; but like that masterpiece it was and remains a noble effort. It has been misunderstood and misrepresented largely because of its evocation of Christian legend and symbol. But it is not in essence a Christian tract; it is an attempt to embrace in artistic terms the religious spirit *per se*, non-dogmatic and non-sectarian. Its basic postulates – Love, Faith, Hope; Redemption and Salvation – belong not to one religion but to all religions, in one form or another. And in that it accords exactly with the innermost spirit of Romanticism. The 'Good Friday Music', though it appears to refer directly to Christian ritual, even to Christian historicism, is in fact a typical Romantic beatification of Nature. Similarly, the confrontation of spirituality with sensuality, though again inherent in Christianity, or rather in Pauline Christianity, is also a leading motif of the Romantic movement and its idealism. Nietzsche, who rebelled finally against Wagner because of *Parsifal*, came to see the central truth in the end. Though it did not accord with his own philosophical tenets, Nietzsche was perceptive enough, and honest enough, to see that *Parsifal* did not really represent a capitulation at the foot of the Cross but a profoundly existential attempt to penetrate the spiritual and artistic life from a standpoint that had long become inevitable in the overall context of Wagner's personal evolution.

Parsifal is the least dogmatic and most ritualistic of all Wagner's works. Both musically and metaphysically the resolution of discordant elements is avoided. In this, as in much else, *Parsifal* is essentially modern in its psychological and intellectual approaches. With the late nineteenth century breakdown of the long European tradition of optimism and the certainty of faith, the old assurance of man's place in the universe, the strong affirmation of tonality in music, the Beethovenian insistence upon tonic and dominant as a form of life affirmation, was no longer possible. It had begun philosophically with Schopenhauer; but it took time to percolate through into the broader social and emotional mainstream. The process of non-resolution, as it might be called, had emerged in its decisive form in *Tristan und Isolde*; but in *Parsifal* it became farther extended and carried into another, though again related, dimension.[12] *Parsifal* thus represents an inescapable development from *Tannhäuser* and *Lohengrin* via *Tristan und Isolde*. The lack of certainty and resolution was, as always, both musical and metaphysical. And inevitably, some of the absurdities came with it: there is always some 'point of improbability'. In the earlier opera Lohengrin is one who could not reveal his identity; in the final drama Parsifal is one who does not know who he is. Lohengrin was sworn to keep his history secret; Parsifal did not know he had a history. And Lohengrin, as it eventually transpires, is the son of Parsifal. It is all interrelated and very complex.

As early as the late 1850s Wagner's mind had taken a decisive mystical–metaphysical turn. On the other hand, it can hardly be doubted that from the outset it was a mind of that particular cast; it simply took necessary time to settle into its proper orbit. The crudity and longeurs of *Tannhäuser* were largely the result of his creative faculties combining to come into their true estate; the man and the artist were in a condition of fermentation, with the primary elements not yet correctly blended and balanced. With *Lohengrin* the first blend and balance were achieved; but then it became necessary for the product of the fermentation to take a fresh direction. It could not stand still, be content to repeat itself, either in degree or in kind. The links between *Lohengrin* and *Parsifal* are far more significant than the common use of the motif of the Holy Grail: they confirm the fundamental unity of Wagner's spiritual and artistic evolution, beginning to end. And in between stands *Tristan*, the musical and metaphysical pivot, with its central character who has inherited the 'sin' of *Tannhäuser* and passes it on to Amfortas to be redeemed by Parsifal, the father of Lohengrin, that the world might become like *Meistersinger* with its spirit of a free mankind liberated by art and love, after the failure of Siegfried. In a manner of speaking, of course.

The idea that *Parsifal* represents the ultimate Romantic pessimism and life negation, as Nietzsche at first proclaimed, can only be in part sustained. There are more ways than one of affirming the value of life and of the world than by a self-conscious lauding or the ambitions of a conqueror. As the French composer Charles Koechlin once remarked: 'In the human soul there is a whole range of sentiments beyond the "affirmations" of the so-called classical period, beyond the romantic outpourings of a Schumann and the dominant-seventh passion of a Beethoven. There is a certain disarray, a certain lack of equilibrium, even a certain indifference (which goes farther than sorrow). And sorrow too . . .'

Wagner was one of the first musicians to see and understand this; that is why to many of his contemporaries his music appeared chaotic, monotonous, ambiguous, lacking in firm foundations or positive direction; a music that seemed to undermine the very foundations of music. In the same way his metaphysical premises seemed to challenge both established faiths and the sense of life to be lived directly and without complication according to accepted and acceptable laws. Schopenhauer had long since fatally undermined that idea, as Kant had called into question the dominance of 'pure reason'; and Wagner was nothing if not Schopenhauerean. The essence of Schopenhauer's philosophy had been distilled into music in *Tristan und Isolde* and in much of *The Ring*. But the influence of Schopenhauer did not end there. In *Parsifal* it reached its apogee. Yet by a curious paradox, instead of a final resignation into life-negation *Parsifal* sought to open other and more profound doors into the future. It represented perhaps a moment of pause in the spiritual evolution of Europe, also taking in elements of the philosophies of the East, elements which were essentially non-assertive, non-dogmatic, non-possessive. But Europe would not pause: it had to plunge on, Siegfried-like, bent upon its own destruction and its foreseen and foreseeable nemesis.

Wagner called *Parsifal* a 'Sacred Festival Drama'.[13] He intended that it should only be performed at Bayreuth, not as a public celebration like *Meistersinger* but as a public communion, or meditation. Neitzsche charged Wagner with trying to turn a theatrical performance into a religious service without public participation and therefore only as 'contemplation'. But that argument misses two important points. In nineteenth-century Romanticism the artist tended to be elevated to the position of high priest, replacing the officers of the Church as the ultimate mentor; and, largely as a consequence of this, it placed a new emphasis on art as ritual. Certainly, at a performance of *Parsifal* there is no public participation in the active and direct sense, as there is for example in Bach's Passions, notably the *St Matthew Passion,* where the congregation was originally intended to join in the singing of the chorales.[14] But that is hardly decisive. Much sacred music does not invite congregation participation, as in, to cite an obvious example, Beethoven's *Missa solemnis*. Art as ritual has an even longer history; and the element of ritual in *Parsifal* is an essential part of its nature; it might be called the primary element. Yet this again is by no means unusual or remarkable. W. B. Yeats saw this, and also touched on another aspect of the totality of *Parsifal* when he wrote, '[Lionel] Johnson's favourite phrase, that life is ritual, expressed something that was in some degree in all our thoughts, and how could life be ritual if woman had not her symbolical place'?[15] This throws light on the figure of Kundry, the redeemed seductress who failed to corrupt the saintly Parsifal. For Wagner woman certainly had her 'symbolical place'. If the world was to be redeemed, woman had to be redeemed too. The Kundry/Mary Magdalene figure has often seemed one of the false notes in *Parsifal*; but it can only be so seen by misrepresentation of Wagner's entire conception of woman and femininity.

The extended time sequences of *Parsifal* were inherent in all Wagner's works; but here they are elevated to a new level of meaning. Wilhelm Furtwängler once said of Bruckner that it was 'his natural destiny to make the supernatural real'. Something of the same might be said of *Parsifal*; and that is why, despite its theatrical and humanistic elements, the charge that it is 'unrealistic' is both erroneous and irrelevant. It is in this sense, and this sense alone, that Bruckner can legitimately be called a 'Wagnerian symphonist', not upon any meaningful technical or aesthetic grounds. It is the mystical element that counts.

One might say that *Parsifal* is fundamentally a contemplative work, extolling the virtues of contemplation against 'action'. That may be so. On the other hand, it represents a supreme crisis, not only for Wagner himself, but more importantly for European civilization on the brink of either its own destruction or its rejuvenation. History has recorded which, for the next century, it was to be.

Wagner set so great a value upon *Parsifal* that during his last years he gave his all to its preservation and production as he wanted it, even to the extent of abandoning his determination that *The Ring* also should only be given at Bayreuth and under his personal supervision. He had to let *The Ring* go, to take its chance in the world, even at the cost of inferior production, partly because his health was beginning to fail, partly because as a consequence he needed to secure a future for Cosima and his children (and von Bülow's, who had also fallen to his charge), partly because *Parsifal* had become his main preoccupation. As *Tristan* had been his principal concern during the 1860s, so *Parsifal* became in the late 1870s and into the 1880s and to the end of his life. After the Munich production of *Tristan* (1865), finishing *The Ring* and seeing its production through had been his major interest; it was in fact the principal reason for the founding of Bayreuth and the Festival Theatre. But once the first festival production of *The Ring* in 1876 had taken place and he had become absorbed into the task of realizing *Parsifal*, he appears to have transferred his allegiance, out of necessity it could be argued, from the former to the latter. It is not that he lost interest in *The Ring*: that would have been impossible after all the years of work and idealism, all the heart- and mind-searching that had gone into its making. All the same, once into *Parsifal* that task took over his entire creative being so that all that had gone before was relegated to the second if not to the back row of his attention.

In designating *Parsifal* as 'Sacred Festival Drama' and laying down that it should never be performed anywhere except at Bayreuth, he laid up all manner of problems and litigations for his successors when Cosima relentlessly tried to uphold that edict. But the real point lay in the designation itself. It established the central truth about *Parsifal*, that its spiritual and metaphysical premises went far beyond the requirements of a theatrical entertainment, even of the most elevated kind; that it had to be judged not as artwork only but as a profound meditation on the deepest meaning of life and the world. To accept only the art and avoid the metaphysics is to evade all the real issues. Wagner was not a systematic philosopher, and nearly all his works are in the nature of exploring potentialities rather than proposing dogmatic answers. Nowhere is this more true than in *Parsifal*. His language was art, and it was in artistic terms that he made his explorations. But the idea that all artworks can only be judged in terms of pure art, that music 'means' nothing but music, that poetry means nothing beyond forms and patterns of words, that painting is colour and draughtsmanship only, maybe tenable in certain contexts: in those contexts, in fact, where that is the specified objective. But it is totally invalid in the larger areas of creative activity.[16] It is certainly in no sense applicable to the life and work of Richard Wagner. It could not be farther from the truth. It is not necessary to accept any 'message', Christian, Buddhist or other, from *Parsifal* or any other Wagner work, or to applaud or disapprove the implied sexual or homosexual implications some have discerned in it and which unquestionably do form a constituent part (inevitably, since like all true and 'altogether' works it embraces the totality of experience and does not shun any aspect of it that may be relevant to the matter in hand) in order to penetrate to the heart of Wagner's last drama and its music. All that is necessary is to tune the mind to Wagner's own and accept what he did upon his own terms, not in a spirit of uncritical adulation or passivity, but in that of genuine enquiry uncorrupted by personal prejudice or preconceived ideology.

The sense of 'sin' from Tannhäuser via Tristan to Amfortas hangs heavy upon *Parsifal*. But so does a kind of wide-eyed innocence inherited from the joyous aspects of *Meistersinger*, notably the young love of Walther and Eva, the essential corollary of the chastity of Parsifal and the redemption of Kundry. But the sense of sin is informing; and an exaggerated sense of sin is one of the major aberrations of officialized and evangelized Christianity. It was in this form another tangential issue of nineteenth-century Romanticism. But it is not, for all that, what puts certain persons off *Parsifal*. That, as with *Tristan* (and it is a further example of the unity of Wagner's *oeuvre*) is a bias of sexuality, overt and explicitly heterosexual in *Tristan*, ambiguous in *Parsifal* – and any hint of sexuality in a 'religious' context is sure to set a number of teeth on edge. Yet it was once again an inevitable consequence. The relationship of *Parsifal* to *Lohengrin* is direct and in the Wagnerian context comparatively uncomplicated; and between *Tristan* and *Parsifal* considerably more oblique but no less relevant.

It may be argued that a sense of sin is necessary if the human conscience is to be sharpened and kept active. Much evil has ensued from the lack of it. On the other hand, an exaggerated and too exclusive, too self-conscious obsession with it devitalizes the energies and aborts all imaginative and creative aspiration. In the end, a preoccupation with sin becomes another kind of dogma and so suffocates all true and meaningful religious feeling. Yet those who hold that in comparison with Wagner's earlier works *Parsifal* is devitalized cannot base their contention on the prevalence of a sense of sin. To some extent this sense was another concomitant of Romanticism, in reaction against the rationalism of the eighteenth century and the inhumanity of the new industrial processes that were everywhere taking the place of the old handcrafts, themselves grossly sentimentalized,[17] which had hitherto prevailed and determined the pattern of human labour. But it was also a precognition of Freud's uncovering of the unconscious, which revealed that, far from being a kind of virgin blank, man at his birth was already full of violent inherited passions and instincts that conformed much more closely to the Christian idea of original sin than to the rationalist conception of a clear-unwritten-on page. Faced with this dilemma the Romantics attempted to split the difference by extolling the divine innocence of the child and contrasting it with the 'corruption' of the adult world. But Freud demolished this hope, too, with the theory of infant sexuality, especially undermining in view of the curious but apparently ineradicable equating of sex with sin. Thus the sense of sin began to take on a twofold meaning: the specifically religious and the scientific or psychoanalytic, which answered more closely to a sense of guilt. And the dichotomy deepened and widened as the inferences were drawn, on the one hand that salvation lay only through the grace of God, on the other that people were not responsible for their own actions. Of the two, the former is the more potent and elevating, for although it postulates dependence on a higher power and can thus lead to enervating subservience, it at least opens the way for a release of potential, whereas the latter notion, that we are never responsible for our actions, precludes any autonomous achievement or creative realization. It is dehumanizing and demeaning in a way that can lead only to an extreme form of nihilism and the most destructive forms of neurosis.

When a particularly troublesome piece of work on producing a vocal score of *Fidelio* was completed, Ignaz Moscheles, who had been primarily concerned with it, wrote at the bottom of the last page: 'Finished with God's help'; whereupon Beethoven immediately scribbled underneath: 'Man, help thyself!' Richard Wagner would have echoed Beethoven's words, though perhaps in a slightly different, more sorrowful spirit. Although he often felt his genius as a burden laid upon him by a relentless destiny, he was the last man to try to avoid responsibility for what he did, had done, or was doing. Indeed, no man acted with more absolute deliberation, or stood more ruthlessly by the outcome of it.

The temptation to regard the 'passivity' of much of *Parsifal* as a result of the ageing process on Wagner's creative energies has to be resisted. It is easy to accept *Parsifal* as an old man's capitulation to the ravages of time, as evidence of declining powers and resignation to it. Certainly *Parsifal* is not a young man's work: it bears the wisdom of years and the distillation of a lifetime's experience. The weaknesses in *Parsifal* are the passing misjudgements of a man ruthlessly and insistently determined to question not only established ideas and values but if necessary even his own formerly cherished ones. It continues the process that runs all through Wagner's work of demonstrating Kierkegaard's 'truth is subjectivity'. A man at the end of his days may see life as comedy or tragedy, and he may look upon encroaching death either as blessed relief or as necessary termination of his legitimate activities on this earth. If he is of a religious nature he may see life as a preparation for an afterlife to which death provides the transition. There are of course endless permutations of these basic approaches; but as Schopenhauer intimated, anyone who is interested in life must also be interested in death.

Verdi ended his long life with a sparkling comedy, *Falstaff*, a work of astonishing spirit and vitality written in extreme old age. Brahms approached death with a mixture of disquiet and resigned sadness, much as he approached life. Beethoven, though he died comparatively young, had already passed in all but physical presence beyond wordly life by the time of his death and in so doing demonstrated that, contrary to the more lugubrious romantic assumptions, joy can be at least as profound as tragedy. (Tragedy, as a joy to him who dies, is in no way synonymous with pessimism: it is in fact the opposite, which is not optimism but something beyond both optimism and pessimism.) Wagner in his last years showed signs of world weariness, and it is reflected in *Parsifal*. He longed for personal redemption and salvation; to contemplate the battle from the outside rather than staying directly engaged. From his middle years onwards his mystical/metaphysical temperament had been more and more filled with pity for the sufferings of existence and all living creatures. To a certain extent it could have lain near the frontiers of self-pity. But in the depths of himself, of his true subjectivity, that was not at all what motivated him.

In any case, he still had plans and projects to further. He had no more music dramas in mind; it is possible to see *Parsifal* as his intended final contribution to that form of art, though it must be a dangerous assumption. But in his final years he discussed with Franz Liszt the idea of writing one-movement symphonies. If he had lived, that idea might well have taken firm root; and if it had, the results might have been remarkable. His music dramas are permeated with 'symphonic' thinking; but he intended to return to the symphonic ideals of Beethoven (which he had largely emulated in his early Symphony in C), not, so far as can be judged, to anticipate the massive autobiographical symphonies of Mahler. More likely, he would have anticipated in his own manner of thinking and working the symphonic evolutions of Sibelius, notably the Seventh symphony with its single continuous texture achieving true organic growth through interrelation of themes and motifs. It would possibly have taken its immediate direction from Liszt's symphonic poems, though upon different structural principles. We do not know. It came to nothing because death supervened; but it leaves a number of inviting speculations open.

He feared at one time that he might not live to complete *Parsifal*. He was suffering from recurrent heart attacks, and it is clear that his physical strength was failing. Continual struggles to keep Bayreuth going, now almost exclusively in the interests of *Parsifal* since he had surrendered right to *The Ring* to other hands and to other theatrical locations, put huge strains on his remaining resources and stamina. He knew he had not long to live, that he could not continue at his strenuous pace of living and working. But he would not give in. Through all the nearly seventy years of his life he had never given in; and now that the end was near he kept his will firm, and his determination to see *Parsifal* completed and produced undiminished. He refreshed himself with periodic visits to Italy for rest and to revive his strength in the sun of the south.

But there was life in the old dog yet. In 1878 he had founded, after difficulties, the *Bayreuther Blätter*, a journal designed to propagate the Bayreuth gospel. He found a sympathetic editor in Hans von Wolzogen and himself contributed forcefully to its pages until the end of his life. And true to form, he managed a late flowering of his amorous proclivities. The object of his rekindled romantic aspirations during these late years was the beautiful Judith Gautier,[18] who had often visited Triebschen and left a touching account of life there in the pre-Bayreuth days. She was the wife of a leading French man of letters, Catulle Mendés, and she had fascinated Wagner from the outset. Now she was one of the Bayreuth faithful. An affectionate relationship smouldered between the ageing Wagner and the young Judith, more than thirty years his junior. Just how far it went and how intimate it really became is not known for certain; but it is clear that Wagner was again intent on indulging his need as well as his taste for feminine comradeship, much as he had with Mathilde Wesendonk and a fair number of other ladies. Nor is it known how far, if at all, Cosima was aware of what was going on. Cosima is a somewhat enigmatic figure. Utterly devoted to Wagner and his interests, she was also a woman of formidable strength of will and character who, especially after his death, presented a virtually impassable barrier upon any ground that she believed endangered his interest, his reputation and his memory. How self-sacrificing she was in the matter of indulgence towards Wagner's extramarital adventures is a pretty question. She remained, at the time and in her recently published diaries, ominously unforthcoming on the subject of Judith. Judith herself declared after Wagner's death that they had never been lovers. Maybe; maybe not. For Wagner it made little difference. In his old age he still sought and needed what Doctor Johnson rather engagingly called 'the endearing elegance of female friendship'.

All this seems like another example of Wagner's personal egotism, in apparent contradiction of his proclaimed Schopenhauerean belief in the submission, even the annihilation of the self to the universal will, leading to Nirvana. However, the situation is not quite as clear-cut as it may look. Although he declared allegiance to Schopenhauer, Wagner did not swallow him whole or adhere in every respect to the detailed implications of his philosophy. For Wagner, Schopenhauer was central but not exclusive to his own thought and feeling. He deviated when it suited him.

Certainly Judith Gautier, who also assisted him to obtain the luxurious silks and satins and perfumes upon which his bodily and emotional well being depended, did not play a part in respect of *Parsifal* in any way directly analagous to that played by Mathilde Wesendonk in respect of *Tristan*. But she did play some part. Wagner always needed some feminine involvement to supercharge his creative horsepower; and even in his last years his marital arrangements did not entirely suffice. Probably no single arrangement of this kind could have sufficed. He was a man of a particular constitution and he needed the 'pairing' of a complementary sexual passion to release his full powers, whether within or outside a permanent union. It is a condition by no means unusual in men of abundant energy and creativity. Social convention often limits its uninhibited deployment; but at the deeper subjective level it remains operative. It certainly did with Richard Wagner.

His turning to religion at the end of his life was neither a sign of exhausted vitality nor a radical change of direction on the part of one whose previous life and work is often wrongly thought of as predominantly profane, not to say pagan. The crypto-Christianity/Buddhism, as upon the surface it appears in *Parsifal*, was no more a diversion, certainly not in any sense a 'sport' in Wagner's total output, than *Meistersinger* had been. He longed at the end for salvation, conscious that, like Falstaff, he owed God a death; and conscious too that deep in the existential core of the world and humanity was a fatal lack of harmony and unity, a hard pitch of suffering the nature of which was always near to him and which had first been given intellectual clarification for him by Arthur Schopenhauer. He himself had faced up to it: in *The Ring* he had made a mighty effort to solve the obstinate riddle; in *Parsifal* he made another and more overtly 'spiritual', if no more ultimately successful attempt. He was trapped in the cauldron of his age and in the flawed assumptions of that Romanticism of which he was one of the foremost representatives and which at the deepest level gave his art and his life both its real meaning as well as its final flaw. Yet if he failed in the end, he saw with increasing clarity that the world must be redeemed or perish. He had sent forth Siegfried with his sword; but Siegfried had proved not the inaugurator of the new and redeemed world, as he had originally intended, but as a last idealization of historical man. And historical man was doomed. Historical man is a natural phenomenon, and therefore a warring, aggressive, essentially unredeemed animal, ultimately self-destroying. Re-released into Nature, freed from the constraints of civilization, Siegfried as historical man can only become more completely his unregenerate self, as Freud, Jung and the psychologists and psychoanalysts have understood. The redemption of historical man can only come on the spiritual plane; it can never come within Nature alone.

But historically religion has not done much better. Religion is concerned with salvation and redemption; that is its essence. Yet too often religion has operated only by negativing the fullest creative potential by insisting on 'sin' and frailty instead of aiming to release latent strength and the inner power of regeneration. The falsity of the religous façade has betrayed the inner force of true spiritual reality, the 'contemplation of God face to face' as Kierkegaard intimated, the 'true inwardness'.

Wagner turned at the end away from the hero image to that of the Pure Fool.[19] And it is precisely in this that Nietzsche and he parted philosophic company. For Nietzsche *Parsifal* was the last straw, a descent into a form of incense-burning degeneracy which deprived the human will of all strength and purpose. The Nietzschean future lay with the Superman – with, that is, a revitalization and new idealization of the hero who would conquer pessimism through affirmation of the value of life derived from a fresh orientation of his concept of Greek 'tragic optimism'. In *Parsifal* Nietzsche could see nothing but the ultimate negation of all optimism and life-affirmation; and he farther saw, correctly, that it was no last despairing gesture of a dying man but a consummation of everything that had gone before in Wagner's work. The denouement of *Parsifal*, the healing of Amfortas's wound by the touch of the Sacred Spear and the 'conversion' of Kundry, was inherent not only in the Redemption motif of *The Flying Dutchman*, *Tannhäuser* and *Lohengrin*, but also in *The Ring* and *Tristan*. For Nietzsche, who had worshipped at the Wagnerian shrine, it provoked the final apostasy. And that apostasy was all the more complete and furious precisely because he saw in *Parsifal*, and therefore in the totality of Wagnerism, a central truth he could not, dared not, admit without a fatal undermining of the whole of his own philosphic position. Nietzsche's doctrine of courage, adventure and domination of the will to live led him into more, though opposite dangers than the 'degeneracy' of *Parsifal*. He could not see that, as Wagner would have put it, the world had to be redeemed before it could be reanimated. More than that, he failed to see, as many have since, that a radical change had taken place, a change which carried the central metaphysic of the earlier works from the natural into the spiritual. Death and transfiguration had turned into life and transfiguration. Only in the most crude and naturalistic sense could that be equated with life-negation. Even Wagner hiself may have been only in part aware of that conclusion.

All this leads into the deep and often sullied waters of Romanticism, specifically of German Romanticism. *Parsifal* remains Wagner's final attempt to break the circuit. Its religionism may be condemned; its metaphysic may be muddled; but its more profound penetrations cannot be so easily dismissed. If it is objected that the idea of redemption through love is in one form or another no more than the message of Christianity and most other religions, Wagner would no doubt have retorted that not only Christianity but all religions had been corrupted by dogma and institutionalism, the Christ-figure in whatever form betrayed by enforced orthodoxy and temporal authority.[20] And it would be difficult to deny him. He himself once wrote that 'when religion becomes artificial, it is the task of art to save the crux of it'. It is in this sense, as well as several others, that *Parsifal* has to be seen first and foremost as a work of art, art consciously directed to the redemption of religion itself. Art is paramount: that too is a crucial Romantic standpoint; and the consequence is no less indisputable – art is religion. And that in its turn has led to charges of art as illusion, as magic. And magic and illusion confound the rational mind.

Wagner at one time proclaimed himself an atheist; but what he was disbelieving was precisely the form rather than the substance: he was rejecting a God and a way to God that all but the most unimaginatively orthodox also reject. If he seemed once to lyricize to Nietzsche over the Protestant communion service, it is clear from the work he eventually produced that he was looking far beyond the outward form to some deep existential truth away on the other side. He was acutely aware of suffering, his own first of all but spreading outwards from that centre to embrace the whole of the created world. And he had come to profound knowledge that only through renunciation could even the beginnings of the alleviation of that suffering be reached. And it had to be reached in the realm of spirit, not of nature. To that extent the charge that *Parsifal* in particular is unrealistic can be sustained. The hero had gone; the fool been elevated. No wonder Hitler banned performances of *Parsifal* during the Second World War.

But it was not a matter of pessimism versus optimism in any meaningful sense. Still less was it the opposition of his pessimism versus Nietzsche's optimism, loosely if inaccurately so called. In the deepest metaphysical and existential sense the two, Wagner and Nietzsche, parted precisely where they most nearly coincided. Only out of a Schopenhauerean pessimism could the new optimism be born and made to proliferate. Romanticism, beginning in optimism, in a spirit of a sense of joy and wonder, had declined into a existential pessimism that had to be exorcised before the New Order, foreseen but aborted in *The Ring*, could even be contemplated. But its time was not yet. Historical man still clung to his props and practices, and a new pessimism in the form of post-1945 existentialism had to be lived out before the ghosts could be laid. And even then they continued to haunt men's imaginations, to feed their greeds, fear and follies. Siegfried may have been dead at the end of *The Ring*, betrayed as well as betraying. But he lived on in the minds of succeeding generations who were called upon to bear the full brunt of Nothung's tempered steel.

Parsifal finally exhausted Wagner. The worry and labour that went into its completion and production drained his remaining strength. He was utterly determined that it should be produced to standards only hinted at in the first Festival with *The Ring* in 1876. Since it further extended and increased the subtlety of his musical and dramatic principles, now far from those laid down for his contemporary self-guidance in *Opera and Drama*, it required a corresponding extension of its means of production and performance.[21] It made huge demands on everyone concerned, Wagner himself not least.

Parsifal at last came to production, thrice, in 1882. The conductor was Hermann Levi. But at the third performance Wagner took over conducting the final part himself.[22] It required all his determination and strength to 'will what is necessary' to see it through. At the end, amid great applause, he thanked not the audience for their support and attendance but the singers and orchestra for their labours. He had achieved something more than presenting another masterpiece; and he knew it. What he had done was the most difficult of all: he had created not only a wholly new art form in all his post-*Lohengrin* work;[23] he had also created a public for it and a place for its proper presentation. It was a labour and an achievement beyond any but the most gigantic of human wills and constitutions. But he had done it; and he was content.

He died in Venice, where he had gone with Cosima and the children after the third *Parsifal* performance. Utterly worn out, he succumbed to a final, fatal heart attack. He had laboured superhumanly for half a century; and he left his lasting monument in his work. What manner of man he really was remains a subject of controversy, like most other things about him. That he traduced established custom in his life as much as in his work; that he ignored or dismissed social convention by his way of life and his dealings with the world is not to be disputed. It has often been held against him, has led to charges that he was, though generous in many ways, predominantly a bounder and a cad. The charges can be substantiated, according to social conventions and properties that have in any case themselves to be constantly and severely questioned. It is not in the end important. He was in his life as well as in his art stretching out beyond accepted boundaries to a new, freer, more potent way of life and art. He may have been clumsy, even ruthless about it; have ridden rough-shod; have caused distress to those around him. But if so, he would no doubt have replied that he was sorry but in battle there are always casualties, and if some fell in the service of art as he saw and understood it, that could not be helped. Yet he was not often wilfully callous. He was simply consumed with a particularly raging kind of fire. Whether he was a 'good' man or a 'bad' man in the end is irrelevant. The terms are meaningless.

Let the last word rest where it belongs. Napoleon said that no man is a hero to his valet. Peppino, Wagner's man in Italy and Bayreuth, said after his death, simply and honestly: 'No man had a better master.'

CHAPTER NINE

CODICIL: BEYOND
THE THRESHOLD

'The Wagnerian note,' wrote George Steiner,[1] 'sounded throughout social and political life and had its mad echoes in the ruin of modern Europe.' By going back to German medieval literature and folk mythology Wagner had drawn upon a source that had its origins deep in the European as well as the uniquely German psyche. And that gave the whole of his work its particularly compelling density and specific gravity. Without it he could not have created his mythological world with its direct relevance to his own and later times. He was one of the very few who even came near to translating a private insight into a universal principle. Steiner again: 'By the enormous strength of his personality and by his cunning rhetoric, he nearly instilled his concocted mythology into the general mind.'[2]

Yet this is not an accurate deduction. It was precisely because at bottom Wagner's mythology was not 'concocted' but drawn via the creative imagination from the magical centre of folk myth itself, a myth and legend already in existence and part of the general mind, that it could strike so deep and so far in response when translated into modern, i.e. nineteenth-century, terms.

Although it had, as Wagner himself insisted, its political relevances, the Wagnerian mythology was not, nor was it ever intended to be, contemporary and 'practical' only. 'The questions are a matter of metaphysics'; that is to say, it came from the deeps, and to the deeps it returned.[3] If it had been merely topical, contemporary, 'concocted', it could never have taken more than superficial root.

All political mythologies take only that superficial root. They have no depth, no true background in the popular mind. They are essentially intellectual, or concocted. Thomas Mann once said that 'in our time the destiny of man presents itself in political terms'. In so far as that is true, it lays the finger of superficiality on our own time, on the twentieth century; it signifies a triumph of the inessential, a retreat from the metaphysical, the ontological, the truly existential. The classic modern political mythology is

Marxism; and because Marxism is concerned with injustice, exploitation, social enmity and disarray and those aspects of philosophy which evade rather than confront the necessary existential questions, it often has the allegiance not only of sympathetic intellectuals, but also of those whose proper vocations lie elsewhere. Horrified by the suffering and injustice of the world order they see about them, even churchmen are tempted to extol the Marxist creed, despite its proclaimed atheism, forgetting perhaps that whatever the immediate cause and its possible justice, no one can sup with the devil with a short spoon. A primarily political concern with the condition of the world constitutes a reversal of priorities: politics and political theory represent a consequence, not cause of that condition, which always is, and must be, metaphysical and spiritual, the evolution of consciousness in the material world.

If, as has been said, Wagner's music dramas, like all true works of art, are concerned to explore possibilities rather than to propound answers, they run against the political and economic determinism of contemporary society in the Western world but alongside the great folk and communal mythologies, those, in fact, which have made all true great art possible, including Greek tragic drama, because they are in immediate touch with the popular psyche at different levels. They do not rule by a priori law; they may expound moral prerequisites, draw inferences, warn by precept and example; but they do not lay down rules of conduct. No genuinely creative art does, or can do that. Art as dogma and didacticism is invariably bad art; art 'used' for dogmatic purposes denies its innermost nature. Art may demonstrate or it may infer; but it cannot deal in policies or panaceas. If it tries to do so it becomes no more than the shabby handmaiden of propaganda.

This is in no way to argue on behalf of art for art's sake. That leads to an equal, if opposite, denial of essence and potentiality. As W. B. Yeats put it, 'Art, in its highest moments, is not a deliberate creation, but the creation of intense feeling, of pure life.' Art for art's sake is better than art for the sake of propaganda, for the latter demeans and diminishes everything it touches. Art, as Beethoven understood, is essentially revelation; it reveals, at whatever level and in whatever direction, the inward energy and purposiveness of life. On the other hand, to dissociate art from the currents of life in the world it inhabits is to devitalize and deny its value in ways that must in the end prove no less fatal. Art that arises in a fundamentally unhealthy society, a left-wing or right-wing authoritarian or totalitarian state or one breaking apart from some hollowness or rottenness at the centre, is likely to be itself an unhealthy, superficial and non-creative art, though in certain contexts it may transcend its material emotional situation and by the force of its own integrity reduce, even reverse, the demands of triviality. But most true artists, faced with such a society and such a dilemna, have opted to leave and carry on their creative work elsewhere, in some other society, itself no doubt imperfect but sufficiently malleable for their accommodation, where freedom is not a total mockery and travesty.

That was precisely the situation in Nazi Germany. By using Wagner's dramas as a kind of 'soul centre' for their movement, the Nazis sought to tap the mythological aspects and ended by corrupting and perverting them all through. Yet the move was astute, even if it was only half conscious in respect of what it affected, for it gave the party line the appearance of a true mythology, an unarguable national appeal and foundation, and so immeasurably strengthened its 'pull' and popular mesmerism.

The Nazis were not stupid; at least not in this. If they fed off the Wagnerian achievement, used it to propagate their idea of a national revival and a new emotional as well as material glory, they did not make the inference too rigid or direct. They used it, in fact, as mythology rather than as crude propaganda. And this only served to enhance its value to them and weaken opposition to what they stood for. Hitler's patronage of Bayreuth was subtle enough not to outrage too many of those who valued Wagner as a great and profound artist but disliked and distrusted him as a slick and dangerous political figurehead.

There is little doubt that Hitler did identify himself with both Lohengrin and Siegfried. In fact, however, he was much nearer to Alberich, one willing to give up everything, including love, in exchange for the power to rule the world. If Hitler was in one sense a hobgoblin of the German unconscious, he was also the Alberich of European politics between 1918 and 1945. And it was the way he represented a penetration of and an emanation from the collective unconscious, far more than his political theories and practices, that gave him his great power and enabled him to propel a whole nation along the road of its own insanity.[4]

Kant believed that it is the will of nature that right shall in the end prevail, even if it is slow in coming and causes great inconvenience along the way before it does. This may be true, but it is still a dangerous doctrine, if only because it encourages those who are convinced they are right to pursue their course with a rugged determination that is both ruthless and full of the sense of their own rightness. It can too easily become a kind of carte blanche for national dictators and militarists. It can too easily become, and historically has been made, a licence for tyrants and persecutors, a legitimization of those who, whether in the religious or the political fields (and especially where they combine), relentlessly persecute all who oppose them, all dissidents and contrary spirits. And that, of course, was precisely the situation that confronted Europe during the first half of the twentieth century. Kant could have argued that his proposition was correct in this particular respect as well as in the general one. Right did prevail with the defeat of Nazi Germany in 1945, but at the cost of much 'inconvenience'. Hitler, convinced that he was right, was proved wrong.

It is clear that Wagner himself had much of the nature of one who is convinced that right is on his side. He ruthlessly imposed his will and had his way. And it is likely that this personal determination also influenced his nation and its leaders, not only under Hitler but under Kaiser Wilhelm II as well. The irony is that without that unyielding determination, that irresistible belief in his own rightness, there would have been no Bayreuth, no Wagnerian emergence in the fullness of its flowering at all.

But we move away from the essence of true tragedy. Greek tragic drama was not based upon any moral conception of 'right' and 'wrong' but upon the operation of some capricious, frequently malicious force of destiny outside and beyond the control of those who suffer and die. True tragedy cannot be averted by more reasonable behaviour or more intelligent conduct. It is literally in the lap of the gods, indifferent to the fate of those whom they manipulate. That is why the Nazi aberration, though it was tragic in its results for those who suffered under it and because of it, cannot properly be called tragic on the larger scale and in the proper meaning of the term. Hitler and Nazism could have been averted by more sensible political arrangements. The European débâcle, which took place between 1914 and 1945, was self-induced; it thus lacked true tragic stature and grandeur because it was the result not of some implacable destiny but of human duplicity, greed and enmity. It cannot be called nemesis because it was avoidable.

I have called Wagner a true tragic artist; and that remains substantially true. There are dark forces of destiny at work in Wagner's music dramas, sometimes made manifest, sometimes obscured by the theatrical devices of potions and magic. But the central tragic impetus is there, most notably of all in *Tristan und Isolde*, where the protagonists are driven remorselessly on towards death by some unseen and essentially irrational destiny over which they have no control, and do not desire control, and in which death comes as an elevated kind of joy. It is not what the Christian would call the Will of God, because the Will of God is concerned with right and wrong. It is nearer to Schopenhauer's conception of the universal Will, which drives men and women and events on when they are caught up in a tragic situation.

To a certain extent, necessary in the nineteenth century when the dichotomy between rationalism and faith was at its strongest, Wagner modified and in so doing weakened the purity of tragic art as the Greeks conceived it. On the other hand, he had already argued in his writings[5] that it was no task of modern man to seek to resuscitate the art of the Greeks but rather to transform and project it into his own times. By introducing the note of redemption through love, Wagner diminished the full tragic impact. In pure undiluted tragedy there is no redemption, no recompense or justice beyond death. But for Wagner, living as he did in the Romantic, at least nominally Christian nineteenth century, of which he was in the profoundest sense a part and its foremost representative, the situation was not the same as it had been for the Greeks. Their gods were not our God, the God of Jehovah concerned with righteous anger and hard-line justice, or the God who mediated through Jesus Christ with mercy and the forgiveness of sins.

It was Wagner's explicit intention to return the theatre, his own theatre in particular, to a position analagous to that of the Greek theatre, that is to a central place in social and communal life. But for complex contemporary man the situation was different.

If the redemption motif led Wagner away from the central essence of pure tragedy as the Greeks understood it, it thereby led to other conclusions. Nietzsche argued that the Greeks stood for life-affirmation while Wagner degenerated, most of all in *Parsifal*, into life-negation. But this is a curious argument, especially in regard to *Parsifal*. Late Romanticism, and Wagner with it, did decline into various forms of world weariness and disillusionment, a kind of soul-sickness which led eventually to social disintegration and ethical collapse, frequently expressing itself through a mixtue of nostalgia and debauchery.[6] The heroic hypothesis was by no means dead, and at least one major composer, Gustav Mahler, turned it inwards with passionate existential results. For Wagner that hypothesis had died with Siegfried. Yet Nietzsche and many who followed him missed the salient point about *Parsifal*, that it moves not towards redemption through death but to redemption into new life. The wound of Amfortas, symbolically spiritual as much as physical, is healed by the touch of the Holy Spear. Indeed, this forms yet another link, and perhaps the most important of all, between *Parsifal* and *Lohengrin*. Of all Wagner's 'tragic' dramas, *Parsifal* and *Lohengrin* are the only ones in which the eponymous 'hero' (accounting both the Flying Dutchman and Siegfried in that category) does not die. The Dutchman Vanderdecken, Tannhäuser, Tristan and Isolde, Siegfried (and Brünnhilde) are all redeemed through love (in *The Ring* Brünnhilde more or less performs this office on Siegfried's behalf) and transfigured in death in their different and various ways. But death is not the end of *Parsifal* and is only incidental to it. Kundry dies; but Kundry's cycle is completed. Titurel dies of old age; but that is the lot of every man. Parsifal not only does not die but goes on to beget Lohengrin. The charge of life-negation is increasingly hard to sustain.

Nietzsche broke finally with Wagner after the original staging of *The Ring* at the first Bayreuth Festival in 1876, and he did so largely because he was repelled by what he had come to see as Wagner's excessive 'theatricality'. But even here he was led into error. He discerned in that theatricality as it presented itself before him evidence of an overriding femininity in Wagner, in its turn derived from what he took to be Wagner's half-Jewish ancestry. Nietzsche believed both that Wagner was the natural son of Ludwig Geyer and that Geyer was a Jew. It has long been accepted, as Wagner himself came to believe, that Ludwig Geyer was his real father; but later research has confirmed that Geyer was not himself of Jewish origin. It is not in itself all that important either way.[7] On the other hand, it gave Nietzsche a false handle with which to twist his sense that Wagner had betrayed the great ideal of a revived Hellenism to which he, Nietzsche, looked for the salvation of life and art. Wagner was unquestionably a total man of the theatre; and Ludwig Geyer was an actor and also a deep-dyed theatrical character. It is therefore likely that Wagner's own sense of the theatre was inherited from his father. But the charge that it was of Jewish origin is both unsubstantiated and irrelevant. Coupled with his anti-Christian paranoia, it led Nietzsche down a barren trail.

Besides his return at the end to Christian symbol and legend, which he abhorred, there was much in Wagner that Nietzsche came genuinely to deplore, and not altogether without reason. His dictatorial egotism, his persistent Francophobia, his 'democratic' concern for the *Volk*, his antagonism towards Brahms and his supporters (as much simulated in the factioneering of the period as real) – all this deeply offended the sensitive and aristocratic spirit of Friedrich Nietzsche. And much of it was what helped the Nazis to fix upon Wagner and use him for their purposes; for they fixed not only upon his dramas for their sustenance but also upon aspects of his theories as adumbrated in his prose writings, in the 'poison' he had to get out of his system, most notably his anti-Semetic tirades,[8] and his general attitudes as they appear from a cursory glance at his biography.

Except in a few incidental areas, it is no more just to blame Wagner for the crimes and tyrannies of the Nazis than it is to blame Jesus for the crimes and sectarian bigotries of the churches and the clergy.[9] On the other hand, it can hardly be disputed that Wagner did expound certain ideas and theories, and give expression in his dramas to certain psychological and emotional states, which lay him open to the kind of distortion that Hitler and the Nazis were able to build into their creed, and then to justify it, however far from the real cores of Wagnerism it turned out to be. And a good deal of this was inherent in Romanticism itself, both as consequence and as reaction.

In many respects, Hitler and the Nazis were a throwback to the nineteenth century and its political romanticisms. The particular brand of aggressive nationalism invoked by Nazism was far more prevalent up to 1914 than in the 1920s and 1930s: it belonged to the Kaiser's rather than to Hitler's Germany, was endemic to the Second rather than the Third Reich. In the latter it was whipped up deliberately; in the former it was spontaneous. It was more superimposed than natural after 1918. In other words, the entire ethic and national arousal of Nazi Germany belonged to the nineteenth century more than to the twentieth. Like Marxism, Nazism was never a specifically modern manifestation. And that places it still more firmly, if not in the direct Wagnerian orbit, at least in an adjacent one of the period of Wagner's ascendancy. Wagner represented the apex and consummation of German Romanticism. He rose with it and foresaw its decline. *Tristan und Isolde* was perhaps its highest single peak, Nazism its lowest degeneration. Wagner was involved in both. It cannot be denied, and it is no use trying to deny it. No proper understanding of either Wagner himself or of what in historical terms his work led to is possible by evading that crucial issue. It cannot be argued that without Wagner there would have been no Hitler and Nazism; but equally it cannot be denied that Wagner, even if by reflex and against all his real will and intention, did 'inspire' much that was most distasteful in Hitlerism and gave aid and comfort to the Nazi movement by exposing in his works as well as in some of his theories precisely those elements in the German psyche, most of all that 'dark deposit of saga' in the German soul of which Thomas Mann spoke with trepidation, that made Nazism possible.

The distortion and perversion of Wagnerism by the Nazis, however, raises more and larger questions. It serves to pinpoint the whole problem of the perversion of art to political ends. Art does not lay down rules of conduct or support practical theories of society in any significant sense. Art as propaganda is always a debased and sacreligious art. To see or use art in that way is as fundamental an error as to see religion as solely, even principally, concerned with conduct and behaviour. The idea that to be a Christian is simply to behave in a certain manner towards one's fellow human beings is true as far as it goes; but it does not go anywhere that has profound meaning. Christianity is not, to adopt a useful American colloquial expression, a straightforward matter of 'good kidism'; that is, a concern primarily with rules of conduct. To be a Christian in the fullest sense is to believe in the depths of one's being that Jesus Christ was the Son of God, spirit made manifest in nature, the penetration of the natural by the supernatural, the mediation between the one and the other. However it may be named, that is the essence. And it remains true in some form or other of all religions and all religious feeling. All rules and patterns of behaviour are derivatives, not essentials; conduct and behaviour, even in the loosest terms, are consequences of belief, not primary components of it. To have pity and compassion for the sufferings of the world, and to act upon it, is at most only half the equation. It is again a consequence rather than a cause.

Art is even less concerned with conduct and behaviour, except occasionally in ways that are wholly incidental. Art may, in particular cases, support or encourage belief; it is never the cause of it or the reason for it. Even in the most direct cases this is still true. The *St Matthew Passion* is in no sense a tract even though it is obviously a 'Christian' work. It is a dramatic meditation on the innermost meaning of the Passion of Jesus; it fosters emotional and spiritual responses in its audiences; but it has no propaganda value whatsoever, and it can never be used as such. In the same way, Elgar refused to allow *The Dream of Gerontius* to be taken as in any way sectarian. All true religious art is addressed to all men in all places at all times. It is never either a substitution or an act of proselytizing. Nor can the division between 'sacred' and 'profane' art be too easily or unthinkingly maintained. All art is to a greater or lesser extent 'religious', or rather a manifestation of the religious spirit in action. Even artists who, like Delius and D. H. Lawrence, appear to have no religious belief in the accepted sense, confirm this, though not in any dogmatic or orthodox, let alone sectarian, sense.

Thus Wagner's works, whether 'profane' as in *The Ring*, or 'sacred' as in *Parsifal*, have an indelibly 'religious' foundation. It is a question of bias and emphasis rather than of essence. In Yeats's phrase, already quoted, 'Art is the creation of intense feeling, of pure life'. And that implies a certain 'religious' basis, not as doctrine or dogma, but as the apprehension of the deepest, most far-reaching, most penetrating of the ontological realities, beyond the material and the naturalistic. To create 'intense feeling', 'pure life' is in itself a religious undertaking. And to say that certain types of art only seek to confirm the values of art itself does not alter the essentials of the argument. There is always a penetration, a breaking of the mould, a recognition of the deeper realities, no matter what the immediate terms of reference.

Where politics become paramount, art is debased. Politics is a flight from the existential realities. When art is placed at the service of politics, then there is a debasement of the quality and potency of life. Politics is the enemy of 'pure life'. The Nazis' debasement of Wagner was legitimate according to their own terms; but at the same time it exposed the hollowness of all they were and stood for. And that is no less true of what is usually, though erroneously, taken as its opposite – the socialist/communist/Marxist emanation. The use and corruption, from whatever side, of art for political purposes is always corrupt, always a solecism. On the other hand, when art lays itself open to this kind of perversion and distortion, the charge returns upon the artist. And it is not a question of the particular artist's beliefs. Most artists are politically naïve; when they turn their attention to political matters they are invariably turning to matters of which they are not masters. This does not imply that artists should (necessarily) have no political beliefs; only that their politics carry no more authority than anyone else's, whereas their artistic, and therefore their proper, activities do carry authority.

For Wagner, immersed as he was in the totality of that nineteenth century of which he was a foremost representative, the question was not and never could be straightforward. Concerned as he was in the evolution of his nation towards unity and identity, he could not escape the manipulation of his life and works not only irrelevant to his own preoccupations but actively inimical to them. But he would never have accepted the primacy of political authority for one moment. His whole life was a protest against such an assumption. Rather the reverse: he constantly 'used' politics for the furtherance of art and its practical interests – the proper provenance of politics.

The existentialists complained that life was meaningless and that there was nothing to tell them how they should conduct their lives. They complained that philosophy did not perform that service for them. Kierkegaard laid that precise charge against Hegel, his original philosophical mentor. But philosophy, no more than art, is concerned primarily with instructing men how to act and behave. It is an extreme and radical search for the truth; and as Herbert Read wrote in a penetrating essay on Kierkegaard, 'every philosopher or lover of the truth is an extremist'. To say that the same is true of art might be dangerous and lead to a number of invalid conclusions. Yet at the deepest level, art too is essentially extremist, a search for the truth that may be particular or may be universal;[10] but unless it is dismissed as mere decoration the act of artistic creation is both a quest for and an analysis of truth and is therefore in the richest sense extreme. It is seldom the seach for a solution; and when it is, it becomes 'politicized'.

Wagner's work was neither a systemology nor a blueprint. It was, like all true art, an exploration of possibilities. And one of those possibilities, though he would not have recognized it and only by a process of distortion, was Nazism. Everything that exists can be perverted, stood upon its head, reduced to its diametrical opposite. This was certainly true of Romanticism, which, beginning in high hopes and a bright dawn, collapsed through its own inherent flaws. From the beginning, as we can see now, the hope was forlorn, the dawn false. Romanticism declined into a mixture of disillusion and nostalgia in which increasing violence became indigenous. And it did not have within it the power to regenerate itself in a new and more potently existential form. Or rather it, like Wagner's earlier heroes, had to die to be reborn; and in its dying it had to turn to total corruption and degeneracy, both in the public and the private domain, its primary figures twisted into deformity for the sake of a false new dawn that in fact proved to be a haunted dusk. Richard Wagner, because he was a central figure of that distortion, also had to suffer perversion and corruption. And he cannot be wholly exonerated. The possibilities he explored and loosed upon the world contained within them, like Romanticism itself, the seeds of destruction. He would no doubt claim that he had foreseen the danger, and in *Parsifal* had attempted to subvert it; that in the death of Siegfried the false hero image had been laid to rest, redeemed. But in creating Siegfried in the first place, in sending forth the 'hero' with a sword, he had opened possibilities that were both ominous and negative. And Germany being Germany, and the European situation being what it was, the outcome was probably inevitable. By the time it might have been averted it was already too late, as by the time of Siegfried's final awakening it was too late. The tapping of the collective unconscious had indeed let loose a formidable set of goblins.

It may be argued, and as Jung intimated, that we all have to live through our 'Siegfried phase'. But if Siegfried does not die, both inside ourselves individually or within the body politic, or is not killed, but is allowed to continue on his way with his sword and his 'fearlessness', his arrogance and his elemental primitivism, the consequences are bound to be dire. They were. Nazism was the ultimate Romantic disaster.

NOTES

INTRODUCTION

1 The difference between early and late Liszt is not as marked as it may seem. The 'ascetic' Liszt of the last years was inherent in the flamboyance of his early excesses. Stripped of their virtuoso decorations, the early piano pieces contain the essence of the economy of the late ones.

2 'Sufferings and Greatness of Richard Wagner', in *Essays of Three Decades*, trans. H. T. Lowe-Porter, London (Secker & Warburg)/New York, 1947.

3 Ibid.

4 New York, 1945; London (Putnam), 1947.

1 EARLY YEARS

1 This is, of course, also linked to romantic nationalism, which is the collective search for and aggressive assertion of identity.

2 OPERA AND TRANSITION

1 Bellini was also a formative influence on Glinka, and so spread his net even farther than the main Italian and German operatic evolutions.

2 In Cardus's graphic phrase: 'The mind of Wagner worked on two planes. He saw with his ears and heard with his eyes.' In mature Wagner the orchestra is in a very real sense the protagonist. This, however, does not mean that 'Wagner without voices' is in any way admissable.

3 A SOLITARY VOYAGE

1 In *Fidelio* the influences are predominantly French, stemming from Cherubini; in Wagner they are predominantly Italian, mostly from Bellini.

2 There is another version of the story noted by Sir Walter Scott in *Rokeby* but not relevant in the context of Wagner. According to this the Dutchman's ship carried great treasure and a horrendous murder was committed on board; whereupon the crew became afflicted with plague and no port would accept the vessel, so she became a ghostship condemned to sail the seas for ever. The motif of the treasure, at least, is common to both versions.

3 In his later life Wagner for some reason tended to play down, if not actually reject, the influence of Heine's book. Why he did so remains something of a mystery.

4 'From here begins my career as *poet*, and my farewell to the mere concocter of opera-texts.' – *A Communication to My Friends*.

5 It is possible that Heine regarded this as his own interpolation and therefore thought himself entitled to payment for its use by Wagner. There was some talk of an 'arrangement'. It could have been why Wagner tended to dismiss the Heine connection.

6 This tends to be emphasized by the necessity of making the three-act version, in which the conventional elements were unavoidably exaggerated.

7 See George Steiner's *The Death of Tragedy* (Faber & Faber, London, 1961).

4 TOWARDS THE VORTEX

1 *A Communication to My Friends* – the source of Wagner quotations, except where otherwise stated.

2 'Tradition is only laziness' – Gustav Mahler.

3 In England it was a particularly Victorian vice – but that, of course, is simply another aspect of Romanticism.

4 'Arbeiten wir rasch. Heben wir Deutschland sozusagen in den Sattle. Reiten wird es schon konnen.' – 1867.

5 It has been revived and recorded, on RCA ARL 2 1104, with Anna Moffo and Dietrich Fischer-Dieskau in the lead roles.

6 See specifically Freud's paper on *The Most Prevalent Form of Degradation in Erotic Life*.

7 It does not, of course, occur only in Romantic opera. It is an integral part of much fiction, and applies particularly to all forms of opera, classical perhaps even more than romantic, if in a somewhat different form. Improbability is the stuff of which operas are made.

8 This applies only to Hitler himself, not to the Nazis as a whole. The others – Goering, Himmler, Goebbels, Borman – were in general political racketeers who took advantage of the situation created by Hitler. Goebbels was the most talented of them, a man with sharp enough wits to understand and propagate the myth.

9 Not only the Romantics, naturally. All artists to some extent have this dream quality somewhere in their creative faculties. The common, though not quite accurate term is 'inspiration'.

10 The term is in fact meaningless. Every man, or woman, who achieves anything memorable, in any field, automatically becomes a 'legend' in the public mind. The words 'legend in his lifetime' as it is familiarly used is a crude journalistic cliché.

11 It is by no means the same thing as a simple repetition for the sake of emphasis or exaggeration, a device resorted to as much by political orators and pamphleteers as by composers.

190

5 THE RING AND THE EVOLUTIONARY THRUST

1 This can easily be misunderstood. It does not mean merely the private whim or egotistical 'desire', but a profound probing into the depth of one's being, to understand oneself in one's total existence.

2 For a comprehensive analysis of the genesis of *The Ring*, and indeed of all Wagner's dramas, see Ernest Newman's *Wagner Nights* (Putnam, London, 1949).

3 He might well have sympathized with Dr Johnson's jibe against opera as 'an exotic and irrational entertainment', taking the condition of opera which he found and to which he most strongly objected.

4 'Vocalized tone' is quite common in music, especially in folk and popular music. It is a leading ingredient in jazz, where the instrumental inflections are closely related to African language patterns.

5 *Art and Revolution*.

6 See Sigmund Freud, *Group Psychology and the Analysis of the Ego*.

7 *Memories, Dreams, Reflections*, recorded and edited by Aniela Jaffé, translated by Richard and Clara Winston (Collins and Routledge & Kegan Paul, London, 1963; Random House Inc., New York, 1961, 1962, 1963).

8 Ibid.

9 It was the same with Kant a generation earlier. 'He has influenced even you, although you have never read him,' Goethe said to Eckermann in 1827; 'now you need him no longer, for what he could give you you possess already.' *Conversations with Goethe*, which Nietzsche once called 'the best German book there is'.

10 The theme of retribution and penance in the wake of incest (though not only that) lies behind Thomas Mann's novel *The Holy Sinner*.

11 *A History of Western Philosophy* (George Allen & Unwin, London, 1940).

12 Levi held Wagner in the highest esteem, calling him 'the finest and noblest person. It is natural that the world misunderstand him . . . but posterity will some day acknowledge that Wagner was as great a man as he was an artist. Even his struggle against what he calls 'Jewry' in modern music arises from the noblest motives.' Levi may have been dazzled by Wagner, as many were; but the tribute was sincere.

13 *Aspects of Wagner* (Alan Ross, London, 1968; Panther Books, London, 1972).

14 *Wagner's Ring and Its Symbols* (Faber & Faber, London, 1963, 1969, 1974).

15 This idea of genius as a kind of 'sickness' was another Romantic conceit. In post-Romanticism it lies at the root of Thomas Mann's *The Magic Mountain*, where the inhabitants of the sanatorium form a microcosm of the toiling, warring world in the lowlands; but it is also implicit in *Buddenbrooks*, *Death in Venice* and *Tristan*. In Mahler the contrast between the special atmosphere of the highlands or mountainscape of 'genius' and the 'normal' world below, looked back on in affection in the sound of cowbells and the pastoral scene, is particularly notable in the Sixth symphony. In plainer form it may even be said to appear in Richard Strauss's *Alpine Symphony*.

16 This is true of nearly all Wagner, not just *Tristan und Isolde*. The implications are far ranging: Brünnhilde's Immolation, which ends *Götterdämmerung* and so *The Ring* cycle itself, is simply another form of Liebestod.

17 Shaw's term.

18 The two, the musical and the metaphysical, are of course closely related in this context. A metaphysical impasse would inevitably create a corresponding musical one.

19 Brünnhilde's disobedience in trying to save Siegmund was the expression of Wotan's real, as opposed to his political, will. Hence Wotan's extreme anger and his despair at having to reject her.

20 Those, especially producers, who try to impose their own unimportant left-wing (or right-wing) political views on *The Ring*, or declare that they are not interested in the cosmic or the metaphysical, are the worst of the anti-Wagnerians. They falsify Wagner in the same way that Hitler did, and deserve no better fate. That does not mean that Wagner has no meaning for the contemporary world; it means the exact opposite, that his meaning for us, as it was for his own time, is infinitely deeper and more significant than temporary political manipulations.

6 TRISTAN AS WILL AND IDEA

1 In 1803, the year of the *Eroica*, disillusion had not set in; Napoleon was still abroad and at his exercises. But Beethoven's judgement was accurate, and as usual ahead of its time.

2 Academicism was, as usual, out of touch with the world beyond the cloisters.

3 *Tristan* has been called 'Schopenhauer set to music'; an exaggeration, of course, but there is truth near it, and the influence of Schopenhauer on this and subsequent Wagner works can hardly be overrated.

4 That is no excuse for performing Wagner's works in any language but their own. There is an argument for it, but it is not one that can immediately be comprehended. Most performances do not allow the words to be heard clearly in whatever language they may chance to be. The close relationship between the music and the word structure requires that any reasonably ideal performance be in the original German.

5 *The French Revolution*, Book V, Chapter V.

7 LIGHT AND LIFE IN C MAJOR

1 That is why it is legitimate to listen to *Tristan* on records or radio while *Meistersinger* should always be heard 'live', or at least via a recording or transmission taken from a public performance. *Tristan* can be heard without the stage matter, even though that contravenes Wagner's principle of total art and destroys the configuration of all the arts; but not *Meistersinger*. Even that, however, is not the real point. If *Tristan* is essentially private ecstasy with death a joy to those who die, *Meistersinger* is no less essentially a public celebration and a joy to those who live.

2 They never do, of course. The duc de Sully (1560–1641) was only one among many who tried to bring about a federated Europe and eliminate war. He called it the Grand Design and he saw that it was perfectly practical 'if only the nations would agree'. They did not agree and the plan foundered. Rousseau tried a similar idea; and also failed, for the same reason. And Romantic nationalism made, and has made, it even less likely. The sovereign state is the enemy of any form of federation, even real cooperation.

3 Perhaps 'pessimism' is not the right word here. 'Doubts and questioning' might be more appropriate.

192

4 Individualism is not the same as personalism. Individuality implies separateness, personality unity and wholeness.

5 It is no use arguing that revolutions turn to militarism to defend themselves against outside hostility or counter-revolutionary movements. Militarism is inherent in the process of revolution itself; it is not a by-product but a primary ingredient.

6 *Reflections on the Revolution in France, 1790.*

7 Quoted by Natalie Bauer-Lechner in *Recollections of Gustav Mahler* (London, Faber Music, 1980; original E. P. Tal & Co. Verlag, Leipzig, 1923).

8 I am indebted to Colin Wilson for the useful analogy of the boy and the elephant. The boy represents the left side, the 'self', the intellectual and scientific capacity; the elephant represents the right, the instinctive, the intuitional, the source of creative power. The boy is much less powerful than the elephant; but so long as he remains active and alert, he can direct the huge strength of the elephant to valuable ends. If he does not, if he either neglects the elephant so that its strength is wasted, or keeps it well but allows it to become complacent and indolent, the potential of the partnership is lost. If, on the other hand, the boy and the elephant become separated, both lose some part of that combined power. Each continues to exist and function independently, but with the link broken the potential is dissipated. In most people the boy and the elephant are both idle and do not exert themselves. It is invariably the boy's fault. If the elephant runs amok, madness ensues because the boy has lost control.

8 THE TWILIGHT OF AN AGE

1 This is in direct contrast to the essentially non-selfseeking 'hero' of the *Eroica* symphony. All the same, the comparison is not entirely fair; the *Eroica* (1803) could not have been written seventy years later: too much had changed. The post-French Revolution optimism had by then declined into the pessimism of the later Romantic period. Wagner can hardly be charged for not having created another *Eroica*-type hero in an age that could no longer support it. The late-Romantic hero figure was inevitably different from, and in many respects in opposition to, that of the immediate post-French Revolution period.

2 He had originally intended to write a *Trauersymphonie* in honour of the German dead; but since this was officially frowned upon for drawing attention to the disasters rather than the glories of war, he contented himself with the somewhat vacuous *Kaisermarsch* instead.

3 There is no warrant for playing the *Idyll* with full, or even reduced, orchestra. Most specious of all is the argument that Wagner wrote it for thirteen players simply because there was no room on the Triebschen staircase for more. If Wagner had intended it for the orchestra he would have specified it; and if physical limitation was the reason for its particular form and texture, that only means that Wagner wrote it for those circumstances, as all true artists accommodate their work to the specific needs of the occasion. Orchestral performance undermines the essential character and intimacy of the *Idyll*: it is a solecism as great as that of performing Ravel's Introduction and Allegro in an orchestral distortion.

4 Nietzsche later turned against *The Birth of Tragedy* himself as well as against Wagner.

5 The Nietzsche/Wagner relationship has been admirably analysed and expounded by the singer Dietrich Fischer-Dieskau in *Wagner and Nietzsche* (Deutsche Verlags-Anstalt GmbH, Stuttgart, 1974; translated by Joachim Neugroschel, Seabury Press, Inc., New York, 1976; Sidgwick & Jackson Ltd, London, 1978).

6 Nietzsche was a passionate devotee of French culture. This was another cause of the rift between him and Wagner.

7 So did Beethoven, like Wagner a fundamentally honourable man and artist under the surface.

8 Hanslick understood virtually nothing about Wagner's art *per se*; and he committed the classic critical solecism when he proclaimed that for 'modern music' the Beethoven Ninth symphony and *Missa solemnis* stood at the gates saying 'No farther', as though art were not essentially evolutionary and can never say 'No farther', whether with Beethoven, with Wagner himself, with Schoenberg and Webern, or with Boulez and Stockhausen. But on one point Hanslick was right, when he saw that Wagner's methods were valid only for Wagner himself. Wagner's influence on later generations was frequently deplorable, demonstrating that emulation is empty and pretentious if it does not embrace a total matching of means to ends. Wagnerisms without Wagner were indeed inimical to 'musical tradition and continuity', except in incidentals. But then so is the work of all great and truly original artists, Beethoven included.

9 This again was by no means unusual. All truly creative artists show some deepening of spiritual and existential awareness at the end of their lives, in the light of experience. If they do not, they are not true artists. It is certainly the case with Beethoven (more than any other), with Bach, Mozart, even the agnostic Brahms. It is also true of Shakespeare. It does not mean that their late work is necessarily 'better' than their early work; often it clearly is not; but they cannot, unless they are mere mechanics of their art and craft, remain unchanged in the light of a lifetime's experience.

10 Nietzsche's attitude to Christianity was in fact ambivalent, despite his proclaimed hostility. He once said that there had only ever been one true Christian and he died on the Cross; a sentiment by no means unique and frequently reiterated.

11 Shaw's phrase again.

12 See quotation from Charles Koechlin on page 168.

13 *Bühnenweihfestspiel* is the precise German term used by Wagner.

14 An old lady at the first performance of the *St Matthew Passion* is reported to have exclaimed, in some horror: 'Heaven help us! We are at the opera!'

15 Book IV, 'The Tragic Generation' section of *The Trembling of the Veil* (1922) from *Autobiographies*.

16 This does not necessarily imply a 'value judgement'; it is simply a distinction in kind, which may perhaps best be described as that betwen the existential and the academic.

17 Hence the romanticizing of the Middle Ages, as much in the William Morris type of 'socialism' as in the movement towards a revival of German unification in the nineteenth century.

18 The daughter of the poet Théophile Gautier, also a friend of Wagner.

19 The name Parsifal, or Parzival, comes from the Arabic; from *parsi* meaning 'pure' and *fal* meaning 'fool'. See Fischer-Dieskau, *Wagner and Nietzsche*, page 154.

20 See quotation from Kierkegaard on page 166.

21 It is the most difficult of all Wagner's works to stage satisfactorily. That is one reason why he decreed that it should be given nowhere except at Bayreuth.

22 It is often said that Levi fell ill and that is why Wagner had to take over. But apparently Levi remained in the orchestra pit while Wagner conducted and wrote a moving account of it afterwards in a letter to his father. The audience did not know that Wagner had taken over until afterwards, as Wagner would not show himself.

23 From *The Flying Dutchman* on in reality, although *Lohengrin* remains the turning-point. As with all essentially 'existential' artists, each new work created a particular universe of its own. *Parsifal* represented the final evolution, not only technically but metaphysically. In *Parsifal* there was at least one major modification of the basic Wagnerian principle. Gurnemanz acts not only as Narrator, necessary because so much of the action lies in the past, but also as something analagous to the Greek chorus, commenting on the action and seeing it from the other side, as it were. Thus whereas in the earlier dramas the orchestra expresses the feeling behind the action while the singers carry it along, in *Parsifal* that role is split between the orchestra and at least one of the voices, that of Gurnemanz. There is thus an even richer and more subtle combining of voices and orchestra, a continual interplay which alters the bias without undermining the essential Wagnerian principle of dramatic tension between two planes, the conscious and the unconscious. The figure of Gurnemanz, by 'crossing the bar', gives the dramatic technique a still closer and more cohesive integration. Gurnemanz is sometimes seen as little more than a rather long-winded old bore; but that is to miss the entire point of the work's structure and realization.

9 CODICIL: BEYOND THE THRESHOLD

1 *The Death of Tragedy*, page 322.

2 Ibid.

3 'The only two powers that trouble the deeps are religion and love, the others make a little trouble upon the surface.' — W. B. Yeats. Wagner would have assented.

4 The 'Alberich syndrome', as it might be called, is not peculiar to Wagner. It has universal relevance. The 'murder' of love and the degradation of human relationships in the pursuit of power, position and self-advancement is a central theme in the novels of Dickens and also of Franz Kafka. Cf. Mark Spilka: *Dickens and Kafka* (Dennis Dobson, London, 1963; Indiana University Press, Indiana, 1963).

5 See page 86.

6 Despite the 'strength through joy' and open-air element in Nazism, there was also a strong sense of nostalgia and debauchery, partly inherited from the Weimar Republic but more indigenous, especially with Roehm's S.A. (the original 'brownshirts'), the Nazi party stormtroopers.

7 The idea that Wagner's anti-Semitism originated from his knowledge and consequent resentment that he was himself half-Jewish is not convincing. It contradicts rather than supports his theories in *Judaism in Music*.

8 As I have said, if a man gets rid of the poison in his system he must be careful where it goes. It is rather like atomic waste matter; it must be disposed of, but if care is not taken it may contaminate the earth for generations.

9 No comparison between Wagner and Jesus is intended. It is simply an example.

10 This remains true even where the search is for truth about art itself.

SELECT BIBLIOGRAPHY

Wagner literature being so extensive and apparently inexhaustible, it is not possible to give here more than a brief selection; nor, in all probability, is it desirable to attempt further explorations and excavations. A whole book could, and possibly should, be devoted to the subject; but even that might not cover all the possibilities. I therefore concentrate here on books and writings with a particular relevance to the matter in hand.

The most comprehensive Wagner biography remains Ernest Newman's great four-volume work, published between 1933 and 1946. Though further data has come to light since Newman's day and continual research still unearths further material, this remains the standard biography. Newman also wrote other books on Wagner, notably *Wagner Nights*, which is strong on fact and on the literary, historical and legendary background to Wagner's music dramas but not so strong on the psychological and existential meaning of them. Robert Donington's book on that subject supplies the need, at least in so far as *The Ring* is concerned, though here too the approach tends at times to become a little one-sided and to treat Wagner in a supporting rather than the primary role in the matter of psychological theory. Cosima Wagner's recently published diaries, skilfully translated and edited by Geoffrey Skelton, are an invaluable new mine of primary source material; and Skelton's *Richard and Cosima Wagner: A Biography of a Marriage* is another admirable and essential piece of work, filling in many details. Among smaller and more general books, Bryan Magee's *Aspects of Wagner* stands out for clear thinking and lucid writing, while Robert L. Jacob's volume in the Dent 'Master Musicians' series is also excellent. *The Wagner Companion*, edited by Peter Burbidge and Richard Sutton, is a thoroughly useful symposium.

The standard works of the European philosophers, notably Schopenhauer, Kant, Hegel and Kierkegaard, are essential reading, and Bertrand Russell's *History of Western Philosophy* has a special value in its alert and sharp-minded coverage of the totality of the subject, which bears, directly or indirectly, upon Wagner and his works. Shaw's *The Perfect Wagnerite* treats the subject from the political angle in a manner that is at once witty, illuminating and outrageously (but quite unrepentently) biased.

All this, however, is very well. The prime reading source is and must always be Wagner's own voluminous writings. The task may be formidable,

196

the undertaking enough to daunt minds less formidably constituted than Wagner's own; but it has to be faced. Without that immersion, however great the incipient danger of drowning, Wagner will remain at a distance, an even more complex enigma than he was – and that is in itself enough to strike all manner of sparks of terror and apprehension. The standard translation in bulk remains that made for the Wagner Society in the 1890s by W. Ashton Ellis. This is often said to be faithful but virtually unreadable. The judgement is over-harsh; and to what extent it is justified may be laid to Wagner's own door. For the rest, the following list must suffice.

WAGNER'S OWN WRITINGS

Richard Wagner's Prose Works, translated by William Ashton Ellis (London 1892–99).
Mein Leben, edited by Martin Gregor-Dellin (Munich 1963); as *My Life* (London 1963).
Letters of Richard Wagner, translated by M. M. Bozman (London 1927).
Letters of Richard Wagner: The Burrell Collection, edited by John N. Burk (New York 1950).
Richard Wagner to Mathilde Wesendonk, translated by W. A. Ellis (New York 1905).
Family Letters of Richard Wagner, translated by W. A. Ellis (London 1911).
Richard Wagner's Letters to his Dresden Friends, translated by J. S. Shedlock (London, New York 1890).
König Ludwig II und Richard Wagner, 5 vols, edited by Otto Strobel (Karlsruhe 1936–9).
Richard Wagner and Minna Wagner (Berlin, Leipzig 1908, London 1909).
Three Wagner Essays, translated by Robert L. Jacobs (London 1979).
Beethoven, translated by Edward Dannreuther, with a supplement from the Philosophical Works of Arthur Schopenhauer (London 1880).
Judaism in Music, translated by Edwin Evans (London 1910).
Opera and Drama, translated by Edwin Evans (London 1913).
Stories and Essays, selected and edited by Charles Osborne (London 1973).
Wagner Writes from Paris, selected and translated by Robert L. Jacobs and Geoffrey Skelton (London 1973).

BOOKS ON WAGNER

Adorno, Theodor W., *Versuch über Wagner* (Frankfurt 1952).
Barth, Herbert, Mack, Dietrich, & Egon, Voss, *Wagner: A Documentary Study*, Preface by Pierre Boulez; translated by P. R. J. Ford and Mary Whittall (London 1975; original, Vienna 1975).
Barzun, Jacques, *Darwin, Marx, Wagner* (New York 1958).
Bekker, Paul *Richard Wagner, Das Leben im Werke* (Stuttgart 1924).

Bélart, Hans, *Richard Wagner in Zürich* (Leipzig 1900–1).

Bory, Robert, *La vie et l'oeuvre de Richard Wagner par l'image* (Paris 1938).

Boucher, Maurice, *The Political Concepts of Richard Wagner*, translated by Marcel Honoré (London, New York 1950).

Burrell, Mary, *Richard Wagner, His Life and Works from 1813 to 1834* (London 1898).

Chamberlain, Houston Stewart, *Richard Wagner* (Munich 1896), translated by G. Ainslie Hight (London, Philadelphia 1897).

Culshaw, John, *Reflections on Wagner's 'Ring'* (London, New York 1976).

Curzon, Henri de, *L'oeuvre de Richard Wagner à Paris et ses interprètes (1850–1914)* (Paris 1920).

Donington, Robert, *Wagner's 'Ring' and its Symbols* (London, New York 1963, 1974).

Ellis, William Ashton, *Life of Richard Wagner*, 6 vols (London 1900–08).

Fischer-Dieskau, Dietrich, *Wagner and Nietzsche*, translated by Joachim Neugroschel (London, New York 1976, original, Stuttgart 1974).

Gal, Hans, *Richard Wagner*, translated by Hans-Hubert Schönzeler (London, New York 1976).

Garten, H. F., *Wagner the Dramatist* (London 1977).

Gutman, Robert W., *Richard Wagner: The Man, His Mind and His Music* (London, New York 1968).

Hutcheson, Ernest, *A Musical Guide to 'The Ring of the Nibelung'* (New York, Toronto 1940).

d'Indy, Vincent, *Richard Wagner et son influence sur l'art musical français* (Paris 1930).

Jacobs, Robert L., *Wagner* (London, New York 1965).

Kietz, Ernst Benedikt, *Richard Wagner in den Jahren 1842–1849 und 1873–1875* (Dresden 1905).

Magee, Bryan, *Aspects of Wagner* (London, New York 1968).

Newman, Ernest, *Life of Richard Wagner* (London, New York 1933–46).

—, *Wagner as Man and Artist* (London, New York 1914).

—, *Wagner Nights* (London, New York 1949).

—, *The Wagner Operas* (London, New York 1949).

—, *A Study of Wagner* (London 1899).

Osborne, Charles, *Wagner and His World* (London, New York 1977).

Panofsky, Walter, *Wagner – A Pictorial Biography* (London, Ontario, 1963).

Petzet, Detta and Michael, *Die Richard Wagner Bühne König Ludwig II* (Munich 1976).

Shaw, G. Bernard, *The Perfect Wagnerite* (London, New York 1898).

Skelton, Geoffrey, *Wagner at Bayreuth* (London, New York 1965).

—, *Richard and Cosima Wagner: Biography of a Marriage* (London 1982).

Stein, Herbert von, *Dichtung und Musik im Werk Richard Wagner* (Berlin 1962).

Stein, Leon, *The Racial Thinking of Richard Wagner* (New York 1950).

Taylor, Ronald, *Richard Wagner: His Life, Art and Thought* (London 1979).

Wagner, Cosima, *Diaries*, translated and edited by Geoffrey Skelton (London, New York 1978, 1980).

Westernhagen, Curt von, *Richard Wagner: Sein Welt, sein Wesen, seine Welt* (Zürich 1956).

—, *Wagner* (Zürich 1968).

GENERAL WORKS

Abraham, Gerald, *A Hundred Years of Music* (London 1938, 1949, 1964).

Conrad, Peter, *Romantic Opera and Literary Form* (Berkeley 1978).

Dunlop, Sir John K., *A Short History of Germany* (London 1965).

Einstein, Alfred, *Music in the Romantic Era* (London, New York 1954).

Freud, Sigmund, *Collected Papers* (London, published over a period).

Grout, Donald Jay, *A Short History of Opera* (New York, London 1947).

Hanslick, Eduard, *Vienna's Golden Years of Music, 1850–1900*, translated by Henry Pleasants (New York, London 1950).

—, *Music Criticisms, 1846–99*, translated and edited by Henry Pleasants (London, New York, 1950, 1951).

Jung, Carl Gustav, *Memories, Dreams, Reflections,* recorded and edited by Aniela Jaffé, translated by Richard and Clara Winston (London, New York 1963). Also general works.

Kaufmann, Walter, *Nietzsche: Philosopher, Psychologist, Antichrist* (Cleveland, New York 1962).

Kerman, Joseph, *Opera as Drama* (New York, Oxford 1956).

Mann, Thomas, *Essays of Three Decades*, translated by H. T. Lowe-Porter (London, New York 1947).

—, *Doktor Faustus*, translated by H. T. Lowe-Porter (London, New York 1949).

Mellers, Wilfrid, *Man & His Music*, Vol.3 (London 1962).

Russell, Bertrand, *A History of Western Philosophy* (London 1940).

Searle, Humphrey, *The Music of Liszt* (London, New York 1966).

Schweitzer, Albert, *Civilization and Ethics* (London 1946).

Steiner, George, *The Death of Tragedy* (London, New York 1961).

Stern, J. P., *Hitler: The Führer and the People* (London, New York 1974).

Taylor, A. J. P., *Europe: Decline and Grandeur* (London 1950, 1952, 1956; 1957 complete).

Terraine, John, *The Mighty Continent* (London 1974).

Voigt, F. A., *Unto Caesar* (London, Toronto 1938).

INDEX

Hitler, Adolf, 3, 4, 6, 9, 12, 73–4, 90–2, 95, 98, 102ff, 114, 131, 152, 153, 181, 182, 184, 190*n*
Hoffman, E.T.A. 50, 62, 65
Homer, 72
Human, All Too Human (Nietzsche), 161

Ibsen, Henrik, 21
Iphigénie en Aulide (Gluck), 71

James, Henry, 59
Johnson, Samuel, 174, 191*n*
Joyce, James, 25, 147
Jung, Carl Gustav, 97–8, 114, 188

Kant, Immanuel, 75, 116, 169, 181, 191*n*
Katz, Adele T., 8
Keats, John, 94
Kierkegaard, Søren, 82, 115, 166, 176, 187
Klemperer, Otto, 105
Koechlin, Charles, 168
Kullervo symphony (Sibelius), 100

Lachner, Franz, 60
Lamark, Jean Baptiste, 15, 96
Laube, Heinrich, 26
Laussot, Jessie, 83–4
Lawrence, D.H., 94, 186
Levi, Hermann, 1, 103, 178, 191*n*, 195*n*
Lincoln, Abraham, 74
Liszt, Franz, 1, 2, 54, 82–3, 84, 93, 94, 118–9, 140, 144, 173, 189*n*
Logier, J.R., 23
Ludwig II of Bavaria, 83, 112, 130, 139, 140, 142, 143, 144, 145, 161, 162, 163
Lytton, Bulwer, 38–9, 41

Magee, Bryan, 103
Mahler, Gustav, 1, 2, 8, 21, 52, 105, 138, 153, 158, 173, 183, 190*n*, 191*n*
Maier, Mathilde, 129, 140
Mann, Thomas, 2–3, 7, 18, 53, 74, 90, 94, 179, 191*n*
Manson, Mrs & Miss, 41
Marschner, Heinrich August, 31
Memoirs of Herr von Schnabelewopski (Heine), 52
Mendelssohn, Felix Bartholdy, 20
Mendés, Catulle, 174
Meyer, Friederike, 129
Meyerbeer, Giacomo, 16, 31, 35, 39, 41–2, 61, 101
Möller, Abraham, 40
Moscheles, Ignaz, 172
Mozart, Wolfgang Amadeus, 9, 18, 24, 35, 48, 50, 89
Mussolini, Benito, 74

Napoleon (Bonaparte), 14, 70, 74, 126, 136, 151, 178

Newman, Ernest, 53, 142, 191*n*
Nietzsche, Friedrich, 5, 68, 87, 110, 111, 117, 121, 160–1, 166, 167, 169, 176, 177, 183, 184, 194*n*

Orff, Carl, 88

Pachta, Count (& daughters), 30, 32
Palestrina, Giovanni, 18
Paul, St, 122
Pitt, William, 136
Plato, 81, 115, 116
Puccini, Giacomo, 44
Purcell, Henry, 125

Ravel, Maurice, 18
Read, Herbert, 187
Richter, Hans, 83
Ritter, Julie, 83, 84
Ritter, Karl, 83
Rossini, Gioacchino, 46
Russell, Bertrand, 101

St Matthew Passion (Bach), 169, 185, 194*n*
Satie, Erik, 5
Sayn-Wittgenstein, Princess, 118, 140
Scherchen, Hermann, 49
Schlesinger, Moritz Adolf, 42–3
Schnorr, Ludwig, 143
Schoenberg, Arnold, 48, 89, 105
Schopenhauer, Arthur, 87, 96, 98, 99, 114, 116, 117, 121, 123, 124–5, 132, 139, 148, 160, 167, 168, 174, 175, 178
Schröder-Devrient, Wilhelmine, 24, 33, 35, 62–3, 64–5, 70
Schumann, Clara, 29, 54
Schumann, Robert, 3, 168
Scott, Sir Walter, 189*n*
Scribe, Eugène, 41
Shakespeare, William, 19, 21, 32, 89
Shaw, George Bernard, 67, 191*n*, 194*n*
Shelley, Percy Bysshe, 37, 38, 116, 139
Sibelius, Jean, 5, 21, 100, 173
Smart, Sir George, 40–1
Socrates, 166
Solti, Sir Georg, 105
Sophocles, 21
Spontini, Gasparo, 39
Stalin, J.V., 102
Steiner, George, 179, 190*n*
Strauss, Richard, 8, 191*n*
Stravinsky, Igor, 5, 8, 21, 88, 128

Tichatscheck, Josef, 65
Tieck, Ludwig, 65
Tragical History of Doctor Faustus (Marlowe), 53
Tsykiewicz, Count Vincenz, 26, 30

Uhlig, Theodore, 83

201

202